Rabindranath Tagore

Titles in the series Critical Lives present the work of leading cultural figures of the modern period. Each book explores the life of the artist, writer, philosopher or architect in question and relates it to their major works.

In the same series

Antonin Artaud *David A. Shafer*
Roland Barthes *Andy Stafford*
Georges Bataille *Stuart Kendall*
Charles Baudelaire *Rosemary Lloyd*
Simone de Beauvoir *Ursula Tidd*
Samuel Beckett *Andrew Gibson*
Walter Benjamin *Esther Leslie*
John Berger *Andy Merrifield*
Leonard Bernstein *Paul R. Laird*
Joseph Beuys *Claudia Mesch*
Jorge Luis Borges *Jason Wilson*
Constantin Brancusi *Sanda Miller*
Bertolt Brecht *Philip Glahn*
Charles Bukowski *David Stephen Calonne*
Mikhail Bulgakov *J.A.E. Curtis*
William S. Burroughs *Phil Baker*
John Cage *Rob Haskins*
Albert Camus *Edward J. Hughes*
Fidel Castro *Nick Caistor*
Paul Cézanne *Jon Kear*
Coco Chanel *Linda Simon*
Noam Chomsky *Wolfgang B. Sperlich*
Jean Cocteau *James S. Williams*
Salvador Dalí *Mary Ann Caws*
Guy Debord *Andy Merrifield*
Claude Debussy *David J. Code*
Gilles Deleuze *Frida Beckman*
Fyodor Dostoevsky *Robert Bird*
Marcel Duchamp *Caroline Cros*
Sergei Eisenstein *Mike O'Mahony*
William Faulkner *Kirk Curnutt*
Gustave Flaubert *Anne Green*
Michel Foucault *David Macey*
Mahatma Gandhi *Douglas Allen*
Jean Genet *Stephen Barber*
Allen Ginsberg *Steve Finbow*
Günter Grass *Julian Preece*
Ernest Hemingway *Verna Kale*
Victor Hugo *Bradley Stephens*
Derek Jarman *Michael Charlesworth*
Alfred Jarry *Jill Fell*
James Joyce *Andrew Gibson*
Carl Jung *Paul Bishop*
Franz Kafka *Sander L. Gilman*
Frida Kahlo *Gannit Ankori*
Søren Kierkegaard *Alastair Hannay*

Yves Klein *Nuit Banai*
Arthur Koestler *Edward Saunders*
Akira Kurosawa *Peter Wild*
Lenin *Lars T. Lih*
Pierre Loti *Richard M. Berrong*
Jean-François Lyotard *Kiff Bamford*
René Magritte *Patricia Allmer*
Stéphane Mallarmé *Roger Pearson*
Thomas Mann *Herbert Lehnert and Eva Wessell*
Gabriel García Márquez *Stephen M. Hart*
Karl Marx *Paul Thomas*
Herman Melville *Kevin J. Hayes*
Henry Miller *David Stephen Calonne*
Yukio Mishima *Damian Flanagan*
Eadweard Muybridge *Marta Braun*
Vladimir Nabokov *Barbara Wyllie*
Pablo Neruda *Dominic Moran*
Georgia O'Keeffe *Nancy J. Scott*
Octavio Paz *Nick Caistor*
Pablo Picasso *Mary Ann Caws*
Edgar Allan Poe *Kevin J. Hayes*
Ezra Pound *Alec Marsh*
Marcel Proust *Adam Watt*
Arthur Rimbaud *Seth Whidden*
John Ruskin *Andrew Ballantyne*
Jean-Paul Sartre *Andrew Leak*
Erik Satie *Mary E. Davis*
Arnold Schoenberg *Mark Berry*
Arthur Schopenhauer *Peter B. Lewis*
Dmitry Shostakovich *Pauline Fairclough*
Adam Smith *Jonathan Conlin*
Susan Sontag *Jerome Boyd Maunsell*
Gertrude Stein *Lucy Daniel*
Stendhal *Francesco Manzini*
Igor Stravinsky *Jonathan Cross*
Rabindranath Tagore *Bashabi Fraser*
Pyotr Tchaikovsky *Philip Ross Bullock*
Leon Trotsky *Paul Le Blanc*
Mark Twain *Kevin J. Hayes*
Richard Wagner *Raymond Furness*
Alfred Russel Wallace *Patrick Armstrong*
Simone Weil *Palle Yourgrau*
Tennessee Williams *Paul Ibell*
Ludwig Wittgenstein *Edward Kanterian*
Virginia Woolf *Ira Nadel*
Frank Lloyd Wright *Robert McCarter*

Rabindranath Tagore

Bashabi Fraser

REAKTION BOOKS

My father, Bimalendu Bhattacharya
William Radice
Indra Nath Choudhuri

Published by Reaktion Books Ltd
Unit 32, Waterside
44–48 Wharf Road
London N1 7UX, UK

www.reaktionbooks.co.uk

First published 2019
Copyright © Bashabi Fraser 2019

All rights reserved

No part of this publication may be reproduced, stored in a retrieval system, or transmitted, in any form or by any means, electronic, mechanical, photocopying, recording or otherwise, without the prior permission of the publishers

Exclusively distributed in India by Speaking Tiger

Printed and bound in India by Replika Press Pvt. Ltd.

A catalogue record for this book is available from the British Library

ISBN 978 1 78914 149 8

Contents

Introduction 7
1 The Tagores of Jorasanko 16
2 Growing Up in the Tagore Household 35
3 English Interlude 51
4 Loss and the Journey to the Banks of the Padma 67
5 The Abode of Peace 100
6 From Shantiniketan to the World Stage 117
7 The Renunciation of Knighthood 136
8 Where the World Meets in a Nest 145
9 'The Call of Truth' and 'The Great Sentinel' 160
10 Waves of Nationalism and *The Religion of Man* 176
11 Tagore's Modernity 192
12 The Legacy: At Home and in the World 207

References 219
Select Bibliography 237
Acknowledgements 242
Photo Acknowledgements 245

Rabindranath Tagore, *c.* 1916.

Introduction

Rabindranath Tagore became the first non-Westerner to win the Nobel Prize in Literature, when he was awarded the prize in November 1913. He was immediately catapulted onto the world stage, much to his and the world's surprise. In a lecture in 2014 on the artistic output of Tagore, Mijarul M. Quayes said that by conferring the Nobel Prize on Tagore, the Prize was transformed from a European award to an international one.[1] Though there is a general belief that Tagore was awarded the Nobel Prize on the basis of *Gitanjali* (1912, Song Offerings), the poet's own poetic prose translations of 103 songs, with an ecstatic introduction by W. B. Yeats, this study notes that the Nobel Library had several other works by Tagore and had a full account of his illustrious family, his multifaceted talents and his pioneering work in education and rural uplift (which are mentioned in the Nobel citation). In 1913 Tagore was already a household word in his native Bengal for his writing, and was well known for his early association with the Swadeshi movement – a nationalist struggle in the early twentieth century promoting home-grown industries and goods – his public lectures, his educational project at Shantiniketan and as a remarkably talented son of the highly respected Tagore family. With the Nobel Prize, Tagore became a global figure and was recognized as a bilingual writer, as he took to writing several of his essays and lectures in English while continuing his creative output in Bengali. He soon became internationally known as, simply, the Poet. He continued writing and working on his various projects right up to his death in 1941. No other poet has had his songs adopted as national anthems of two countries (India and Bangladesh) and inspired a third one (in Sri Lanka).

Tagore's body of work remains staggering, as he wrote not only poetry, but novels, short fiction, plays, essays, dance dramas, lyrics, lectures, primers, innumerable letters, science pamphlets and sermons. He was a lyricist, a composer, a critic, a translator, an artist, a historian, a philosopher and an environmentalist. He was also an educationist who established a school, an international university, Visva-Bharati at Shantiniketan, a rural reconstruction centre at Sriniketan and cooperatives on his estates, in what is a remarkably comprehensive programme of creative achievement.[2]

In order to understand Tagore's creativity and vast output, he needs to be placed against his familial background. The Tagore family was exceptional not only because of its sociocultural dominance and its economic contribution to Bengal, but because of the multiple talents of its various members through the generations, who provided the rich cultural atmosphere that marked Tagore's early years at his family home at Jorasanko, north Calcutta. Jorasanko was a veritable hive of creativity and experiment, where tradition and modernity, Eastern and Western modes of thought, culture and art forms, were cultivated and transfused at the time of the Bengal Renaissance, in which the Tagore family played a leading role. The close family relations who nurtured and encouraged Rabindranath in diverse spheres and at different periods of his life, whose impetus and influence shaped and facilitated his creativity, become crucial to an engagement with the times and the man himself: his father, Maharshi Debendranath; his fifth brother, the dynamic Jyotirindranath, and his wife, Rabindranath's sister-in-law, Kadambari, who was his muse and literary critic; his wife and companion Mrinalini; his artistic niece, Indira Devi; and his agriculturist and environmentalist son Rathindranath – all

A contemporary image of Jorasanko Thakurbari.

were important to Rabindranath Tagore's life. The Tagore family's significant socio-political role as India moved from the position of a subservient nation to one rediscovering, reviving and reaffirming its heritage becomes the backdrop in an assessment of Tagore's unswerving belief in freedom at all levels, emotional, political and creative.

This inherent sense of freedom can be traced back to the socio-religious ostracism the family suffered as Pirali Brahmins. It is believed that their ancestors had inadvertently compromised their caste status, and thus fallen from grace, during an unfortunate incident when they were guests in a Muslim house. The resulting social aspersion accounts for the entrepreneurial diversions made by the Tagore family, as they sought their fortunes and an anchor beyond their native place, beyond constricting social boundaries. Tagore's questioning of orthodoxy and authoritarianism, both patriarchal and political; his attacks on superstitious beliefs, social evils and divisions; and his transformation of his educational institution from a Bramhacharya institution to a modern one, marked by its secular curriculum and activity, can be seen as an inevitable result of his upbringing and environment.[3]

With Tagore's love of freedom came an abhorrence of violence, which can be seen in his firm belief in dialogue as the true solution to the smoothening of differences between sociocultural groups and nations. This is evident in his writing, as well as his turning away from the later violence of the Swadeshi movement; his public debates with Gandhi on the problematic nature of using non-violence as a political weapon; and his lectures and talks as a self-appointed Peace Warrior after the Nobel Prize, as the First World War destroyed a known, familiar world and a generation. It is also apparent in his choosing to speak against narrow nationalism, militarization, imperial expansionism and the dangers of unfettered capitalism during the interwar years. While Gandhi adopted non-cooperation as a political strategy for effective decolonization, Tagore practised cooperation in his own familial estates and through his rural reconstruction centre, and urged for cooperation between the dominant and subservient, powerful and beleaguered nations. Tagore was the first Easterner who took on the global ambassadorial role of bridging the gap that existed between the West and the East. He asserted that the East had something to offer the West which could prove beneficial, and that nations could come together through mutual respect, cooperation and exchange.

Tagore, like Gandhi, saw India's strength and unity in diversity, and believed that India had survived over centuries through accommodation, and could continue to thrive through social inclusion and acceptance, which found a voice in his writing and his pragmatic projects. This sense of accommodation finds expression in Tagore's belief in continuing the Indian tradition of hospitality, welcoming the visitor/foreigner and engendering an atmosphere of interchange. However, Tagore was beset by a restlessness which marks the Tagorean family members, both women and men, who challenged social boundaries, political subjectivity and cultural narrowness. In Tagore's case, he moved from house to house, from land to river, traversing the country and setting sail across the ocean, making multiple journeys which made him aware not only of his nation's and the world's diversity, but of the similarities between people, between like-minded individuals. He reached out and communicated with leading intellectuals, artists and leaders of his time and interacted with students at various universities. The luminaries he interacted with were national and international, including Sir Jagadish Chandra Bose, Mahatma Gandhi and Jawaharlal Nehru (independent India's first Prime Minister) at home, and Thomas Sturge Moore (who nominated him for the Nobel Prize), William Rothenstein, Romain Rolland, Albert Einstein, William Butler Yeats, Ezra Pound, Patrick Geddes, Margaret Noble (Sister Nivedita), Count Keyserling, John Maynard Kaynes, Helen Keller, Victoria Ocampo, Carlo Formichi, Benedetto Croce, Ananda Coomaraswamy, Kakuzo Okakura, Yone Noguchi, Tan Yun Shan, Tan Seyn and Zhu Peong abroad. He worked with Sylvain Lévi, Moriz Winternitz, Leonard Elmhirst, W. W. Pearson, Edward Thompson and Charles Freer Andrews, who met him in his own domain. As a transnational citizen and writer, he strove to create a less divided world through mutual understanding, building on national and international friendships and journeys, signifying his cosmopolitanism. He was both a national and an international figure and writer, embracing his home and the world.

Tagore was further distinguished by his rootedness. At an early age, entrusted with the responsibility of looking after his family estates by his father, he encountered the apathy and sense of hopelessness and helplessness among the rural folk in his native Bengal. He was shocked into action to bring social justice and economic improvement through his *zamindari* (landlord) role and through rural regeneration programmes which he hoped would be a stimulus for similar programmes across India. At another level, he worked to free young minds in his own institution through freedom of thought and creative activity, adopting an interdisciplinary system that sought to bring the humanities, social sciences and sciences together in a holistic education, in an international university where he initiated knowledge exchange.

Yet, though he was hailed first as the Eastern sage/mystic and as a poet-philosopher, his reputation and reception have been erratic, swerving from adulation to rejection, and even indifference. The interest in Tagore has come in waves, the first being soon after the Nobel Prize in 1913, then around his seventieth birthday in 1931, resulting in Ramananda Chatterji's edited volume *The Golden Book of Tagore* published that same year, in which great minds from across the world wrote paeans to the Poet. The centenary of Tagore's birthday in 1961 saw a small flurry of celebrations spearheaded by the government of India and in his native Bengal. However, in 2011–12, during the 150th anniversary of Tagore's birthday, the government of India took on the task of reviving global interest in Tagore. This has seen a resurgence of interest in Tagore's work and ideas, which remain more powerful and relevant than ever today, as the world is riven by divisive politics, violence and the rise of right-wing ideology. So Tagore's appearance on the world stage has been like a comet – he appeared like a spark of illumination and then disappeared, almost forgotten. In his time, Tagore was an international phenomenon, as his meetings and friendships with national and international figures, his unstoppable pen, activism and practical projects portray.[4] Yet there have been moments of near silence and even ignorance in the decades since his death, not just of his writing, but of his very person and legacy. This sliding scale of response to Tagore's person and work is what needs to be revisited, explored and reassessed.

Even during his time, he was often a lonely, isolated figure, working and speaking against popular beliefs and ideas. He was knighted in 1915 by the British Crown, but relinquished his knighthood as a mark of protest against the Amritsar Massacre in 1919 (a resignation which was never accepted), after which he was never held above suspicion. He had his literary detractors at home and abroad, and at various points in his career he was considered a dangerous radical by the government in India, which warned government employees against sending their wards to study at his institution and funders from supporting his pragmatic projects. The government machinery was sometimes responsible for the cold response by the press in Britain and America, and affected official opinion, which created obstacles to his acceptance on his lecturing journeys abroad. His audiences could move from unbridled enthusiasm to undisguised hostility when he continued to speak his mind against heady modernization, fast-paced industrialization, materialism and foreign political domination. And Tagore was acutely sensitive to scathing criticism. He could be prickly about responses when his message was misconstrued, and he could suddenly cut short his scheduled lectures and meetings when confronted with negative reports of his mission and purpose. What are of interest here are considerations such as how this widely feted Nobel Laureate became unfashionable in the post-war years. How have the interim years between the resurgent waves of interest in Tagore seen a near oblivion of his work? Was it, as Jawaharlal Nehru has said, because he was decades ahead of his time?

This biographical study reassesses this Renaissance man, a polymath, who embodies the modern consciousness of India, engaged as he was in nation building and contributing to the narrative of a nation. Tagore's life and work are inseparable, so an analytical reappraisal of the familial, socio-political and cultural background provides a prism through which one can understand Tagore as a writer, artist and pragmatist. The fact that he draws on his Indian past, uses the Upanishadic tenets, weighs the contingency of the current times and is eclectic in the way he values and imbibes Western values and technological and scientific development shows how he provided within himself an infusion that embodies progress.

Tagore was open to new ideas and trends in literature, art and music, which he transformed and informed with his own mastery and style, and introduced into Bengali literature. His writing, songs and art carry the burden of the times as they convey the changing role of a thinker and activist who related to and worked with the world as it evolved around him. A large body of his work has been translated into India's several languages and into European and Asian languages. Leading poets translated him in his time, such as André Gide, Juan Ramón Jiménez and his American wife, Zenobia Camprubí Aymar, Frederik van Eeden and Raden Mas Noto Soeroto. More recently scholars like William Radice and Martin Kämpchen have translated him into English and German, respectively, validating the power of his writing. *Gitanjali* remains one of his most translated books and has never gone out of print.

His work is multifaceted and progressive, which becomes apparent in an evaluation of his life. For a fuller understanding of the poet's ambivalences and misreadings or misjudgements, the unfolding events in his life in regard to the world need to be scrutinized in order to throw light on some of his apparently puzzling actions and responses. In this connection, the most striking aspect of Tagore is his willingness to revise his opinion when proven wrong by the confrontation with 'truth', as is evident in his conflicting estimations of Mussolini, which shows how he was unwilling to compromise his intellectual integrity.[5]

Tagore was much more than a writer; he was a composer and musician, having established his own brand of songs, Rabindra-sangeet. His contribution to the enrichment of the Bengali language, his modernization of Bengali literature – as he minimized the gap between classical and spoken Bengali – and his gathering, recording and refining folk tales, verse, popular rhymes and songs all point to his role as a national bard. He was an innovator, creating the dance drama, the prose poem, the short story in Bengali and his own brand of opera, and he was a remarkable artist who took to his brush late in life, leaving a body of work that is both disturbing and powerful as he responded to the climate of conflict in the interwar years. He was, as he himself said, modern, acutely conscious of and willing to reassess and adjust to the changing times.

Jawaharlal Nehru said he had two gurus: Mahatma Gandhi and Rabindranath Tagore. Ashis Nandy has observed that what Nehru did not say was that while Gandhi was Nehru's political guru, Rabindranath was his intellectual guru.[6] Both men stood by the tenets of truth, love and compassion as central to their deep humanism. Today Gandhi and Tagore are considered India's greatest thinkers and leaders, who have shaped modern India and, in Gandhi's case, influenced several political leaders, such as Nelson Mandela. India's debt to Tagore is immense, and together with Mahatma Gandhi he remains one of the architects of modern India and India's primary soft power. Tagore's liberal humanism and modernity make him relevant today and his place in world literature can be endorsed by a close study of his life, times and work.

IMPORTANT NOTE: In this book I have referred to 'Shantiniketan', keeping in mind the palatal 'sh' (as in 'Shanti' in Sanskrit), which is the way it has always been pronounced. However, wherever references are made to 'Santiniketan' in quotations, I have retained the spelling which pertains to Tagore's times and official references.

1
The Tagores of Jorasanko

Rabindranath Tagore was born 7 May 1861 at Jorasanko, the family seat of the Tagores, in Bengal, in the Mechhuabazar area of north Calcutta (now Kolkata), the capital of British India until 1911–12. He was the fourteenth child of Debendranath Tagore and Sarada Devi and their youngest surviving son (the fifteenth child, a son, died very young). Though his birth seemed insignificant, as his mother was by then very tired after her multiple pregnancies, he was born after a major watershed in Indian history, following the Indian Revolt (1857–8) and the assumption of power by the crown from the East India Company of the Indian Presidencies in 1858, which then became the British Provinces. The Bengal Province included Orissa, Bihar and Bengal, and Calcutta was considered the second city of Empire. In a speech he made to Chinese students years later, Tagore recalls his birth as occurring on an epochal cusp of change: 'Our house was a huge, sprawling traditional house . . . I did not witness all the customary bustle of festivities through the seasons. When I came, the old times had just receded as a new era descended, though its paraphernalia had not yet arrived.'[1]

It is important to understand the family background of the Tagores in the perspective of changing times. Jorasanko, known as Thakurbari, the House of the Tagores, was founded by Tagore's ancestor, Nilmoni Kushari, in 1784. As a leading family of Bengal, the legends around it are numerous and part of the popular imagination. The Tagores are called Pirali Brahmins, who were ostracized by Brahminical Bengal. Rabindranath's story begins with Maheshwar Kushari's son, Panchanan Kushari, who, with his uncle Sukdev, came to Gobindapur on the Adi Ganga river, a distributary of the Ganges, looking for a livelihood. This was at the time of Job Charnock, who had bought the three villages – Kalikata, Sutanuti and Gobindapur – which would become the nucleus of Calcutta, the main trading port in East India, where the Dutch, Portuguese, French and English collided in a global market. This brisk trading station was home to fishing castes, like Jele and Malo, and some business castes. They welcomed Brahmins amid them and in reverence addressed them as 'Thakur', the revered Brahmin. Panchanan Kushari picked up French and English in his dealings with the dominant traders, as he supplied the vessels with provisions, thus amassing a fortune. The English assumed that 'Thakur' was his surname and their mispronunciation altered it to Tagore. This is how Panchanan Kushari was transformed into Panchanan Tagore.

Panchanan Tagore's two sons, Jayram and Ramsantosh, learnt English and French from trading with English and French businessmen and on their father's recommendation to the Collector, Ralph Seldon, were appointed as Amins (Pay Masters).[2] Jayram had four sons: Anandaram, Nilmoni, Darpanarayan and Gobindaram. In 1756, when Siraj-ud-daula attacked Calcutta, the Tagore family suffered financially. After 1757 Mir Zaffar, whom the British instated as Siraj-ud-daula's successor, gave Nilmoni Tagore Rs 18,000 as compensation. Nilmoni was a Dewan of the East India Company, which controlled the Bengal Presidency of Bengal, Bihar and Orissa. He later became Record Keeper for Orissa's Collectorate, sending money to his brother Darpanarayan. Darpanarayan was the Dewan of Wheeler. The death of Jayram's son Gobindaram led his wife, Rampriya Devi, to ask for the division of the property at the Supreme Court and won two houses in Radhabzar and Jackson Ghat. This led to a schism in the Tagore family. This is when an established businessman of the area, Baishnabcharan Seth, gifted one bigha (approximately ⅓ of an acre) at Mechhuabazar to Nilmoni – where Jorasanko was built.

This triangular confluence of Muslim, Hindu and English shaped the history of the Tagores, their social isolation leading to their wandering spirit, their entrepreneurship, their intrepid ventures into fresh business projects, as they searched for an anchor, which made them what they were, cosmopolitan in outlook, at home in the world.[3]

However, the socio-religious ostracism meant that the Tagore family found it difficult to find husbands for their daughters and daughters-in-law for their sons. As the family hailed from Jessore, most of their daughters-in-law came from this district where the Tagore family had influence. It was customary for girls in those days to marry when they were very young and come to live in their in-laws' home, to be moulded by the family that became theirs. The Tagore household was no exception and maintained this practice. The Tagore family had the practice of keeping their sons-in-law resident as part of this teeming household and their wealth was an effective enticement.

Nilmoni's son Ramlochan, who had no male heir, adopted his brother Rammoni's son, Dwarkanath (1794–1846).[4] At his family home, Ramlochan was known for the musical soirées he held, where he invited classical singers and poets, an atmosphere into which Dwarkanath was born and raised. Ramlochan set up a Trust consisting of his wife, Aloka Devi, and his brother Radhanath, who on Ramlochan's death in 1807 managed the estate for the thirteen-year-old Dwarkanath until he came of age.[5]

Unleashed from orthodox social boundaries and driven from close social associations with the known, familiar world, the Tagores experienced an unsolicited freedom, which perhaps explains their exploits beyond existing 'norms' set by Hindu Brahmin strictures of social acceptability. With hindsight, this was probably the climate that created Dwarkanath Tagore's boundless spirit, which led him to build a business empire that was rooted in the local but embraced the global. This contact with the world beyond narrow walls of rigorous ritual, dictated by caste and fears of 'pollution', opened up the horizon for a family that was lively, imaginative and creative, living the Renaissance, as they participated in and led the debates on sociocultural change.

Ramlochan's faith in Dwarkanath's mettle and vision proved to be canny and prudent. Ramlochan had admitted Dwarkanath to Sherbourne's school in Calcutta, embracing the new by initiating his adopted son into an English education. Dwarkanath showed his gratitude to his English master, Sherbourne, by granting him a monthly income until his death. Dwarkanath was also taught by several Scottish teachers: William Adams, J. G. Gordon and James Calder; later on he became well versed in law under the guidance of Barrister Fergusson. However, the Tagores maintained their traditional education. Dwarkanath was conversant in Pharsi and Bengali.

The title of Krishna Kripalani's biography *Dwarkanath Tagore, A Forgotten Pioneer: A Life* (1981) sums up Dwarkanath's achievements and contribution to modern India. His business career started with him working for Mackintosh & Co, which owned Commercial Bank. He became Record Keeper for the 24 Parganas Collectorate in 1818 and in 1822 he was appointed the Dewan of Plowden's Collectorate. In 1829 he established the first Indian bank – the Union Bank. When Mackintosh & Co failed in 1833, he was the only solvent shareholder there. He resigned from his government position and set up Carr, Tagore & Co, the first Indo-British company with equal partnership between European and Indian businessmen. His company was the trading agent of the Steam Tug Association. Dwarkanath's business acumen led him to succeed in diverse ventures: he had coal mines and sugar factories; he traded in silk, indigo, sugar, salt and saltpetre; he was on the Opium and Tax Board and had several steamboats

Dwarkanath Tagore, undated.

which traded with other countries. He even set up a factory to repair steamships. Alongside his business enterprise, he continued to invest in land and added to the family estates in Shahjadpur, Birahimpur, Kaligram, Shelidah and Pandua, thus strengthening the Tagores' landholdings, which proved to be a prescient move. Many years later, his youngest grandson, Rabindranath, would inherit the responsibility of looking after these family estates, which he did with his dedicated humanist approach.

At home Dwarkanath was a Vaishnava who followed a strict diet of abstinence from meat and alcohol. Outside, Dwarkanath met the world on its own terms. Dwarkanath continued his father's tradition of holding musical soirées and feasts for invited guests. There was an *andarmahal* where the Tagore women dwelt, and there was the outer house, the *bahirmahal*, where guests came and business transactions were made. In order to entertain his foreign friends, Dwarkanath furnished his Baithakkhana house with luxurious furniture, using it as a public meeting place where he invited, among others, Miss Eden, Governor General Auckland's sister, and Lady Bentinck. Here the best of classical Indian vocal and instrumental music and Western instrumental music found expression, and lavish meals were served while the wine flowed freely. However, Dwarkanath's compatriots complained that he was more solicitous towards his foreign guests, which he immediately rectified by inviting his Indian friends to taste his remarkable hospitality. (His philanthropy and lavish hospitality earned him the title of Prince Dwarkanath Tagore.) Indeed, his spurning of superstitious beliefs and rituals and his adoption of Western-style food habits in his life outside Jorasanko alienated his wife, Digambari, who decided to cut off all ties with her husband. Dwarkanath then removed himself from his household and took up residence in his Baithakkhana House.

Dwarkanath's business success enabled him to amass vast wealth, which was not just spent on lavish entertainment. On meeting the socio-religious reformer Raja Rammonhan Roy (22 years his senior), who was a visionary and modernist, and who is now considered the 'Father of Modern India', Dwarkanath became his greatest supporter and admirer. With Raja Rammohan Roy, Dwarkanath spearheaded the Bengal Renaissance, a reform movement which influenced socio-religious, cultural and educational spheres that would transform Bengal and have a pan-India effect.

He helped with the establishment of the Bramho Sabha, a movement advocating Monotheism, that rejected rituals and idol worship, resisted Brahminical dominance and held debates on Vedanta. With Raja Rammohan Roy, he worked to abolish the act of widow immolation, Sati, and succeeded in seeing legislative acts against many social evils passed – including the Sati Abolition Act of 1829.[6] Their advocacy for widow remarriage bore fruit under Dwarkanath's son Debendranath's leadership in an act passed in 1856.[7]

In order to safeguard the interest of landlords, Dwarkanath founded the Landholders' Society in 1838, which later became the British Indian Association, and his son, Debendranath, was the secretary of this association between 1851 and 1854. The British Indian Association had a broader class base, lobbying for diverse interests. Dwarkanath also sought to amend the Chaukidari Act, the Land Reforms Act and the Salt Act. He was instrumental in sending a dispatch to the British Parliament seeking greater representation of Indians in the proposed self-governance scheme on local councils.[8]

Rammohan Roy was also a strong advocate of an English education, which the British East India Company had not invested in or shown any interest in developing, as it allowed the Sanskrit Toll-Madrasa style of education (vernacular education) to continue. But Rammohan Roy saw that English education would open doors to a world of global knowledge, of science, justice, philosophy and literature, and thus urged the government to introduce English education in Bengal. Rammonhan Roy had established the Anglo-Hindu School in 1831, where Dwarkanath sent his son Debendranath.

With Roy, Dwarkanath became intricately involved in establishing and supporting multiple pioneering educational institutions, which included Hindu College and the Medical College and Hospital. His powerful position lent impetus to these institutions, and he took on the task himself of addressing ingrained Hindu reservations against dissection by being present at some such sessions. Dwarkanath's philanthropic generosity was overwhelming. His financial support touched various aspects of Indian society. He gave stipends to medical students and paid for two students to accompany him on his first voyage to England in 1842; he even supported their further medical training. His example encouraged the Indian government to fund two more medical students on this voyage. Several organizations like the Calcutta District Charitable Trust and the Hindu Benevolent Institution benefitted from his benevolence.[9]

With Rammohan Roy, Dwarkanath was a leading light of the Bengal Renaissance. He was a member of the Asiatic Society, founded by Sir William Jones in 1784, and subsequently Dwarkanath was involved in the establishment of the Archaeological Survey of India, the Zoological Survey of India, the Botanical and Geological Survey of India and the Agricultural and Horticultural Society.[10]

Dwarkanath was probably feeling restless as his mentor Raja Rammohan Roy had left for England, crossing the feared 'black waters'. Dwarkanath's estranged wife, Digambari Devi, died in 1839. His bonds had now been broken. He set sail on 9 January 1842 for England with his nephew Chandramohan. In the West he was feted with fanfare by royalty, aristocracy and other dignitaries. He was received by Queen Victoria, and the Duke of Norfolk made him Armourial Ensign. The Municipality of Edinburgh made him a Freeman of the City, a unique gesture towards someone who was from a subject nation. In France Emperor Louis Philippe welcomed him. He returned all these honours in style, fulfilling his appellation of 'Prince'. In fact, in Paris he is known to have hosted a dinner, draping the walls with Kashmiri shawls, which he then gifted the guests when they were departing.

Once he returned home to Calcutta, Dwarkanath met with disapproval and hostility from certain quarters of Hindu society. Moreover, he did not feel the same enthusiasm and energy with which he had expended his many businesses before his departure to England. It is perhaps because of this inability to feel settled that he started once again on 8 March 1845 for England. This time he took his youngest son, Nagendranath, his nephew Nabinchandra Mukhopadhyay and four medical students, whose expenses were covered by Dwarkanath. Before his departure he made a will, dividing his property between his sons, leaving his Jorasanko house and his share of Carr, Tagore Company with Debendranath and Rs 100,000 for the welfare of the poor. This was a judicious move as Dwarkanath was not to return home from England this time, as he died in Surrey on 1 August 1845 at the age of 52, thus ending an era. Dwarkanath had built bridges between the past and the present in India, opening the way to a future of global contact and enterprise for Indians. He carried his forefathers' association and exchange with foreign traders and businessmen to a level of equal entrepreneurship with the colonizer, as he won their respect and admiration. He addressed and overcame the hiatus between home and the world on a personal level.

His son Debendranath was initially drawn into his father's world of sparkle and splendour. But he was close to his grandmother, a deeply religious lady and a strict vegetarian whose life was measured out in rituals, fasting and abstinence. From her, Debendranath heard the sacred verses and spent a lot of his time in the women's quarters. The Tagore women remained in purdah during Dwarkanath's time, confined to the *andarmahal*, while all the transactions with the outside world were conducted by the men in the outer house, the *bahirmahal*. Debendranath was torn between these two worlds.[11] He attended Hindu College from 1831 after the teacher Henry Derozio had been dismissed. The influence of Derozio's followers, a group called the Young Bengal, was still strong in their vociferous dismissal of traditional Hindu ways and Bengali culture and literature; the group espoused Western ways, symbolized by eating beef and drinking alcohol. Debendranath's response to this aggressive brand of anglicization was a staunch avowal to support Bengali language and literature. He set up the Sarvatattwadipika Sabha, an association where the proceedings were conducted solely in Bengali, unlike the Derozians' Academic Association where all discussions were in English. When he later established the Tattvabodhini Sabha, one can detect its nucleus in Debendranath's earlier Sabha. Debendranath's love of and dedication to Bengali literature and culture would be central to Tagore's creative experience and expression.

Debendranath was very different from his father, his otherworldliness in sharp contrast to his father's robust enjoyment of life; however, there is no evidence of any hostility between the two. Rabindranath seems to have struck a balance between the two in his own social engagement with life, his romantic attachment to nature and society, his spirituality and secularism.

Dwarkanath was aware of his son's lack of interest in the business world. He tried to induct him as the assistant cashier at his Union Bank, where Debendranath was punctual, diligent and efficient, but his enthusiasm for his father's various investments was not ignited by this experience. When his father died in 1845, Debendranath was 29 years old. His father's untimely death meant that the extent of his debts as a result of his lavish lifestyle and philanthropy led to Carr, Tagore & Co. shutting down. Debendranath called all his father's creditors and told them that he knew that legally they had no rights over the Tagore property, but he was handing it over to them until he had paid off the debts with interest. His integrity astounded them, as the decision made the Tagore family penniless. The creditors arranged for the family to receive a monthly allowance and soon after handed the management of the landed estates back to Debendranath's capable hands – a responsibility which he fulfilled with high moral principles, paying back all his father's debts to the last penny. Debendranath never returned to the business and trade that his father had invested in, but ensured that the Tagore family was comfortably well off with the income from the landed property. Rabindranath, whom his father entrusted later with the management of the Tagore family estates, inherited his father's ability to sustain his family, while bringing his own social commitment to the betterment of his tenants.

Debendranath was troubled as he observed the practices of the Hindu religion, however. One day, while he was sitting at home, a torn page from a book flew near him which he reached out and caught. On it were Sanskrit words he did not understand.[12] He sent for the famous Sanskrit scholar Ramchandra Vidyabagish, the preceptor of the Bramho Sabha founded by Rammohan Roy. Vidyabagish identified the source of the verse as from the *Ishapanishad*, one of the Upanishads, and explained the meaning: 'All this, whatever moves in this moving world, is enveloped by God. Therefore find your enjoyment in renunciation; do not covet what belongs to others.'[13] After that, Debendranath took lessons in reading the Upanishads, a knowledge and regard he passed on to Rabindranath, who, like his father, was deeply influenced by their philosophy. Debendranath was also a Persian scholar and a great lover of Hafiz, whose work he read regularly alongside his reading in English and Bengali.

The great Hindu Bengali religious festival dedicated to Durga, the mother goddess, is Durga Puja, celebrated annually in late autumn.[14] It is held with great pomp and splendour, and is the highlight of the year in a five-day celebration. Debendranath, who felt that the truth had been revealed to him about divine creation and the meaning and purpose of human life, gathered his family together and announced that henceforth the Tagore household would give up idol worship and rituals, and instead practise and propagate the Bramho way: its monotheism, its freedom from superstition and its liberal values based on the Upanishads. It was a bold step and drove a wedge through the Tagore household as one section of the family segregated itself from the Bramho ways and continued to hold Hindu festivals. The move further isolated the Tagore family from mainstream society. It was a benchmark decision and a difficult one, but this very special family rallied around the patriarch's decision and the Tagore household became the seat of the religious reform movement that was to seep into the sociocultural consciousness of Bengal, rejecting and resisting orthodox Hinduism. The dissenting voices of the Bramho activists expressed in the journal *Tattwabodhini Patrika* (established in 1843), which was to play a central role in confronting the challenges of transformation on the socio-religious front, took forward the ideas of Raja Rammohan Roy and Dwarkanath, under the leadership of Debendranath at the high tide of the Bengal Renaissance.

Debendranath set up self-funded Tattwabodhini Pathsalas (primary schools) in Calcutta and in the adjoining districts of 24 Parganas and Nadia, which taught the tenets of the Bramho faith alongside other subjects. The impetus lent by Dwarkanath to education was thus continued, albeit in a different vein by Debendranath. The two influences of the East and the West, Indian tradition and English studies, respectively, would find expression in Rabindranath's educational institutions at Shantiniketan, continuing the Tagore family's contribution to education.

Shantiniketan needs a mention here. Debendranath was close to the Sinhas of Raipur in Bengal, and often visited their property in Bolpur. On one of his travels he was fascinated by a vast tract of land called Bhubandangar Math, which had a few mango groves and straggling bushes. A solitary *chhatim* tree drew his attention. He asked the palanquin bearers transporting him to stop and he sat under the tree to meditate. An inexplicable peace descended upon him and he sought to buy twenty bighas of this land from the Sinhas; he named it Shantiniketan, the abode of peace. It was here that he built a *mandir* (temple) for Bramho worship and in 1886 he set up a trust with three trustees, charging them with setting this land aside for an ashram serving as a Bramho retreat. This would become the nucleus of Tagore's school and international university where the Bramho way of life would be initiated. Religious festivals were replaced by folk festivals like the spring festival (Basanta Utsav) and the autumn festival (Sarat Utsav), and folk customs like Briksha Ropan and Halakarshan (tree planting and ploughing ceremony, respectively).

Debendranath and his wife, Sarada Devi, had fifteen children. Sarada Devi had the responsibility of the sprawling Tagore home and the Tagore household, consisting of her own children, the extended family, numerous helping hands and a stream of visitors

Maharshi Debendranath Tagore, undated.

to look after. Her supervision was meticulous and efficient, but it did not leave her time to care for her children in this bustling household. However, her tact and intelligence kept this family of kith and kin together, qualities which her daughters-in-law would have to imbibe in order to keep alive the Tagore household's tradition of familial living and hospitality. In spite of having a troop of servants, the women of the Tagore household cooked, served meals and were actively involved in various creative activities in the household. In fact, the Tagore household's cuisine was distinctive for its excellent flavours and variety. Sarada Devi personally saw to the procurement of food items and supervised and helped in the busy kitchen. While Debendranath went on his many long journeys, Sarada Devi was left as the eldest daughter-in-law to look after the complex household and hold it together. When her husband took up the leadership of the Bramho Samaj and introduced religious reforms at home and society, it must have been difficult for Sarada Devi to give up her long-held beliefs and rituals, but she remained a close, supportive companion of Debendranath, bravely giving up celebrating Durga Puja and other Hindu festivals, which had punctuated Bengali life over generations, as she accepted the Bramho way of life. Her multiple pregnancies left her little time to look after her children personally. She also suffered the tragedy of seeing some of her children die prematurely.[15] Her surviving children's contribution to the Bengal Renaissance emphasizes the atmosphere of creativity, debate and change that Tagore was born into and experienced as he grew up.

Sarada Devi's second child, a son, Dwijendranath (1840–1926), was a poet, lyricist, composer, mathematician and philosopher and a specialist in Western philosophy. He translated the Sanskrit *Meghdut* by Kalidas into Bengali. His experiments with poetic verse deeply influenced Tagore. His allegorical long poem *Swapnaprayan* (Dream Journey) remains a classic in Bengali literature. He invented Bengali shorthand (writing a manual for it) and musical notations.

He wrote several articles on serious issues for *Tattwabodhini Patrika* and was the first editor of the journal *Bharati*, established by his brother Jyotirindranath in 1877, whose editorship Tagore was to take up some years later. He dedicated his life later on to the educational institution Tagore founded at Shantiniketan, and was a much-loved and valued presence there. In fact, many of Tagore's nephews and grand-nephews, some descended from Dwijendranath, worked with dedication at Tagore's ashram – the school at Shantiniketan – enriching it with their creative talents.

Sarada Devi and Debendranath's second son, Satyendranath (1842–1923), retraced his grandfather's journey to Britain when he was eighteen. He was the first Indian to enter the ICS (Indian Civil Service), joining it in 1868. Like his eldest brother, he was well versed in Bengali and Sanskrit. His Bengali works include translations of *Gita*, the first translated verse into Bengali of Marathi poetry (the fruit of his first posting in Bombay), and his autobiographies, *Amar Balyakatha O Bombay Prabas, Bombay Chitra* and *Raja Rammohan Roy*. He also translated his father's autobiography into English with his daughter, Indira Devi.

The Tagore women lived in the *andarmahal*, the inner house, practising *aborodh*, purdah. The Tagore family was one of the first to encourage their women to step over the threshold – from the home into the world, breaking years of seclusion. Satyendranath was the intiator of freedoms for women, setting the trend as he groomed his young bride, Jnanadanandini, to join him in his life in the public sphere. He had observed and imbibed various ideas about women's education and independence from his stay in England. He educated Jnanadanandini in Bengali and English, and taught her the deportment of Victorian women. The story goes that he took Jnanadanandini in an open horse carriage through the streets of Calcutta without her veil, which startled and scandalized the city. Earlier, daughters-in-law of the Tagore household stayed at Jorasanko if their husbands travelled or worked

Sarada Devi, mother of Rabindranath Tagore.

away from home. When Satyendranath was posted to Bombay, he sought Debendranath's consent to take Jnanadanandini with him. At first Debendranath resisted. No daughter-in-law of the Tagore household had left its precincts to live elsewhere. But Satyendranath's insistence to spend his professional life in his wife's company – as his postings would always be away from home – compelled his father to give his consent.[16] Satyendranath was responsible for ushering in a new era into the household, his experiences in England having opened his horizon to the reality of modern times.

In fact, the Tagore house was witness to change as each generation expressed itself, its personal beliefs and attitudes affecting the very ambience of the rooms of Jorasanko and the dress of its inhabitants. From Dwarkanath's time, Western furniture – tables, chairs, sofas and so on – adorned both Jorasanko and the Belgachia garden residence. Dwarkanath was well known for his princely attire. When Debendranath inherited his father's debts, he adopted austerity to counter poverty and the luxurious lifestyle of the Tagore household was altered to one of simplicity at every level. Debendranath himself dressed like a sage. His sons responded in different ways to the question of personal dress and furnished their rooms with a mix of East and West, as Hindu, Muslim and Western styles found expression in their daily life. The men wore pyjamas, an upper tunic called an *aachkan*, a *choga*, a *chapkan* (a long sleeved, long skirted cloak and a long coat, repectively) and a *pugree* (turban). At home, the furnishings included traditional four-poster beds, beautiful mats, bolsters, Mughal-style hookahs and Western carpets. An organ had been bought in Debendranath's time. The syncretism born of a triadic confluence was thus evident in every fold of life in the Tagore household.

Debendranath's third son, Hemendranath (1844–1884), is best known for his love of the Bengali language. While the waves of English education surged through the city, Hemendranath set up tuition at home in Bengali for his younger siblings and cousins, engendering a love of the Bengali lanaguage and literature in the younger generation, something for which Rabindranath would be always grateful to this brother, who was, as he said, 'a hard task master'.[17]

Debendranath's fifth son was Jyotirindranath (1849–1925), also known as 'Jyotidada' or 'Natunda', as Tagore called him.

Dwarkanath's flamboyance seems to have skipped a generation and found expression in this grandson who dressed in style, tried several business ventures and had a zest for life like his grandfather. However, he did not have his grandfather's business acumen, so his various projects, like shipping and the making of home-grown matchsticks, failed, and his debts mounted. In his autobiography, *Jibansmriti*, he says that after his second brother Satyendranath came back from England, it was as if a flood of change had swept through the Tagore household, as modern furniture, dress, attitudes and behaviour were introduced, a change that Jyotirindranath embraced willingly. He initiated the Tagore family journal, *Bharati*, of which Dwijendranath was an editor. He was a talented playwright and feverishly wrote plays based on Indian history, myth and legend, directing them himself and having them enacted in the Tagore household for his family and friends, in which his family members, including the women, acted – another innovative move for women in the Tagore household. Rabindranath was fascinated as a child by the stage performances (which he watched surreptitiously from a distance, as he was not allowed to be part of these night-time revelries). Later he acted in them, an experience which ignited his own creativity in playwriting, the composition of dance dramas and his own role in them. Jyotirindranath was a gifted musician who played the violin and piano and composed music. He was also an artist, and many of the portraits of the Tagore family are attributed to him.

Though thirteen years older than Rabindranath, Jyotirindranath, with his young wife Kadambari, took young Tagore into their circle, and he became a valued companion. They urged him to sing, write and compose with Jyotirindranath and his talented friend Akshay Chaudhuri. The trio of men spent hours at the piano, singing and composing as Bouthan (as she was called by Tagore, meaning 'brother's wife') watched, appreciated and nurtured them, plying them with her delicious, imaginatively prepared snacks and *paan* (betel leaf).

Tagore's eldest sister, Saudamini (1847–1920), was a motherly figure, who cared for little Rabindranath after the birth of his mother's fourteenth child and the birth and death of her fifteenth child had left the matriarch exhausted. Saudamini later devotedly looked after Debendranath in his old age.[18]

Sarada Devi's fourth daughter, Swarnakumari (1856–1932), was the first Bengali woman novelist. Well known in Bengali literary circles, Swarnakumari's novels have been translated into English. She also wrote short stories, poetry and plays and was an accomplished musician. Her marriage in 1867 was conducted using the Bramho rites newly improvised by Debendranath, a bold step in his time. She was married to Janakinath Ghoshal, a liberal Bengali who broke the Tagore tradition of a live-in son-in-law and the Bengali tradition of living in an extended family, and set up his own establishment with his nuclear family. Swarnakumari attended the meetings of the newly formed Indian National Congress at its inception over 26–28 December 1889. Her two daughters, Hiranmoyee Devi (1868–1925) and Sarala Devi (1872–1945), a writer and a musician, distinguished themselves through their service to the Indian nation – which was finding a voice in the political sphere as the Indian national movement gained momentum. Sarala Devi was an active participant in the national movement while Hiranmoyee was a dedicated social worker.

This is an account of Rabindranath's immediate family and does not go into the details of his extended family of aunts, uncles and cousins who were part of this entrepreneurial and creative atmosphere in a vibrant household. At Jorasanko, the men and women rode on the high tide of change and reform that propelled India into the modern era, their powerful voices and beacon embodied in Tagore's multifaceted endeavours.

2
Growing Up in the Tagore Household

As the fourteenth child of a teeming household, Rabindranath Tagore's birth was not particularly significant, though his name, Rabi (sun), had the promise of aspiration.[1] As has been said earlier, Sarada Devi was a tired mother by this time and little Rabi was initially looked after by his eldest sister, Saudamini, and then left in the care of a troop of wily servants, who reigned over their little wards, improvising methods to keep them captive and deprive them of sumptuous snacks and delicacies which they were supposed to procure for the children with funds allocated for the purpose. Rabindranath, with his characteristic sense of humour, called their rule a 'servocracy'.[2] Under the servant regime, Rabindranath, with his adaptable sensitivity, soon learnt that it was best to say 'no' to any delicacy like *luchis* (a light, deep-fried bread made of plain flour, popular in Bengal) and vegetables suggested to them, and opt instead for the humble *muri* (rice crispies) for the evening snack, which pleased their servant Brajeswar who had a penchant for good food himself. Rabi never complained about the inadequate supply of milk or dishes at mealtimes.[3] Since Debendranath had adopted a policy of introducing austerity to overcome his father's debts, the clothes that the Tagore children were given were simple and considered adequate by Tagore. He only complained when the family tailor, Niamat, forgot to put in the right number of pockets that he needed for his modest possessions. The result was that, as he himself observed, he grew hardy and developed a resistance to illnesses that children contract like fever, the common cold or diseases that were prevalent, such as malaria, measles or chickenpox.

One servant devised an ingenious method of confining Tagore for hours as he rushed away on the pretext of being busy. He drew a chalk circle on the floor and warned Rabindranath of dire consequences if he stepped outside the boundary. Knowing full well about Sita's abduction by Ravana, the Demon King, when she transgressed the boundary set by her brother-in-law, Lakshman, in the *Ramayana* (which Brajeswar narrated to him), Rabindranath was cautious not to break this golden rule. Mercifully the circle was beside a window with French shutters which he could lift to view a pond with ducks, observe the regular bathers and see a banyan tree and some palm trees. A canal which had been constructed in Dwarkanath's time brought water from the Ganga at high tide, and little Rabi could hear its gurgling sound from the corner of his veranda. The pond and the attraction of the view would find its way into many of his poems and songs later, such as in his collection *Dawn Songs* (1883). The outside world beckoned and the urge to travel took root in Rabindranath from these early years of confinement and isolation. He felt not just shut off from the world outside, but barred from the *andarmahal* where his mother, aunts, sisters and other women dwelt, for if he ventured there, his youngest sister would shoo him out of the women's quarters.

There were three favourite places in this mansion where the dreamer in Rabi found peace and quiet to indulge in mental escapades to imaginary worlds. One was his father's room on the terrace of the outer building where Debendranath meditated and retreated when he was in the city, but which was vacant for many weeks in the year when the patriarch was away on his many travels. Seated on a sofa opposite the window here, Rabi could view the world outside Jorasanko, see the bangle seller coax his wares onto soft willing hands, watch the kite mount the sky screaming, imagine the hot haze of the desert like a young Livingstone and admire the sunset. The inner courtyard garden, which Rabindranath concedes was not much of a garden with its few neglected trees, was a space where he would wander to with expectancy at dawn on autumn mornings. Another was his grandmother's palanquin, which stood discarded, a relic from the past. In *Boyhood Days* (1940), Tagore said that perhaps his own neglected self drew him to this neglected object in which he was Robinson Crusoe embarking on adventures during the afternoons when most of the household retreated for a siesta.[4] It was perhaps this palanquin that is the subject of his famous poem 'The Hero' (published in *Shishu* (The Child), 1903), in which a little boy imagines he is travelling in one with his mother and when attacked by robbers, he valiantly vanquishes all of them. At the end of the poem, the child says:

> Smeared in blood and drenched with sweat,
> I come to you and say 'Ma, the battle is over'
> Then you descend from the palanquin
> And pick me up in your arms and kiss me
> Saying, 'Thank goodness Khoka was with me
> I can't imagine what would have happened otherwise'.[5]

It embodies the hankering for a mother's company – her caresses, attention and appreciation – which haunted Tagore, finding expression in his poems addressed by a child to his mother in *The Crescent Moon* (1913).[6]

The first escape came when a dengue epidemic affected the city and Rabindranath, with other children, was sent by Debendranath to a house at Panihati. The house was beside the Adi Ganga and had a large garden. Here Rabi tasted the freedom of walking to the river, exploring the garden and being in close communion with nature.[7]

During this time, schools were few. Most Bengali children were tutored at home. The Tagores had a stream of gurus coming to the household to teach various subjects. When Rabindranath's older brother Somendranath and cousin started going to school, he wept for not being allowed to dress smartly like them and be driven in a horse carriage to school. His tutor gave him a resounding slap and told him that now he was crying to go to school, but once he started school, he would cry a lot more so as not to be sent there. This was a prophecy that would come true. It was at this time that Rabindranath was introduced to Krittibas's *Ramayana* and *Chanakyashlok*.

Tagore attended the Oriental Seminary for a short time but had little memory of what he was taught there. He was then sent to Normal School when he was around seven or eight years old. He remembered being made to sing an English song every morning whose full meaning remained a mystery to him later in life. Their version of the song was 'Kallokee pullokee singilling mellaling, mellaling, mellaling . . .', which he later deciphered as probably 'full of glee, singing merrily, merrily, merrily', but he could not resolve what 'Kallokee' could have meant.[8] At school he was shocked by the foul language used by an incompetent school teacher who used cruel methods, like caning, for controlling his class. The Tagore boys spoke a sophisticated version of Bengali, wore tailored clothes (not the indigenous dhoti and *chador*) and arrived in a horse carriage, which made them objects of envy and derision. Rabindranath was fair, handsome, gentle and retreating, which brought him unsolicited attention from other boys. He was then transferred to De Cruz's Bengal Academy, which could not ignite his enthusiasm for school. It was probably here that Tagore, bored by the method of rote learning, composed his long poem *Abhilash* (Yearning), which was published in 1874 in *Tattwabodhini Patrika*.[9]

Though Debendranath had given up most Hindu rituals of worship as he spearheaded the Bramho Movement, he still stood by his Brahminical status, so when Rabindranath was just under twelve years old in 1873, he arranged for him, his son Somendranath and his grandson Satyaprasad to have their sacred thread (Upanayan) ceremony, an initiation into Brahminism with three days of reflection, meditation and retreat as they took their vows. The boys were isolated in a room on the third floor where their shaven heads and gold earrings made them laugh at each other. However, their learning of the *Gayatri Mantra* was something that stayed with Tagore and was a solace to him all his life.

After the Upanayan, Debendranath called Tagore and asked him whether he would like to go with him to the Himalayas. Rabindranath, in his quiet manner, said yes, but inwardly he was ecstatic. This meant that he would not have to go back to school to be teased by the boys about his shaven head. This journey with his father was the first venture for Rabindranath to a world outside Jorasanko, beyond relatives' houses in Calcutta and an opportunity to be with his reclusive, reticent father. Perhaps Debendranath had seen something in this shy, dreaming son of his and wanted to get to know him better and also take personal responsibility for his education. The first stop was at Shantiniketan. Here Tagore was far from the tyranny of 'servocracy'. He had his first taste of unfettered rambling where the little pools of water caused by rainwater and small undulations in the sandy soil became his rivulets and hills – his very own Lilliput where he roamed, gathered stones and imagined he was a conqueror. The sense of peace he experienced, which engendered creativity, would remain with him and Shantiniketan would be the abode of peace he would ache to come back to from his many restless journeys later in life.

From Shantiniketan en route to Dalhousie in the western Himalayas, the Maharshi and Tagore visited Sahebganj, Dinapur, Allahabad and Kanpur, until they reached the Golden Temple at Amritsar. Here father and son joined the Sikhs who believed in the Absolute and did not worship images, which resonated with the Maharshi's own beliefs. Debendranath knew many of the hymns they sang and joined in the singing. This respect for a different religion was something that would stay with Tagore.

Rabindranath at the age of twelve, 1873.

They reached their cottage in Bakrota from the foothills through an arduous climb, partly on foot, partly on horseback or carried in *jhampans* on poles. The beauty of the Himalayas with the tall deodar trees, the spring flowers and the snow peaks mesmerized Rabindranath. His father supervised his lessons in Bengali literature, English and Sanskrit. His astronomy lessons, which started under the stars in Shantiniketan, continued here in a rigorous routine. He was woken up before sunrise and was taught to chant verses from the Upanishads, followed by English lessons, after which he had a cold shower. This discipline prepared Rabindranath for simple living, and a life of healthy routine allowed him in later life to carry out his multiple projects, both creative and pragmatic.

When he came back to Calcutta he was no longer the shy, neglected boy who had dwelt mainly in the servants' quarters, but a hero who could recite from the Upanishads and read Valmiki's *Ramayana* and thus had the privilege of entering his mother's bedroom where she showed off the newly acquired knowledge of her Rabi to the womenfolk. Rabindranath was flattered, but anxious lest his inadequate knowledge and understanding of Sanskrit were discovered. He was horrified when his eldest brother, Dwijendranath, was once called upon by Sarada Devi to appreciate Rabi's reading of the *Ramayana*. Luckily his brother was preoccupied and absent-mindedly agreed that Rabi was very good before he walked away, affirming Rabindranath's exalted place with his mother and her companions in the *andarmahal*. The Upanishads would be a constant fountain of sustenance for Rabindranath on his personal spiritual journey.

Back in Calcutta he was admitted to St Xavier's School, where once again he found the teaching methods insipid and the routine restricting. One teacher, however, a Spanish priest, Father Peneranda, with his gentle kindness, made a deep impression on Rabindranath. Once during a writing class when Rabindranath could not concentrate on the work and his mind was far away, Father Peneranda put his hand on his shoulder and asked him whether he was feeling well. The gesture and words stayed with Rabindranath, who later sought the ideal teacher for his institution, an investment he felt was the first step to a good education. It was here that his teacher, on hearing that Rabindranath wrote poetry, asked him to write a poem and read it out in class. As an obedient child, Rabindranath wrote with easy facility, but reading it out was an excruciating experience for the shy boy. The disbelief that he could have composed it was humiliating and one boy even boasted that he could identify the original and could bring it to prove Rabindranath's plagiarism. The boast never materialized, but the outcome was that Rabindranath, to his great relief, was never asked to write or read his work again.

Learning in the Tagore household began at home even before school started. Woken early, Rabindranath began his day learning wrestling from a wrestler in the courtyard. After this a medical student came to teach him about parts of the human skeleton – an occurrence which found its way into his short story of the same name. At 7 a.m., Master Nilkamal came with slate in hand. Rabindranath was taught all his lessons – arithmetic, geometry and algebra – in Bengali.[10] It was his third brother, Hemendranath, his Shejadada, 'a hard taskmaster',[11] who took his younger siblings and cousins under his wing and inculcated a love of Bengali language and literature in them as he firmly believed that Bengali should be the medium of instruction. A teacher came to teach natural science and simple science experiments were taught at home to the Tagore children. When Rabindranath came home from school, a gymnastics master was already waiting to train him on the parallel bars. His distant but indulgent mother, like most women of her time, would readily grant Rabindranath respite from studies whenever he feigned illness, telling the tutor to excuse Rabi as he was not well. She was not happy with him accruing all the dirt on his body with the wrestling every morning and on holidays she made it a point to scrub him clean with a home-made unguent composed of orange rind mixed in thickened cream and almond paste and other ingredients, a ritual he tried to wriggle out of, but had to endure. In school the boys believed that the fair complexion of the Tagore children was because they were bathed in wine when they were born (which they believed was a European custom).

The walls of St Xavier's proved claustrophobic and its teaching methods unimaginative and unproductive, like all the other schools Tagore had attended; finally, in 1875, when he was fourteen, he stopped going to school. However, his lessons did not stop. He continued in a rigorous cycle of home-schooling, beginning at 5 a.m. and ending with his English teacher, Master Aghor, coming at 9 p.m., by which time his eyes were heavy with sleep. Tagore tells the story of the English teacher whose punctuality made him unpopular with the children. One day when it was raining heavily, they were jubilant thinking he would not come, when to their utter dismay they noted the familiar black umbrella bobbing in the street as Master Aghor picked his way carefully through the flooded streets. At one of the first lessons Tagore had to translate Shakespeare's *Macbeth* into Bengali, and one of his first critiques of English literature was of this play.[12] Other translations from English included Cantos II and XV of Lord Byron's *Childe Harold's Pilgrimage* (1812–18) and four songs from Thomas Moore's *Irish Melodies* (1807).[13]

However, Tagore envied the birds for their freedom from suffering through English lessons, as the nuances of the language – with its inexplicable spelling, pronunciation and grammar – escaped him as a child. This resistance to a foreign tongue at an impressionable age made him a staunch believer in the mother tongue being the ideal medium of instruction for children. Many years later, when he set up his own school at Shantiniketan, he did not introduce English in the early classes, but waited for the children to seek English lessons when they were ready to communicate with the world.

On days when Rabindranath escaped school, he scoured Dwijendranath's bookcase and read voraciously. There was not much children's literature available in Bengali at this time, but Rabindranath read the story of the mermaid and Robinson Crusoe translated into Bengali with interest. Publishing had given an eager Bengali readership a taste of popular prose which was refreshingly accessible in its closeness to the spoken language, making it different from the *shadhu bhasha*, the classical Bengali of written texts. One such serialized journal was *Abodhbandhu*, which was popular but forbidden to the young Tagore, who nevertheless read it with enjoyment. This is how he was able to read the leading poet of the time, Biharilal Chakraborty, whom he longed to emulate. The gap between the written and spoken language was something Tagore went on to remove in his modernization of the Bengali language. His early introduction to Michael Madhusudan Dutt's magnificent Bengali epic *Meghnad Bad Kavya* led him to write a critique of it, which he later regretted as a rash adolescent response.

Amidst all the tutored learning, Rabi came across the line '*jal pare pata nare*', 'the rain patters, the leaf trembles' – a simple but connected truth encapsulated in a lucid rhyme whose beauty and meaning suddenly brought home to Rabi the enchanting possibilities of verse, which for him was 'the first poem of the Arch Poet'.[14] Rabi recollected two other joys: that of listening to the doggerel of a ballad recited by their cashier, Kailash, with its 'rapid jingle of the frequent rhymes', and a popular children's rhyme, 'The rain falls pit-a-pat, the tide comes up the river'.[15] When he was eight years old a cousin pulled the budding poet into a room and explained to him the fourteen-metre Bengali line called *payar* and asked Rabi to write in the metre. The mystery of metre was thus removed for the young poet, who found he could adopt this complex metre without any problem.

Around the time he was fourteen, Rabi was introduced to medieval Bengali poetry in *Vaishnav Padabali*, which filled him with wonder and pleasure like nothing he had encountered before.[16]

The strong impression Vaishnav poetry had on him bore fruit one afternoon when the rain clouds had gathered in the sky and he lay prone on his bed in his brother's Sudder Street house and wrote the first line of a lyric in Maithili, the language of Vaishnav poetry: 'Gahana kusumo kunjo maajhe / mridulo madhuro banshi baaje' ('In the arbour of flowers I hear the sweet tune of his flute'). This pleased the young poet, giving him the confidence he needed to go on to compose his first opera, which he called *Bhanu Singha Thakurer Padabali*.[17]

Rabindranath was fascinated by the eighteenth-century boy poet Thomas Chatterton's fabricated 'discovery' of a fifteenth-century romance written by a monk poet, Thomas Rowley. This story inspired his own collection *Bharati* (1877), in which he invented a lost medieval poet whose newly discovered songs were brought out under the name Bhanu, another word for Rabi, which meant the sun, and Thakur being the Tagore surname. It was hailed as a great discovery and Rabindranath was amused and disturbed by the literary debates that ensued around the once lost, now rediscovered medieval poet's poetic prowess; he was deeply embarrassed when a scholar, Nishikanta Chatterjee, writing his PhD thesis on Bengali medieval poetry in Germany, declared the work's exalted place among poems from the fifteenth century.[18]

When Tagore was thirteen, Sarada Devi passed away. Her daughter-in-law Prafulla Devi wrote that the heavy lid of an iron chest had fallen on Sarada Devi's arm, after which she experienced excruciating pain in the limb, which several doctors could not ease.[19] In Ajitkumar Chakrabarty's biography *Maharshi Debendranath Tagore* (1916), he described the resulting arm pain as developing into cancer which incapacitated Sarada Devi for a long time and led to her death.[20] Her husband had returned to the house only the day before her death from one of his many Himalayan travels. The news of Sarada Devi's death was brought to the sleeping children by a maid who came like a torrent to their rooms, crying and telling them that they had lost their all. The bleary-eyed youngsters were led to pay their last respects to the matriarch, who seemed to young Rabi to be sleeping. One memory for Rabi was that when he looked up at the terrace after the cremation, he saw his father meditating in his usual spot. His calm composure and reflective response made a deep impression on Tagore, who would experience the successive deaths of many loved ones in the years to come. A deep loneliness engulfed Rabi as he realized his mother would not come back. What sustained him was the affectionate company of his brother Jyotidada and Kadambari, his *Chhoto Bouthan*, as their rooms on the third floor became his favourite haunt. Here Kadambari created a terrace garden which bloomed with flowers. Though very young herself, she had a deeply affectionate nature and understood the loneliness and sensitivity of the youngest Tagore son. She acted like his elder sister, scolding him, taking over the supervision and preparation of Rabi, Somendra and Satya's refreshments from the servant, seeing to it that they had delicious and ample snacks. She provided the shelter and comfort the motherless boy needed at a crucial time in his life. She was also his muse as she listened to, appreciated and criticized Rabi's writings and told him that though it was sometimes good, it was not as good as Biharilal's poetry, thus fuelling the young poet's target of perfection. Kadambari was an avid reader and was known for her literary acumen and refined taste in literature. Rabi wrote for her, eager for her praise, finding in her a harsh critic who would not allow his head to be turned by the easy praise and acceptance he found within the Tagore family, or by their friends and visitors.

In the meantime, nationalist fervour was gaining momentum and was given impetus by the Tagore family in their support of the Hindu Mela, which had been established in 1867 under the enterprising leadership of Nabagopal Mitra, who was also the editor of the weekly *National Paper*. It arose as a resistance to the maligning effects of the Christian fathers who had denigrated Hinduism and its culture and had effectively portrayed Hindu society as decadent and its religion as evil. These ideas were responsible for the 'Orientalism' that Edward Said would describe in 1978 as consciously constructed in the nineteenth and early twentieth centuries to create a whole discourse on the Orient and represent it as Europe's 'Other'. The objective of the Hindu Mela was to counter this damaging projection of Hindu society and create a sense of national consciousness and pride in a 'National Gathering', which would create unity in diversity among Bengal's many groups.[21] An announcement about the Mela was made on 10 April 1867 at Rajah Narsing Chunder Roy Bahadoor's Garden House, during an occasion that also showcased gymnastics, athletics, chemical experiments, music, concerts and an exhibition of the works of men and women. Its first secretary was Ganendranath Tagore, with Nabagopal as co-secretary. Its cultural and linguistic focus made it a significant vehicle of nationalist consciousness in Renaissance Bengal. It was at the Hindu Mela that Tagore performed the first public reading of his poetry with 'Hindu Mela's Gift', a poem influenced by Biharilal's poetry and Hemendrachandra Bandyopadhyay's patriotic song, 'Bharat Sangeet'.[22] The leading playwright Nabinchandra Sen was present at this reading and was deeply impressed by Tagore. Soon after, he told Akshaychandra Sarkar that he had heard a powerful poet and vocalist at the Hindu Mela and predicted that this young man would become famous, a prediction Tagore fulfilled.[23] Akshaychandra's immediate response was, 'Is it Rabithakur?' The idea of composing nationalist songs was an attribution of the Tagore family members.[24] Once when Jyotirindranath was agonizing about adding the right lines to his play *Sarojini* in order to depict the story of the self-immolation of besieged Rajput women, Tagore – who had been listening to his efforts from another room – suggested that a poem would perhaps work better. On his brother's encouragement, he produced 'Jal jal chita' (Of the Burning Funeral Pyre), which conveyed the appropriate mood at a dramatic moment in the play. Jyotidada was overjoyed and it was this poem that Tagore recited at the Hindu Mela. At sixteen he was inducted into the editorial staff of *Bharati*, where his first long poem, *Kavi Kahini* (The Poet's Story, 1878), was published.

Tagore was thus inducted into Jyotirindranath's circle. The latter established a secret society, Sanjibani Sabha, inspired by the Italian unification revolutionary Giuseppe Mazzini. His society met in a derelict house on Cornwallis Street and the proceedings were carried out in great secrecy behind closed doors, in a dark room, using a code language. It began with the chanting of a Vedic mantra and was marked by a sense of revolutionary excitement. Later Tagore would recall, 'In this Sabha our main aim was to experience a fiery excitement.'[25] The Sanjibani Sabha, like many of Jyotirindranath's heady ventures, died out without creating any political ripples.

On the artistic side, Rabi and Jyotidada's creative partnership took wing, as the older brother played tunes on his violin while Rabi composed lyrics to the music. Jyotidada bought and installed a piano in his apartment at Jorasanko. Rabi wrote lyrics to fit his brother's tunes, which brought together Indian classical ragas, folk tunes and Western music. Jyotidada's close friend Akshay Chowdhury was a great lover of Western melodies, and introduced these tunes in his musical soirées. On the terrace near Jyotidada's rooms, Kadambari's beautiful garden provided the perfect ambience for the soirées.

In Kadambini and Jyotirindranath's bedroom there was an instrument that fascinated Rabi: a model of a ship in a glass case under which was a cloth of painted waves, which rippled to organ music when wound up. It is mentioned in his novel *Gora* as an image that evoked wonder of the outside world, having the excitement of the foreign.[26] On one occasion Jyotirindranath took Tagore on a boat trip along the river, a liberating event for Tagore, anticipating his many boat trips through their estates and across the sea to foreign climes.

Tagore's creativity continued in diverse streams with his first two short stories, 'Bhikharini' (The Beggar Woman) and 'Karuna' (Pity/Compassion), which appeared in *Bharati* when he was sixteen. This gave him the courage to begin his first novel, *Karuna*, and publish it in the magazine.

This interlude in Tagore's adolescent life at Jorasanko was brought to an end with Satyendranath's last effort to provide some formal education to his youngest brother, who seemed to be flitting through life, writing and composing without any fixed aim in view. Satyendranath had broken with another tradition as he had not only crossed the black waters but had sent his wife, unaccompanied by her husband, to England with her two young children, Indira Devi and Surendranath. In September 1878 Rabindranath sailed to England, his first journey to the 'world' he had dreamt of beyond the Himalayas, far from his Jorasanko family home.

Studio portrait of Rabindranath in Brighton, 1878.

3
English Interlude

Maharshi Debendranath and Satyendranath must have felt that Tagore's creative days were passing without any concrete aim or objective. His future as a man of letters was not considered a viable option. Rabi had to have a prestigious profession. To achieve this end, Satyendranath took his youngest brother to England to study for the Bar. Before crossing the ocean, Rabi had to be prepared in English studies and etiquette in order to be ready for his sojourn. There are records in the Tagore family accounts of English books arriving at Jorasanko from Messrs Thacker, Spink & Co.[1] The names of the books are not known, but we know from Tagore's *Reminiscences* that he wanted to acquire an adequate knowledge of the history of English literature as he wanted to write an essay on it in Bengali and asked Satyendranath to get him the requisite books for the self-imposed task. One outcome was an essay on 'The Anglo-Saxon Race and Anglo-Saxon Literature', which examines the Roman conquest and includes a summary of the Old English epic *Beowulf*, with translations of some sections and poems from the fragment of Caedmon's *Genesis* and *Exodus*. It was at this time that Tagore was introduced to other Western masters and was fascinated by Dante's undying love for Beatrice and Petrarch's lifelong passion for Laura, and was moved by Goethe's life and character.[2]

Satyendranath had been appointed Assistant Collector and Magistrate at Ahmedabad in April 1865. On 19 April 1876 he became the District and Sessions Judge. His residence was the beautiful

Shahibag, which had been the palace of Prince Khurram before he became Emperor Shah Jahan. It was here that Tagore spent four lonely months reading prodigiously in his brother's impressive library, and writing while his brother was away for the greater part of the day, working. This Mughal palace became the inspiration for Tagore's surreal short story 'The Hungry Stones', in which he evoked the historical times in a haunting tale.[3] This appeared in *Sadhana* and was included in *Galpo Guchho*, his collection of short stories. At Shahibag he read Tennyson which would later bear fruit in translations of his poems and an essay on the life of the Victorian poet.[4] He also read Scott, Byron and Shakespeare. From the terrace of this sprawling palace, he could watch the narrow Sabarmati river's easy flow. Rabi's bedroom, where he composed many poems and songs, was on the top floor; some of these compositions appeared in *Bharati*.

Satyendranath felt that Tagore's homesickness could be remedied by introducing him to young women who were familiar with the attraction of the West. So in August 1878 he sent him to the house of his friend, Dr Atmaram Pandurang Turkhud, in Bombay. The doctor's three daughters, Ana, Durga and Manik, had been educated in England. Ana was made responsible for Rabi's anglicization. She was a little older than Rabi, who found her sophisticated upbringing and confidence intimidating. On one occasion, after telling Rabi of the Western custom that anyone stealing a lady's gloves while she was asleep won the privilege of kissing her, Ana promptly fell asleep in an easy chair in the room and woke up sometime later. Casting a furtive eye to her side, she was surprised to discover her gloves untouched. However, not to be deterred by his mentor, Rabi told her that he wrote poetry, which she showed a deep interest in, so the youthful pair spent time with Rabi reading and translating his poems to Ana, who was an appreciative listener.[5] Ana asked Rabi to give her a name. Nalini was a favourite name of his that had appeared earlier in many of his poems and plays. This was the name he gave Ana, which she liked and which she wove into a song, 'Shun Nalini, khol go aankhi' (Listen Nalini, open your eyes). The name haunts other songs, with lyrics such as 'Shunechhi shunechhi ki naam tari / Shunechhi shunechhi taha / Nalini, Nalini, Nalini, Nalini / Kemon modhur aha' – where the poet says he has heard her name, Nalini, and what a sweet-sounding name it is!

Earlier, in 1877, Rabi had spent some time with Jyotidada in his boat on the Ganga, where he started writing his collection *Shaishab Sangeet* (Children's Songs). On his return to Jorasanko, he wrote the poem 'Bhagna Hriday' (Broken Heart), which was the beginning of his collection *Kabi Kahini* (The Tale of the Poet, 1878). Many of the poems in this collection had been written while he was staying in the Turkhud household and published serially in *Bharati* later that year.[6] A copy was sent to Ana by Jyotirindanath. Ana was delighted and wrote a letter to Jyotirindanath thanking him, saying that Tagore had read and translated it to her until she knew 'the poem by heart'.[7]

On 20 September 1878, Rabi sailed for England from Bombay with Satyendranath on ss *Poona*.[8] Tagore's journey and his experiences in England were recorded in his *Letters from an Expatriate in Europe* (1881), which appeared in *Bharati* and was later published as a collection. He later regretted the *Letters* as coming from an ill-considered 'youthful bravado'.[9]

Initially he was quite ill on the boat, but once he had recovered, his observations of his fellow passengers were recorded in his travel records, showing his eye for detail, as he noted human characteristics which would find full expression in his short stories later. His reading on the ship included Richard Chenevix Trench's *Proverbs and their Lessons*. In his letters he notes his progress, stopping at Aden, going through to the Suez where the travellers were covered with a layer of desert dust which, as he observed, made them look like Indian sadhus to their fellow passengers. At Suez, the prospect of riding a donkey, the only available mode of transport, put him off as he was told about the donkey's strong will to do what it liked rather than comply with the directions of its rider. From Suez they took the train to Alexandria, whose busy port impressed the poet. Here he noticed ships belonging to Europeans and Muslims, but the absence of ships from his own country saddened him.[10] From here they set sail on ss *Mongolia* to Brindisi in Italy, travelling overland by train to Paris, where he visited the International Industrial Exhibition – of which he wrote that one month would not have given him enough time to describe it, though he did send detailed descriptions of the Turkish baths in Paris.

He then proceeded to London, from where he went on to Brighton, where his sister-in-law Jnanadanandini was based with her son Surendranath, now six years old, and her five-year-old daughter Indira. This was a time when Tagore would find pleasure in the children's company, an experience which helped him in later years when he had his own children and when he opened his school. He was admitted to a school in Brighton where the headmaster complimented him on his 'splendid head'. In *Reminiscences*, Tagore recalled the shy overtures of the boys in this school, who, far from bullying the newcomer, would surreptitiously put apples and oranges in his pockets and run away. Early in January 1879, he was called outside one day by his excited niece and nephew to see snow falling. The white mantle he encountered, with its magical unfamiliarity, seemed like a dream world. The days that followed in Brighton were a romp with the children and a rollercoaster of social engagements arranged by Jnanadanandini. Music filled Rabi's life once again as he, as the children's Rabi Kaka (Uncle Rabi), sang popular Victorian melodies in his beautiful tenor voice: 'Won't you tell me Mollie darling' or 'Darling I am growing old'.[11] Both children would remain close to Rabi Kaka and Indira would go on to compose music and become an exponent of Rabindrasangeet (Tagore's songs), and a valued expert with her knowledge of her uncle's distinctive yet

Rabindranath with Indira Devi and Surendranath Tagore.

varied repertoire. The English interlude would seal a bond between uncle and niece, evident in the correspondence between the young poet and Indira in the 1920s, which records the uninhibited confidences shared by the young poet, who remained a much-loved uncle to his favourite niece. Surendranath would translate Tagore's letters in *Chhinnapatra* as *Glimpses of Bengal* and Tagore's novels *The Home and the World* and *Four Chapters*. He was later involved with the establishment of Visva-Bharati, Tagore's international university at Shantiniketan, and would become editor of the *Visva-Bharati Quarterly*.

The fun-filled days in Brighton were put to an end to by Satyendranath's friend Taraknath Palit, who took the initiative of bringing Tagore to London and found him lodgings which were unwelcoming and spartan. His room overlooked Regent's Park, where the bare branches of winter trees offered a bleak prospect to a homesick and lonely teenager. The move was made to give Tagore time and space to prepare himself to become a barrister. Tagore had few visitors here and when some Indian friends came, he was loath to let them go. His only respite was a harmonium which he played to relieve the monotony on gloomy evenings. He had a Latin teacher whose threadbare state and lifelong obsession with his global theory that one idea was shared by all civilizations in any particular age struck him in its well-meaning naivety. Tagore had some conflicted memories of his acquaintance with teachers during his English interlude. His Latin teacher's honesty moved the young student, for when he tried to pay him, the master, in spite of his penury, refused payment since he felt he had not taught his pupil anything and had wasted his time – he only received his fees after much coaxing. After this Palit decided to move Rabindranath in with Mr Barker, a classicist, who provided lodgings for students he prepared for examinations. This was a joyless household, where the husband and wife never had any conversations at table and Mr Barker maintained an indifference to his once pretty spouse.

In London, Tagore attended the annual meeting of the National Indian Association with Satyendranath. He also made visits to the House of Commons. He was very impressed with Gladstone's speeches, and compared him with Sullivan. He was present when an Irish member, O'Donnell, campaigned against the Press Act in India. What struck him was the utter contempt with which the Irish members were treated in parliament and how empty the House became when Irish members spoke. He was shocked to see the heckling and hissing that went on in parliament during sessions, the indignity meted out to opponents trying to make a point, making him wonder at how these British decision-makers, whose behaviour was like bickering boys, could govern another nation sensibly and responsibly.

He made an escape from London's pollution in March 1879 on Jnanadanandini's invitation to spend some time with her family at Tunbridge Wells, where he felt revived by the fresh atmosphere and beauty of rural England. It was a welcome break from his bleak London days and was followed by a holiday with Jnanadanandini's family at Torquay in Devon, where they had rented a cottage. The picturesque landscape with its hills, flower-strewn meadows, pine trees and a seashore offering a limitless horizon moved the poet, but when he chose a beautiful spot on the rocky shore to write, he recalls his poetry did not come as easily as it did in his homeland. He did write a lyrical drama, *Magnatari,* later retitled *Bhagna Tari* (The Wrecked Boat), which focused on the theme of unfulfilled love. In his *Reminiscences* he said he would have preferred to have discarded the work without regret, but it was published in the family journal *Bharati* like the other works he wrote during his English sojourn. Later it was incorporated into the collection *Shaishab Sangeet* (Childhood Songs). The memory of this salubrious place would remain with Tagore and would perhaps be the trigger that made him think of this county as the perfect place for his friend and collaborator Leonard Knight Elmhirst, the agriculturalist and rural reconstructionist, to establish Dartington Hall for rural regeneration in the interwar years, implementing Tagore's ideas of replenishing and reviving the arts and crafts, and the creative potential of a depressed community. In England, Tagore, who had been fascinated by the story of Chatterton's life told by Jyotirindranath's friend Akshay Chaudhuri, read W. W. Skeat's edition of Chatterton's *Poetical Works* (1871), which led him to write a critique on 'Chatterton, the Boy-poet', published in the July issue of *Bharati*. During this time he also received gifts from India – the autumn issue of the journal *Abalabandhab*, and Jyotirindranath's play *Asrumati*, which was dedicated to Tagore and included his song 'Gahana Kusuma Kunja Majhe', in the language Brajabuli (one of the songs in *Bhanu Singher Padabali*).

Abanindranath, Tagore's nephew, has described how his father, Ganendranath, decided that the Tagore family women should also see the play, so he rented the whole Bengal Theatre for one day, moving away the benches and arranging for easy chairs, garlands, hookahs, carpets and cane blinds for the women to be taken from

Satendranath Tagore, Jnanadanandini Devi, Jyotirindranath Tagore and Kadambari Devi.

the Jorasanko family home to furnish the theatre for the day. This was a historic event as women in Bengal had never had the opportunity to see a play enacted on a public stage. Thus a social norm was broken for the first time by the Tagore family. It was also the first time that the Tagore women left their private domain en masse and entered the public arena to watch the stage production of Jyotirindranath's *Asrumati* in September 1879.[12] Tagore also received his older sister Swarnakumari's lyrical drama *Basanta Utsab*, which was staged in the Tagore household. Tagore wrote a beautiful letter in praise of his sister's work.[13] So the contact with the world of Bengali literature continued for the young *littérateur* during his period in England.

On his return to London from Devon in June 1879, the most fruitful period of Tagore's time in England was spent in Dr Scott's household at 10 Tavistock Square. He was later told that when Dr Scott's two younger daughters were told that a strange Indian was

Jnanadanandini Devi, undated.

coming to stay, they fled to a relative's house and only came back when they were assured that he was innocuous. It was a crowded but warm household with four daughters, two sons, three maids, a dog named Toby, a kindly father and a caring mother. Here, in the Scotts' living room, Tagore experienced a renewal of the cultural and creative atmosphere that he had known at home in the Tagore household, as he now spent many evenings with the Scott daughters, especially the third one, Lucy, who was close to him in age, singing English, Irish and Scottish songs, many from Thomas Moore's collection, accompanied by Lucy on the piano. He even endeavoured to teach Lucy Bengali on her request in what was an East–West exchange. The Bengali lessons soon made him realize that the rules of Bengali spelling and pronunciation, which he had confidently believed followed a clear logic, were not as straightforward and uniform as he had assumed. At the University College London library, he looked up Bengali dictionaries and made prodigious notes, studying the nuances of Bengali spelling, which he took back to India in a leather suitcase. Unfortunately, these papers were discarded by a little girl in the Tagore household who made the suitcase a receptacle for her doll's belongings. However, Tagore went on to write several essays on the Bengali language. This encounter with the peculiarities of Bengali as a language would inform his own teaching at his school at Shantiniketan at the beginning of the twentieth century.

It was at the Scott household that Tagore encountered the universality of human nature and familial bonding. In Mrs Scott he found a woman fully absorbed in her household – a devoted wife, a diligent housewife and a loving and balanced mother – who approved of singing but was alarmed by the younger ones' conducting seances. She put a stop to it once and for all when she firmly confiscated her beloved husband's chimney-pot hat, which they had decided to use as a tool for the game. In these homes away from home, Tagore experienced the thoughtful and affectionate care of two very kind women in Mrs Barker and Mrs Scott. Mrs Barker, in spite of her spiteful husband, was a meticulous housekeeper who worked around the clock to keep the house clean and tidy and have the meals ready on time. She chatted easily with Tagore and played the piano on his request, until her husband's abrupt entry and admonition one day interrupted these pleasant moments. Tagore reserved his special praise for Mrs Scott, who was solicitous about his comfort and well-being, coaxing him to eat well, scolding him if he was not well wrapped up in the cold weather, giving him hot footbaths before bedtime and administering medicine if she felt he was not well. But he was most impressed by her devotion to her husband, whose every need she anticipated. All his life, Tagore would retain his admiration for her, and all devoted wives.

Early on during his stay in England, Tagore realized that the British ear was not attuned to accept and appreciate Indian tunes, as he discerned the stifled giggles and smiles at gatherings where he had been asked to sing. His grandfather, Dwarkanath, had had the same response during his sojourn in Britain. Tagore had discovered that foreign melodies could seem strange in their unfamiliarity, but they could grow on one with time and association. All through his life Rabi experimented with tunes from his native Bengal, folk and classical tunes from across India, and Arabic and European tunes to create an astounding repertoire of around 2,200 songs in which words and music were woven in a perfect marriage, carrying their mood and emotion across regional barriers.

He was impressed by the honesty he encountered in ordinary Englishmen. In Torquay he saw a man inadequately clad against the cold, his toes sticking out of his shoes, who looked at him silently with pleading eyes, not daring to beg, as it was forbidden. Tagore gave him a coin, but the man came after him saying he had been mistakenly given a gold coin. A similar incident occurred with a porter. In each case he had given a guinea, because he did not have anything smaller.

During this time, Tagore took admission to University College London's Faculty of Arts and Law. Here his classmate was Taraknath Palit's son Lokendranath, who was fourteen years old while Tagore was eighteen. The difference in age did not matter, as his young friend's sharp intelligence and wit brought the two very close. They spent hours in the library discussing various subjects and would burst into laughter every so often, inviting disapproving glances from many blue-eyed female readers. Lokendranath would remain a close friend and associate of Tagore's after his return to India.

At University College London, Tagore attended Henry Morley's lectures on English literature, especially those on Shakespeare. He wrote about Morley's teaching methods and how Morley's expressive readings of Shakespeare or Thomas Browne's *Religio medici* (1642) enlightened students on the meanings of the texts. He encouraged debates about the reading among his students and manoeuvred the discussions in such a way that the analysis seemed to come from them. Tagore read the Shakespeare editions brought out by Clarendon Press, and enjoyed reading *Coriolanus* and *Anthony and Cleopatra* during this period. One particular method of Morley's he admired was the practice of a student leaving an anonymous essay on a particular day of the week, which Morley would take home and come back to discuss and give his comments in class, which were never destructive or unkind, except on one occasion. An Indian student had submitted an anonymous essay which was an adulation of the English in India and rudely dismissive of Indians. Morley was livid and said that no Englishman should be happy about this kind of praise of his character. In his criticism, he tore the essay to shreds. Tagore was mortified. He then felt it his duty to write an essay which was more candid about 'The English in India'. One the day of discussion, he was too nervous to attend Morley's class. After the class, Lokendranath came and slapped him on the back, congratulating him on his brilliant essay. Morley told his students that some of them might go to India later for their careers, and they should neither forget the treatment the English meted out to Indians nor show disrespect for Indians. He also praised the style and the use of the English language in the essay, which affirmed Tagore's mastery of the language that he would continue to use when he chose to address an audience beyond Bengal. Tagore would retain a deep respect for Morley all his life and remain convinced that the model teacher was the first requirement for a good educational system. However, once again, the strictures for formal education could not hold Tagore's attention. Tagore came back without the degree that was much coveted by his family.

His observations on British culture, on certain characteristics, were gathered and recorded in letters he wrote home which were later translated into English as *Letters from an Expatriate in Europe* (1881), which have been mentioned earlier. He was impressed by the free mixing between men and women and the visibility women enjoyed in Britain, comparing their natural behaviour with the constrained Bengali womenfolk at home. He felt that British society had advanced because of the way it treated its women and was critical of the social strictures that confined women to their walled existence in India. Perhaps this memory would stay with him and would lead him to write about the liberal Nikhilesh bringing his beloved wife Bimala from the *andarmahal*, the *zenana*, across the threshold to the *bahirmahal*, the public rooms, in the 1916 work *Ghare Baire* (translated by Surendranath into English as *The Home and the World*, published in 1919).

However, his letters aroused consternation in the Tagore household, and his admiration of Western women was perhaps the reason why his father, the Maharshi, wrote to him hastily to come home when his brother Satyendranath was returning from England. Tagore's reverence for his conservative and ascetic father and his innate shyness made him keep a discreet distance from women all through his life. His romantic nature found expression in his vast creative oeuvre and some of his letters.

Before leaving England, he had a strange experience. One Anglo-Indian widow, whose husband had occupied a high position in India, had retired to England and on meeting Tagore at a party had given him a badly written eulogy by a sycophant to her husband which was meant to be rendered in Raga Behag.[14] She requested Rabi, whom she insisted on calling Ruby, to sing the dirge, which a gentle, malleable Rabi did to his own consternation. This request was repeated at other places until just before he was leaving, the lady asked him to come and sing it to an ill friend. Rabi/Ruby could not refuse an old friend. He describes this hapless journey in *Reminiscences*, of taking the wrong train and then the right one to the lady's suburban house, arriving after the party and being offered a weak cup of tea after a long, hungry day and invited to dance with the ladies on an empty stomach.[15] Then, having missed the last train home, he was bundled off to the nearest inn for the night before it closed. Here the much-awaited meal eluded him and he spent a cold night on an old bedstead in a room where the only other furniture was a washstand. The following morning he was given a cold breakfast of the remnants of the previous night's dinner by the widow, which he says would have sustained him adequately the night before. He was then led to a landing and pointed in the direction of an upper window where the patient slept and asked to sing the dirge to the invisible person one last time. When he returned to the Scott household, they fussed around a famished and exhausted Rabi, assuring him that his experience was not typical of English hospitality, which he agreed was true.

He did not return straight to India, but travelled with Satyendranath and his family to Nice in France for a holiday in February 1880, after which they made their passage to India together on ss *Oxus*, a ship owned by Messageries Maritime, arriving in India in mid-March 1880.[16]

Tagore's notebook was not crowded with many compositions. He called this period one of 'utter disorderliness'.[17] He came back from England with his unfinished manuscript, *Bhagna Hriday* (Broken Heart), which he finished and dedicated to his sister-in-law Kadambari. The reader can only speculate who the subject of these lyrics is; the protagonist is a poet who is not able to recognize the love of the woman he shares his poetry with. The plot is negligible and sentiment overflows. Was he thinking of Ana or one of the Scott girls or Kadambari? Such questions have been posed by many critics who are not happy to accept that 'Beauty is Truth', letting the reader remain 'content with half-knowledge' and not reach after 'any irritable reaching after fact & reason'.[18] Poems written in England were now collected with others he wrote on his return to India in a volume published in 1881.

The book was well received at home, as we see from the response of the Maharaja of Tripura, who sent his Chief Minister to offer his felicitations to the young poet.[19] But Tagore is dismissive of this narrative poem, which he did not try to publish later. In his *Reminiscences* he comments on this period as one in which not only was he eighteen, but those around him seemed to be eighteen as well, caught up in a youthful profusion of artistic excitement and experiment.[20]

Kadambari Devi, wife of Jyotirindranath Tagore.

4
Loss and the Journey to the Banks of the Padma

While Tagore had been away, his readers in Bengal had been reading of his experiences in his *Letters*, so he remained very much in the public domain. The *Letters* were written in popular, everyday Bengali, signalling Tagore's facility with the contemporary modern language, which marked his early contribution to modernizing the Bengali language. The *Letters* were published in the Tagore household journal, *Bharati*. In fact, the years before he left for England and a few years after he came back could be called his *Bharati* years.

A tragic event occurred in the Jorasanko family while Tagore was in England. At the end of 1878 Tagore's brother-in-law, Swarnakumari's husband, Janakinath, sailed for England to study to become a barrister. Just before this, his wife with her four children moved to the Jorasanko house. Jyotirindranath's wife, Kadambari, was childless. She had been like a mother to a lonely Tagore as a boy and more so after his mother died. Once Swarnakumari moved back to her father's house, her daughter, little Urmila, became Kadambari's adored child. Kadambari looked after her like a mother and Swarnakumari was happy to have Urmila live in Kadambari's apartment on the second floor of the familial house. On 31 December 1878, Urmila ventured on her own in one unsupervised moment of childish curiosity to climb down the spiral staircase leading to the granary and lost her balance, dying instantly from the fall. The incident cast a shadow on the Tagore household and Kadambari was stunned. This loss would stay as a deep, unexpressed wound in her mind.[1]

On his return from England, however, Tagore was once again hurled headlong into the heady atmosphere of creativity at Jorasanko. He says in his *Reminiscences* 'we wrote, we sang, we acted, we poured ourselves on every side'.[2] It was as if they were on an unstoppable chariot with Jyotirindranath as the charioteer. This unfettered life gave him the taste of freedom that he had cherished and strove for all his life, born of the sense of a full freedom that his Jyotidada had let him experience, a freedom 'inside and out, in the face of all dangers', unrestrained by 'custom or convention'.[3] Tagore related two incidents indicative of his brother's fearlessness and unconventionality with his characteristic humour in his *Reminiscences*: how while accompanying his brother to the family estate's headquarters at Shelidah, Jyotidada urged Rabi to join him on a tiger hunt. Tagore carried no gun and both brothers left their shoes at the edge of the forest and crept forward on bare feet to waylay the beast in a bamboo thicket, which was mercifully dealt with by his brother.[4] On another occasion, Tagore, who had never ridden a horse, was urged by his freedom-loving and freedom-giving brother to mount a horse and gallop at his side.[5]

At Jorasanko Tagore plunged into the endeavour of establishing a Literary Academy with Jyotirindranath and others to create a platform for Bengali thought and literature and a language that could be adapted to scientific terminology. When they approached the erudite Pundit Vidyasagar to be a member, the sagacious educationist advised them to leave the established men out as they could never agree on any single matter. The Academy did not succeed, like so many of Jyotirindranath's enthusiastic imaginative ventures, but the effort and thought behind it would be put into practice later by Tagore in his writings on science.

In 1880 Tagore's verse novel *Banophul* (Wild Flower) was published in *Gyanankur*. It was 'full of spirit, elegance, and lyrical

Rabindranath as Balmiki in the play *Balmiki Prativa*, staged at Jorasanko House, 1881.

beauty. The style is clear and the versification melodious and unaffected . . . the descriptions . . . very vigorous . . . It is a simple love story.'[6] In 1881 Tagore published an operetta, *Valmiki Pratibha*, which dramatizes the legend of Ratnakar, the robber-chief, who was known for his ruthlessness, but was transformed by a life-changing incident to become the composer of the epic *The Ramayana*. In his story, Ratnakar is appalled to see the plight of a young girl who has been captured by the robber gang as a sacrificial offering to the goddess Kali. He frees the girl, disperses the miscreants and finds himself burdened with remorse for his life of crime. His penitence wins him the blessing of the goddess Saraswati, patron of literature and the arts, and Ratnakar is transformed into Valmiki, who finds himself appointed by divine grace as the scribe of Rama's story, *The Ramayana*. The songs in the operetta abound with Tagore's assorted skills as a composer – he absorbs and mixes tunes with deftness to fit the mood and pace of the story. His one-time introduction to the catchy tunes in Thomas Moore's *Irish Melodies* by Akshay Chaudhuri and Lucy Scott finds expression in some of the songs in *Valmiki Pratibha*, especially the rollicking songs sung by the robbers. At a Jorasanko performance of the musical, Rabindranath played the role of Valmiki and his niece played Pratibha, the little girl who is rescued by the robber chief, which explains the name in the title. This was followed by another musical play, *Kal Mrigaya* (The Fateful Hunt, 1882), which tells the story of a blind hermit whose son is inadvertently killed by King Dasharath, the father of Rama, who mistakes the noise of him filling a pitcher in the river in the forest as that of a big animal drinking water. The death of an only son and carer makes the bereaved and aggrieved father curse King Dasharath, saying that his beloved son would be banished from his kingdom and sent into exile for fourteen years. Once again, Tagore has a key role in the production of the lyrical drama at Jorasanko, playing the blind hermit, his excellent voice bringing the songs to life. Tagore's powerful singing voice, his enjoyment and ability as an actor, his stunningly handsome features, his piercing eyes and expressive face gave these roles a vigorous impetus. These musical plays are not remarkable for their action or plot. The joy of composing heterogeneous tunes that embody Tagore's versatility and carry the burden of the narrative would continue in later compositions which would mark a new genre, invented by Tagore – the lyrical play which would be enacted through dance, his famous dance dramas.

However, a sense of unfulfilment and even failure at not having succeeded in passing the civil service or bar examinations must have goaded Tagore to write to his father in Mussoorie in the Himalayas to let him go back to England to resume and complete his studies. Debendranath complied. But the journey was probably delayed, as Prabhatkumar Mukhopadhyay says, by the turmoil in the Tagore household by Kadambari's attempted suicide. A change of scene was required to help Kadambari recover. Jyotirindranath took Kadambari to the Bombay region to recuperate, so Tagore lost his musical and literary soulmates for a while. He occupied their rooms on the third floor and in his enforced solitude, he discarded pen and paper and started composing poetry on a slate. The opportunity this simple device presented was liberating. He did not have to cross things out or tear off unwanted pages, but could, at one rub, get rid of what he disapproved. Tagore had known his eldest brother Dwijendranath's friend Biharilal Chakraborty, the leading Bengali poet, before he sailed for England, when Biharilal was a frequent visitor and participant at Jyotirindranath's 'Nandan Kanan', a platform for discussing literature and music. It was on Rabindranath's return from England that he grew close to the established poet, walking into his house unannounced at all hours, reciting poetry and singing his songs to him. In Biharilal he found a poet's mind filled with an unalloyed joy. As his poetry flowed, Tagore discovered that he could write what he enjoyed and rely on his own judgement. The result was a collection of poems which he called *Sandhya Sangeet* (Evening Songs, 1882). With this manuscript,

Rabindranath, during the period of composing *Sandhya Sangeet*, 1882, Calcutta.

he realized that at last he had moved away from needing to emulate or be inspired by other poets or poetic forms. He had found his voice, and could write as himself.

There was an incident that Tagore recalled, which he related to the geologist Pramatha Nath Bose, about the wedding of the daughter of the economist Romesh Chandra Dutt. When the host welcomed Bankimchandra Chatterjee, the doyen of Bengali literature, with a garland, Bankinchandra, noticing Tagore's entry, took the garland from his own neck and strung it round Rabi's, saying, 'The wreath to him, Ramesh; have you not read his *Evening Songs*?'[7] This was the leading older writer recognizing the new star who had risen on the firmament, very much like the established Robert Burns welcoming the young Walter Scott onto the literary scene.[8] The poems here are marked by a pervading melancholy: the very first one, addressed to evening – personified as a mysterious woman brooding over the earth – sets the tone for the collection. The poems are sincere and unaffected, but one can still see the young poet struggling with expressing his emotions.

The delayed journey to England was again picked up by Tagore in April 1881. On his way to catch the boat, he stopped upon invitation to give a talk at the Medical College Hall for the Bethune Society, of which Reverend K. M. Banerji was the president. This was his first public lecture, and it was on the subject of music. The poet argued that melody was the vehicle through which to give words expression, rather than the other way round. He made up for the lack of substantial evidence in his argument with multiple examples of songs, which the lecture was interspersed with. It was an opinion he later conceded was wrong and though the lecture was ecstatically received, Tagore felt it was because of his use of songs and his earnestness. He would go on to say that he was always reluctant to publish his songs, for in published form they lacked the soul which was given by the music. On 20 April, Tagore, accompanied by his newly married nephew Satyaprasad, set sail a second time across the ocean from Calcutta. However, this trip was cut short by the nephew's sickness, which was probably a result of missing his young wife, and Tagore felt duty bound to accompany him home from Madras. He went with trembling anticipation to face his father alone at Mussoorie, but was amazed to encounter his father's calm acceptance of his truncated journey.

He came back to join Jyotirindranath and Kadambari at a villa on the Ganga at Chandernagore (now Chandannagar). In *Reminiscences* he says, 'The Ganges again!'⁹ The days here were languid and carefree. Sometimes they ate their meals in the shade of the Bakul trees. Sometimes they spent whole days drifting in a boat on the Ganga, his Jyotidada playing on his violin and Rabi singing along with an intent listener in Kadambari. The day would begin with Raga Purabi and end with Raga Bhag as the sun set.¹⁰ Back at the villa, they would spread a quilt on the terrace and rest under the stars as the river flowed on. In this sprawling house with rooms on various levels, a living room with painted glass and many memorable paintings, Rabi chose for his writing a round room on the terrace, a location he had selected before at his Jorasanko house and his brother's house in Ahmedabad. The uninterrupted aspect of nature was a prospect Tagore always looked for throughout his life. This is why he would, later on, prefer his Shantiniketan, with its wide fields, its far horizon and sweeping sky, to his Jorasanko home. At Chandernagore he continued writing poems, songs and essays on various subjects: *Bibidha Prabandha* (Diverse Essays). Here he ventured working on his first well-known novel *Bou-Thakuranir Hat* (The Young Queen's Market, 1883), a historical narrative of intrigue and vengeance wreaked by a cruel king whose irresponsible governance makes him turn against his son, whose sole fault is his sympathy for the people's suffering. The novel inevitably ends in tragedy. This had been preceded by a novel set in contemporary times entitled *Karuna* (Pity), published serially in *Bharati*, from 1878 to 1879, during his English interlude. It was not considered significant by its author and remains unnoticed by his critics, and has not reappeared in print.

Back in Calcutta, Tagore was still beset by a sense of despondency. As he had done at Jorasanko, he woke up each morning before sunrise so as not to miss anything as the day was revealed each dawn. So he stood one morning on the balcony of Jyotirindranath's

Sudder Street residence, watching the first rays beyond the line of trees down the lane. It was at this moment that Tagore experienced the most startling epiphany:

> All of a sudden a covering seemed to fall away from my eyes, and I found the world bathed in a wonderful radiance, with waves of beauty and joy swelling on every side. The radiance pierced the folds of sadness and depondency which had accumulated over my heat, and flooded it with universal light . . . From infancy I had been seeing only with my eyes, now I began to see with my whole consciousness.[11]

Moreover, 'the invisible screen of the commonplace was removed from all things and all men, and their ultimate significance was intensified in my mind'.[12] The result was a poem that cascaded forth like the very metaphor at its centre, 'Nirjharer Swapnabhanga' (The Awakening of the Waterfall). Like Wordsworth, it was the moment when Tagore seemed to see into the life of things. A screen had been lifted and the poet saw the infinite in the finite, a longing and a search that would continue all his life as his poems and other writings gushed forth like a waterfall from an endless wellspring of creative energy. This sense of marvelling at a world full of beauty, of experiencing the joy of being alive, would stay with Tagore, which never allowed him to falter in his faith in the creative potential of man and the positive reliability of nature. The moment brings to mind Debendranath's epiphanic moment in the Himalayas when life's purpose dawned on him as he watched a waterfall and meditated on its later journey as a life-giving river.

Evening Songs was followed by poems that Tagore gathered in the pages of *Prabhat Sangeet* (Morning Songs, 1883), continuing the chronological, temporal theme expressing the newfound sense of his wonder at the world. However, this joyousness sometimes proved elusive, even when he was amidst stunningly beautiful landscapes – as had happened on the rocky perch on the Torquay seashore in Devon. After the exalting experience at Sudder Street, Rabindranath accompanied his brother and sister-in-law to Darjeeling, where they stayed at Rosa Villa. However, the pristine pine trees, the vistas of mountain ranges and the majestic Kanchanjangha could not bring back that experience of the vision from the Sudder Street balcony. The poem written in Darjeeling that captures his mood is the metaphysical and abstract 'Pratidhwani' (The Echo), which gives voice to an indescribable longing within the poet for something that remains elusive. The poem 'Punormilan' (Reunion), in *Prabhat Sangeet*, epitomizes this new phase of Tagore's work: in it he recalls the child in himself who was close to nature; the adolescent who moved away from nature and the person who has now been led back to nature by a little bird, to claim a space amid her generous expanse. This bond with and understanding of nature stayed with Tagore, whose multifaceted projects were imbued with his passion for environmentalism.

The trio travelled to Karwar in Karnataka on the west coast of India, which was situated on the Malaya Hill tract where Satyendranath was the district judge. Karwar, with its harbour, its semicircular beach, its Casuarina trees and surrounding hills, was where Tagore wrote his play *Prakritir Pratishodh* (Nature's Revenge, 1884). As a stage play it is not strong, but the philosophical debate between reason and emotion, asceticism and social responsibility, self-serving aloofness and human bonding, is played out in this story of a sanyasi keen on renouncing his attachment to the world. The sanyasi finds himself drawn to a little girl, an untouchable, who is orphaned and shunned by society. Alarmed at his growing affection, he leaves her to pursue his life of abstinence, only to be haunted by her presence. He goes back to search for her and finds she has died, leaving him to question his choices, a questioning that would surface in many of Tagore's subsequent compositions.

Back in Calcutta he stayed with Jyotirindranath and Kadambari at a garden house on Lower Circular Road near Chowringhee. It was here that he observed vignettes of everyday life, in the people engaged in their mundane existence in the adjacent slum, the bustee. The pictures that were the result of these observations were the work of an untrained hand – they were, however, sharpened by Rabindranath's artistic eye and published in his collection *Chhabi o Gan* (Pictures and Songs, 1884). This collection also included some of the songs that Tagore wrote on the boat journey from Karwar to Calcutta. Tagore's distinctive style as an artist is evident at this stage; this would develop in later life in his disturbed response to world events during the interwar years. His critical and reflective pen continued to be busy in the essays he wrote alongside his creative work, and which were gathered and published later in *Alochona* (Discussions, 1885).

One day Jyotirindranath came home and announced that he had bought a steamer, which was actually no more than a steel shell, at an auction for Rs 7,000. This was another of Jyotirindranath's impetuous endeavours taken on with zeal, like the earlier pathetic ventures to manufacture matches in a home-grown factory (where not a single match was produced that could be coaxed to burst into flame) and a loom which managed to produce a solitary thin *gamchha*, a skimpy towel. The indomitable optimist in Jyotirindranath believed that all that the steamer needed was an engine and some well-equipped cabins to bring it to life, ready for plying between Khulna and Barishal. He named it *Swadeshi*, furnished it in style with Jnanadanandini's tasteful suggestions and opened it up to the public with a lavish party on board. No funds had been spared to make it stylish and comfortable. It had no shortage of passengers who were ferried gratis and plied with light refreshments, with volunteers carrying the national flag and singing patriotic songs to usher them in. However, he could not compete with the established European Flotilla Company. His accounts showed a total lack of revenue and he was finally saved when the *Swadeshi* sank near Howrah Bridge. It was an example of Jyotirindranath's well-meant but badly planned and executed business and social work ventures. This failed undertaking gave Tagore insight into how carefully any project for India's development had to be thought through and implemented, a lesson that would aid him when he embarked on his lifelong endeavours in education, rural regeneration and social-improvement projects.

The family decided around 1883 that it was time that a suitable girl was found for Tagore. There are many accounts of how the sophisticated Tagore women embarked on scouting expeditions to find the appropriate bride for the youngest Tagore son. It was not an easy job, as the Tagores, being Pirali Brahmins, found it difficult to get suitable Brahmin families to agree to let their daughters marry into the Tagore family. Moreover, Debendranath's adoption of Bramhoism led to further resistance and reluctance from Bengali Hindu Brahmins when it came to tying the marital knot with the Tagores. There was one ridiculous occasion when the head of a principality in Orissa (now Odisha) sent a proposal for marriage with his daughter. The Tagores were introduced to two young women, one very plain and tongue-tied and another who was confident and stunningly beautiful. The latter naturally caught the Tagores' eyes, but they soon learnt that the nondescript girl was the proposed bride, while the ravishing beauty was her stepmother. The hunt for a bride was brought to an end by Jnanadanandini, who pinned her choice on the ten-year-old daughter of a Tagore employee, Benimadhab Raichaudhury, with the rather unfashionable name Bhabatarini. Kadambari was not convinced that the simple, plain-looking Bhabatarini, who had not had much opportunity for an all-rounded education, was the right bride for her talented, sensitive, handsome brother-in-law, but she inexplicably gave in to Jnanadanandini, as most people around her did. Debendranath gave his blessing once he was satisfied that her caste credentials were a suitable match for his family background. It is interesting that Tagore, who was a liberal when it came to women's rights and positions in his writing, was willing, as an obedient son, to agree to his father's adherence to the prevalent orthodox custom of bringing child brides to the house. However, the choice proved to be appropriate, as Bhabatarini, whose old-fashioned name was instantly changed to Mrinalini by Tagore (reminiscent of his favourite name, Nalini), proved to be a practical, devoted wife and companion for Rabindranath with her selfless, self-effacing motherly nature. Mrinalini remained with Jnanadanandini for over a year after the wedding, learning the sophisticated ways of the Tagore women and attending Loreto House, a leading English-medium school in Calcutta. Rabindranath's easy relationship with Mrinalini is captured in his letters to her, his 'Chhuti', which have been published in the first volume of his *Chithipatra* (Letters).

On her return to Calcutta, Jnanadanandini started a journal, from the Tagore household precincts, for girls and boys. She called this *Balak*, and Tagore was the chief contributor. Later he would write several pieces for children, a literary journey which was probably initiated by the responsibility his eldest sister-in-law handed to him with this journal.

As Jyotirindranath's various misadventures met with failure, sinking his fortunes, Debendranath decided to rope in his romantic youngest son and transfer some of the responsibilities of the family estates to his youthful shoulders, two days before his wedding. Tagore's training began under Debendranath's instruction at the Calcutta office, where he was told that he would find out about and make notes on daily expenditure, income, exports and imports from the steward which he would incorporate in a weekly report to his father. Once the father was satisfied with the trust he had placed in Rabindranath's ability and executive powers, he would transfer him

Rabindranath with his wife, Mrinalini Devi, soon after their wedding, 1883, in Calcutta.

to the *moffusil* (provincial) estates belonging to the family. Like any perceptive father, Debendranath must have discerned something in his son's energetic, poetic mind. In Rabindranath he saw someone he could trust to take on the efficient running of the family's landed property with responsibility and imagination. Tagore fulfilled this mission with his sensitive engagement and dedication.

However, the Tagore family's favourite son's wedding was far from a grand affair. It happened without fanfare and in the absence of some key family members. Debenedranath had embarked on one of his restless journeys by river and had reached Bankipur. Satyendranath was away with his family and could not be present. On 9 December 1883, the night of Tagore's wedding, his eldest brother-in-law, Saradaprasad (Saudamini's husband), died at Shelidah, the headquarters of the Tagore landed estate. The news of his death reached Jorasanko the next morning. Saradaprasad had looked after the family businesses with integrity and responsibility and Saudamini, with maternal care, had watched over Tagore as a child.

A few months later, on 19 April 1884, Kadambari, Tagore's *Chhoto Bouthan* (youngest sister-in-law), who had been suffering from depression for many years, committed suicide. A deep gloom descended on Jorasanko. It was a tide-changing incident which seemed to sap Jyotirindranath's enthusiastic engagement with life and left a lasting scar on Tagore.

Before this Tagore had known the losses of his mother; his brother Somendranath; his little niece, Urmila; and his brother-in-law Satyaprasad; but Kadambari's death was to haunt his poetic mind all his life. For over sixteen years, she had been his playmate, literary critic and muse, and though she was only two years older than Rabi, she had saved him, his older brother and nephew from the bullying clutches of a 'servocracy', supervising their meals and well-being. When young Sarada Devi died, Kadambari, who was herself a young girl, looked after Rabi with tender motherly care and he blossomed as a writer, performer and critic as part of a creative trio with Jyotirindranath's affectionate indulgence and under Kadambari Devi's protective watchfulness. She was only 25 when she died.

Kadambari had come as a little girl from a small, close-knit family to this large sprawling mansion teeming with lively family members, busy servants and numerous visitors. This place, with its sophisticated milieu, must have been a daunting and lonely one for a sensitive child from a simple familial background. The *andarmahal* where the women dwelt was a bustle of domesticity where no one had the time or inclination to welcome and protect a frightened lonely girl. Her husband was much older, as was the norm, and though he was kind and gentle, he was too busy with his many businesses, his patriotic and artistic projects, to spend enough time with his young wife. As Kadambari grew up, it became evident that she would remain childless, yet she was a motherly figure as her caring role towards Tagore and his cousin and nephew exemplified. Later her adoption of Urmila, Swarnakumari's daughter, gave her joy and solace, but Urmila's accidental death left her bereft and in shock. Kadambari's nurturing personality found expression in a terrace garden at her apartment with her husband that blossomed under her care, and where Tagore felt free to walk in and feel at home. She had birds which she looked after and loved, showering affection on these colourful, caged creatures. Kadambari was an inventive culinary expert and made delectable dishes and snacks for the Tagore household and visitors. She was adept at making *paan*, betel leaf folded artistically with rare condiments,
and Rabi became an expert in cutting betel nut into fine shreds under her sharp critical eye. At one time, she supervised her father-in-law's repast, keeping to his strict routine when he was at home. She was an avid reader and had a critical acumen which made her an impetus behind the Tagore family journal, *Bharati*. She was the sounding board, with her literary and critical sensitivity, for Rabi's songs and poetry and Jyotirindranath's music compositions. When Rabi left for England, his letters home were covertly, if not ostensibly,

addressed to her. She was happy for Rabi's life taking a direction, but her motherly instincts meant that she was lonely again, without someone to shower with affection.

Jyotirindranath's playwriting, his portrait painting and business endeavours continued unabated. Jnanadanandini played an instrumental role in Tagore's marriage arrangements, and it was she who was the central decisive figure with whom Rabi felt at home, especially after his Brighton days, and it was Jnanadanandini whose advice and help Jyotirindranath sought for many of his ventures. After his wedding, Tagore was busy with managing the family estates with which his father had entrusted him. Jyotirindranath's steamer project, in which Jnanadanandini played a consultant's role, ended in financial disaster, and his continuing preoccupation with the theatrical world contributed to Kadambari's mounting isolation and depression, which finally ended with her decision to end her young life.

After her death, for Tagore even the world of nature, which seemed unchanged, could not sustain him and his whole world appeared meaningless. He was afflicted by a deep despair which seemed insurmountable, the pain being unbearable. This would be the beginning of Tagore's creation of works questioning death, loss and the woman's position in both the family and society.

> When death suddenly came, and in a moment tore a gaping rent in life's seamless fabric, I was utterly bewildered. All around, the trees, the soil, the water, the sun, the moon, the stars remained as immovably true as before, and yet the person who was as truly there, who, through a thousand points of contact with life, mind and heart, was so very much more true to me, had vanished in an instant like a dream.[13]

He wrote a series of poems and lyrics to Kadambari in his notebook entitled *Pushpanjali* (Offering of Flowers), which he did not publish, but which were later included in his *Collected Works*. In his later collection *Lipika* there are many poems which have echoes of *Pushpanjali*. The memory of Kadambari's sharp literary mind, her maturity and responsibility in spite of her youth, would haunt his creative consciousness. Her presence in absence found expression in numerous compositions: in multiple songs like 'Tumi ki keboli chhabi?' (Are you just a Picture?); in poems like 'Shanti' (Peace) and 'Kothae' (Where?); in his novel *Nashtanir* (The Broken Nest); and many more. When she was alive, Tagore dedicated volume after volume to his *Chhoto Bouthan* – his *Letters* from Europe, *Broken Heart*, several songs and poems, and after her death he dedicated *Chhabi O Gan*, *Bhanu Singher Padabali* and *Shoishab Sangeet* (Childhood Songs) to her indelible memory. However, the period after Kadambari's death did not mar Tagore's compositions with any sense of morbidity or hopelessness. What emerged was a man chastened by loss and sorrow, who continued to find meaning and joy in the living world, accepting death as an inescapable reality in life.

Kadambari's death had a tremendous impact on the Tagore household. Dwijendranath resigned from his position as editor of *Bharati* and it was soon announced that *Bharati* as a journal would be discontinued. This was perhaps because of Kadambari's intimate association with the journal, which made it difficult for the members to continue it without her intellectual and critical input and creative impetus. Another journal was founded by Dwijendranath in 1891 called *Sadhana*, of which Tagore's nephew Sudhindranath was editor, and as with *Bharati*, it was understood that Tagore would be its chief contributor. In 1894 Tagore took over the editorship of *Sadhana*, and of Bankimchandra Chatterjee's literary magazine *Bangladarshan* in 1901–5.[14] A few days after Kadambari's death, Tagore's third brother, Hemendranath, who had inculcated a love of Bengali language and literature in him, died. Tagore would continue to encounter many deaths of people he loved, and like a sturdy storm-tossed vessel, he learnt to confront and address this devastating 'truth' of life through his work.

In Calcutta, Tagore, accompanied by his niece Indira on the piano, sang well-known songs that he had heard in England, like 'In the Gloaming', 'Come into the Garden, Maud' and 'Goodbye Sweetheart, Goodbye'. The muse, literary critic and attentive reader/listener he had found in Kadambari could never be replaced or re-enacted in any of Rabindranath's relatives or friends. However, in Indira he found a confidante and a sensitive exponent of his songs. The days in England had sparked an affectionate bond that kept Indira and Surendranath, brother and sister, close to their uncle and his life and work at Shantiniketan.

It is interesting to note that the various collections that were published in the late nineteenth century were called *Songs* – *Evening Songs*, *Morning Songs*, *Pictures and Songs*, *Childhood Songs*, *Kari o Komal* (Sharps and Flats) – yet these were not strung to music, but were definitely lyrics in their rhythmic, personal and emotional appeal. Songs had been and would continue to be composed for musical plays and Tagore's inimitable dance dramas; one he wrote in the last decade of the nineteenth century was *Mayar Khela* (Play of Illusion, 1888), dominated by feeling rather than a discernible storyline.

The year 1884 saw the death of a leading light of Bengal, Keshab Chandra Sen. He had been a passionate leader of the Bramho Samaj, but his modern thinking had led to a parting of ways with the conservative Debendranath. With his astute judgement, Debendranath made Tagore the secretary of Adi Bramho Samaj, which, as he must have anticipated, aroused a fresh religious and spiritual interest in Tagore, who fulfilled his duties as secretary with his characteristic dedication.

In the meantime, both Jyotirindranath and Swarnakumari were deeply involved with their nationalist aspirations. In 1882 the Bengal branch of the Theosophical Society was established, with Swarnakumari as its president. The viceroy, Lord Dufferin, had encouraged Mr Octavian Hume to establish the Indian National Congress (INC) in 1885. In 1887 Jyotirindranath attended the Congress proceedings held in Madras and both he and Janakinath Ghoshal (Swarnakumari's husband) extended their hospitality to the British sympathizers the business magnate George Yule (president of the INC) and barrister Eardley Norton. The governor, Lord Connemara, invited the delegates the next day to the Governor's Palace for tea. After the INC meeting at Allahabad, a lavish party was thrown at the Jorasanko home for Yule and Eardley, an event that was mentioned by Tagore in a letter to his friend Priyanath and the event also finds mention in the news: 'Yesterday there was an evening party at the house of Babu Debendra Nath Tagore, in honour of Mr Yule and Mr Norton.'[15] Tagore remained a spectator to these events from a distance.

His first child, a daughter, Madhurilata, his Bela, was born in 1886 and his son, Rathindranath, in 1888. A restlessness which was characteristic of Tagore seized him to move from his Jorasanko home to Park Street in Calcutta, after which he journeyed to Darjeeling, where he stayed in Castleton House with his female relatives and started writing songs for his lyrical drama *Mayar Khela* (Game of Illusion), which he finished when he was back in Calcutta. It was performed by the Tagore family women – Swarnakumari's *Sakhi Samiti* (Society of Friends), on 29 December 1888.[16]

In 1889 Tagore travelled with his family to Solapur in Maharashtra where Satyendranath was a judge. Here he composed a play in blank verse, *Raja o Rani* (King and Queen), which tells the story of the unmitigated cruelty and violence of King Vikramdeb of Jullunder against his people and his queen and her brother, Prince Kumarsen of Kashmir. Soon after, Tagore sought beauty and peace in the famous rose garden at Ghazipur on the Ganga, but found that this hand-nurtured garden did not have the same effect on him as had untamed nature. On his travels to both Darjeeling and Ghazipur, his sister

Tagore with two of his children, eldest Madhurilata (Bela) and Rathindranath (Rathi).

Swarnakumari accompanied him and we find details of these journeys and experiences in her letters (*Darjeeling Patra* and *Ghazipur Patra*). After a brief period in Calcutta he travelled to Shelidah. In 1888 Tagore published his collection *Kari o Komal* (Sharp and Flat) with some explicitly erotic poems, such as

'Stan' (Breast), 'Chumban' (Kiss) and 'Bibashana' (Naked), which were composed with Tagore's characteristic artistic sophistication and honesty.

Plays, songs and essays flowed from his pen during his restless wanderings. One significant output was a collection of poems from his notebook which was published as *Manasi* (Mind's Creation, 1890). Many of the poems in this expressed the void Tagore felt upon Kadambari's death, for example in 'Shunyo Grihe' (In the Empty House), in which he wonders whether the open sky comprehends the deep pain in the mind of man; the poem goes on to reflect on where the one who was so close to him is now.

On his brother-in-law Saradaprasad's death, the responsibility of looking after the Tagore estate took on a new urgency. In November 1889 Tagore was given the official responsibility of taking over the supervision of the family estates. Initially Tagore embarked on his own to the land of the Padma to take up the role of zamindar that Debendranath had entrusted on him. He toured Shahjadpur, Birahimpur, Kaligram and Patishar, his headquarters being Shelidah, returning at regular intervals to Calcutta to apprise his father (who now lived in Park Street) of the land holdings. Initially he had to stay in his houseboat, which belonged to his grandfather, Dwarkanath, as the house at Shelidah had not been built. The boat was a Dhakai *bajra* (Dhaka-style budgerow), a flat-bottomed houseboat which carried him on the turbulent waters of the land watered by the Padma, through large and small rivers and *bheels* (large water bodies) during the day and stayed moored at night. It was named *Padma* by Tagore. It was here that he could avoid the peopled banks and write undisturbed for hours.

In Calcutta, he had the opportunity to visit his young family and on one such visit to Jorasanko, he found his family members struggling over a drama script that they were trying to adapt from his novel *Bau Thakuranir Hat* (The Young Queen's Market) for a performance. Tagore glanced at the script and found it inadequate.

He told them to desist for a little while. He went away and his sense of social justice, which elicited responses to various prevalent social practices and incidents, found expression this time in *Visarjan* (1890; published in English as *Sacrifice* in 1917), a drama in blank verse against the Hindu practice of animal sacrifice, which he gave to his family to enact.

He then went to Shantiniketan before returning to Solapur to Satyendranath's house. The Shantiniketan Trust had been formed in 1888 with Dwipendranath Tagore (Dwijendranath's son), Priyanath Sashtri and Rabindranath Tagore as the three trustees.[17] Here Debendranath established an ashram as a place for spiritual retreat. An official celebration of the event was held in 1891 on an auspicious moonlit night, with many delegates travelling from Calcutta for the occasion. It was also attended by important people from the surrounding areas – Raipur, Bolpur and Surul – and the audience appreciated Tagore's singing at the event.[18] At Shantiniketan, Tagore wrote two moving poems, 'Meghdhut' (Cloud Messenger), inspired by the Sanskrit poet Kalidasa's lyric work *Meghaduta*, and 'Ahalya' – about a woman who was cursed by her husband when he

Houseboat on River Padma, in east Bengal (now Bangladesh).

discovered that she had been duped and raped by Indra, the
god of heaven, who was enamoured of her beauty. In this poem,
Tagore reflects on Ahalya's oneness with all insentient beings.

While staying at Solapur Tagore had composed *Raja o Rani*,
which, like *Visarjan*, was performed by the Tagore family,
but the former was also staged at the Emerald Theatre in
Calcutta as a commercial production in November 1889.[19]
Both *Visarjan* and the play-script of his novel *Rajarshi* were
written in Shahjadpur.

At Solapur Tagore discovered that his friend Loken Pali was
planning another trip to England. Tagore decided to accompany
Satyendranath and Loken, his old companions, once again to
Europe, leaving by steamer from Bombay on 22 August 1890.[20]
The call of England was to come at various periods in Tagore's
life. His travel diary is full of humorous, satirical and perceptive
descriptions of his fellow passengers. He travelled through Italy
and France where he was charmed by Italian grapes, girls wearing
scarves and the French countryside. But his special appreciation
was reserved for English girls whose blue eyes reflected the sky,
and whose sharp features made them very attractive. Once again
he observed the difference in behaviour between Western women,
with their freedom, and the women at home, confined by more
prevalent social strictures. He did visit the Scott house and was
disappointed to learn that they had moved to an unknown address.
He saw a musical at the Savoy Theatre, *The Gondoliers*, and an
adaptation of Sir Walter Scott's *The Bride of Lammermoor* at the
Lyceum.[21] This time there were no letters home, but he did keep
a diary, which was published as *Europe Jatrir Diary* (The Diary of
a Visitor to Europe). A poignant poem that he wrote in England
was 'Biday' (Farewell), which expresses nostalgia, hopelessness
and pain through the image of a small boat in a vast ocean to which
are wafted memories of sweetness and delight from a known land.
But he soon grew tired of his travels, as the soil and skies of Bengal

beckoned – as would happen many a time in his life. He cut short his voyage, leaving his companions to continue their foreign tour, and returned on his own from the world to his home.

Tagore resumed his zamindari duties on his return to India. His wife Mrinalini, his daughter Madhurilata (Bela), his son Rathindranath and his nephew Balendranath accompanied him in November 1890 to the land of the mighty Padma river. There are some vivid descriptions in Tagore's letters of the landscape viewed from his boat:

> When one is living in Calcutta, one forgets how astonishingly beautiful this world is. It is only when you live here that you comprehend that this sun that sets every day among these peaceful trees by the side of this little river, and the hundred thousand stars that silently rise every night above this endless, ashen, lonely, silent sandbank – what a surprisingly noble event this is.[22]

For the poet 'this sandbank spread across the horizon and the other shore like a picture – this neglected bit at the edge of the world' was a 'large, silent, deserted school',[23] which became his workshop for writing as well as for his pragmatic projects as a conscientious, innovative and benevolent zamindar.

When his family came to stay with him at Shelidah and travelled with him on the *Padma*, they welcomed folk singers, such as Fikirchand Fakir, and Bauls (wandering minstrels of Bengal) like Kangal Suna-Ulla. It was during his stay here that Tagore met the famous Baul singer Lalan Fakir. In the family journal, Balendranath, Rabindranath's nephew, notes how Tagore, with many of the Tagore family members, was instrumental in gathering, noting down and preserving the folk tunes of Bengal. These tunes inspired Tagore to write several songs which used the six-beat rhythmic cycle (*dadra tala*) and reflected universal love and freedom from material bondage. Tagore's 'Amar Sonar Bangla' (My Golden Bengal), with its haunting Baul tune, is the national anthem of Bangladesh today.

Once the house was built in Shelidah, Tagore made it his headquarters and visited his various estates from this zamindari seat. He was greeted by the firing of guns by 'quaintly dressed guards'.[24] Rathindranath describes the entry of the zamindar into an estate for rent collection: women blew conch shells at the bank, from which Tagore would be carried in a palanquin to the zamindar's office building, near which a platform would be awaiting him under a canopy where the village elders and headman, followed by the villagers who offered a token payment, would receive the zamindar's blessing with bowed head. After this, a simple repast of parched rice and yoghurt organized by the tenants would be served to some 2,000 people. This was Tagore's first encounter at close quarters with the rural folk of Bengal. He was appalled by their hopelessness and helplessness, their apathy and despondency.

Rabindranath and his family members at lunch, *c.* 1890, Shelidah.
L–R: Indira Devi serving, Jagadish Chowdhury, Kumudnath Chowdhury, Rabindranath Tagore, Jyotirindranath Tagore, and Sarala Devi holding a fan.

The poverty of his nation became apparent to him during his Shelidah years. He was a conscientious zamindar who took a humane interest in his tenants' welfare, heard their problems, settled their disputes and put in place schemes to alleviate their abject condition and make them self-reliant.[25] He set up an alternative judiciary system based upon the old Panchayati tradition of India: disputes were brought to the village headman, then to five elders of the estate and finally, if unresolved, to Tagore. This legal system was recognized by the government and Tagore's tenants did not have to take a single case to the *mofussil* (provincial) or magistrate's courts. It worked for several years, protecting the people from police harassment and negligence. Tagore set up a cooperative system, visited schools and took on various schemes to inculcate self-reliance in his tenants, many of whom were Muslim. Some of his various endeavours to establish home-grown industries met with failure, like his brother Jyotirindranath's schemes. But Tagore's rural regeneration programme – aimed at instilling hope, self-sufficiency and dignity in his countrymen in his estates, preventing an overweening dependency on government handouts – was appreciated by his father, whose trust in his imaginative poet-son showed the former's canny perception of Tagore's abilities and dedication. The Shelidah days would provide the experience he needed to start his rural reconstruction project two decades later at Sriniketan at Surul in 1922.

The Shelidah days are captured in the letters he wrote to Mrinalini when she was not with him and to his niece, Indira, which were gathered and published in *Chhinnapatra* (Glimpses of Bengal, 1921). He was appalled by the lack of self-worth he encountered in his villagers. They seemed resigned to their fate. In a letter written on 11 May 1893 from Shelidah, he spoke of them: 'Meek and gentle souls shine through their ravaged and wrinkled old bodies.'[26] He developed a deep affection for these people, whom he found to be like 'big children': 'more childlike' than 'little children' who will grow up, the ryots (Indian peasants) 'never will'.[27] These 'helpless foundlings dependent on providence to bring food to their very lips' looked on their zamindar with a 'reverence . . . so unaffected' that 'the simplicity and sincerity of their devotion' made Tagore feel they were greater than him.[28] One time there was a fire in a village and the residents were petrified and helpless. Muslim men from a neighbouring village came running to help them, but had to beat up some of the inhabitants who resisted them when they tried to pull down the thatch to stop the fire. After the fire had been put out, they were grateful that their thatch had been dismantled to stop the flames from spreading.

Tagore was shocked to see the lack of activity once darkness settled in these villages. He arranged for a club to be built where the villagers could gather together, read newspapers, listen to the Indian epics the *Mahabharata* and the *Ramayana*, and find some joy in camaraderie. Once the club was built, however, it remained unused. Nevertheless, people from a Muslim village came to him and said that they were ready for him to build a club in their village.[29]

Tagore met this resistance born of a deep-rooted apathy in many of his villages. In one village where there was a water shortage because the river was far away, he offered to cement a well if the villagers would build it themselves. However, they said that they were not interested in assisting him to go to heaven with his good deed. Another time when Tagore offered to build a road from his estate office to Kushtia and asked the villagers to keep it maintained, they were reluctant to look after a road which would enable the 'gentle folk' to come and go. They did not see their own gain in any such endeavour. These experiences made Rabindranath realize how entrenched the lack of self-respect was, caught as the villagers were between 'tyranny and charity', used as they were to being ruled, exploited and dependent on handouts.[30]

Tagore's letters are full of his variegated experiences during his Shelidah days, told with his intrinsic sense of humour. On one occasion he visited the British magistrate while the young sahib was holding court on the verandah of his tent. Tagore invited the man to his house for a meal, but he declined Tagore's invitation with the excuse that he was going pig-sticking instead. When Tagore returned home, a terrific storm broke out. It suddenly dawned on him that the sahib's tent would provide inadequate shelter during this torrential rain. He sent word to the magistrate to come and stay in his house, but soon realized his folly as the spare room was in a state of total disarray. Then followed a frantic effort to remove servants' belongings, wooden chests and packing boxes full of unused things, and to clear the dust. When the sahib arrived, Tagore dusted down his hair and clothes and received him in the calmest manner, having restored some semblance of order to the guest room.

Tagore was a keen observer of people and life in the *mofussil* and his imagination enabled him to enter their minds, lives and homes, allowing him to write some of the best short stories of his time. He was writing his short stories in Bengali around the same time as Guy de Maupassant and Chekhov were writing in their native tongues; Rabindranath was a pioneer of this genre in Bengali. On his journeys on the Padma he encountered many *ghats* (steps leading to the water) where people came to bathe, and where women washed clothes and utensils and collected water in pitchers. It struck him how the ghat was a witness through time of lives lived on the banks of the river. In his story 'Ghater Katha' (The Ghat's Story), the narrator is a ghat who grows fond of a lovely little girl called Kusum, whose childish feet walk down it to the river everyday. The ghat learns from the chatter of the girl's friends that Kusum has been married off. After her husband disappears and a letter tells her of his death, however, she returns to her parental home. A widow at eight years old, Kusum is changed; she is now pensive and silent. A sanyasi comes and occupies her village's Shiva temple, but he looks very much like Kusum's late husband. Kusum becomes a devotee at the temple, but when she stops coming and on one renewed visit is confronted by the sanyasi, she confesses that she has seen him in a dream as a man she loves. The sanyasi decides to leave the temple and as darkness descends the ghat hears a splash in the river.

Other stories follow, stories which are woven from slight acquaintances, chance encounters and overheard incidents. 'The Postmaster' shows the callousness of the urban intruder and the selfless dedication of a rural orphan girl. In 'Samsya Puran' (The Solution), the insensitive impoverishment by an educated Hindu zamindar, Bipinbihari, of his powerless Muslim tenant Aachimaddi and the complexity of communal relationships are highlighted.[31] 'Sashti' (Punishment) is about the plight of a woman named Chandara who is falsely implicated by her husband for the murder of her sister-in-law, while the crime was actually committed by her brother-in-law. When the husband relents, he is shunned by his convicted wife when he comes to see her. In 'Dena Paona' (The Dowry Death) Nirupama resents her father's efforts to pay the promised amount to her abusive in-laws and dies of illness brought on by suffering and neglect.

Not all of these stories are about rural Bengal. Many are urban tales about women like Giribala in 'Manbhanjan' whose husband is attracted to a stage actress and abandons her for his mistress; when Giribala takes on her role in her absence as the transformed Labango, her husband is livid and bent on revenge. There are historical tales like 'Dalia', set in Shah Shuja's time, and stories where the historical and surreal intermingle, such as 'Durasha', which unfolds amid the mists of Darjeeling; there are other stories in which surrealism dominates, as in 'Skeleton' and 'Laboratory'. Of Tagore's roughly 90 stories, he wrote 44 during his Shelidah years, all of which are written with his characteristic humour, irony and as much sympathy as the characters deserve. His stories emerged from his personal experiences and encounters, for example his story 'Ginni' (Wife) features a schoolteacher, Shibnath Pundit, based upon the Normal School's Haranath Pundit. Pramanath Bishi, the Bengali critic, noted that for the first time in Bengali literature, he found the ordinary, unknown Bengali middle-class depicted in stories.[32] His last story, the 'Mussalmanir Galpo' (The Tale of a Muslim Girl), published a year before his death in 1940, encapsulates his scathing critique of divisive communal politics in a story about human generosity in the face of religious orthodoxy. In his short stories Tagore uses conversational Bengali, which he had begun using in his letters from England and perfected with the confidence of a master *littérateur*. His collection of stories appeared in quick succession in *Chhoto Galpo* (Short Stories, 1894) and *Galpo-Dasak* (1895), and all would later be gathered together in *Galpo Guchho* (Collected Stories).

Tagore was busy gathering Indian legends and stories from Buddhist, Rajput and Sikh sources, which he expressed in a combination of dramatic dialogues and lyrical compositions in *Katha* (Ballads, 1899) and *Kahini* (Tales, 1900). This is also the period when he brought out *Kalpana* (Dreams, 1900), a poetry collection which contained some of his finest poems on nature.

During this period, his poems continued to flow, as did his songs. The two came together in his lyrical play *Chitrangada* (1892), a dance drama which tells the story of a Manipuri princess brought up by her father as a soldier. She falls in love with the great Pandava warrior Arjun. The drama ends with Chitrangada revealing herself as no ordinary girl, but a princess, whom Arjun can know only when he accepts her as an equal. Feminist themes like this would continue to run through Tagore's narratives in poetry, fiction, plays and dance dramas, but somewhere one detects certain ambivalences between the artist and his personal decisions.

Three years after his marriage to ten-year-old Mrinalini, in 1887, he had given a public talk on Hindu Marriage, organized by the Savitri Sabha (an association founded by the Savitri Library) and held at the Science Association Hall in Calcutta. He pointed out the ills of marrying a child to an older man, the practice of dowry which impoverished the girls' families and the incidence of child widows, as he advocated for women's rights. *The Bengalee* recorded 'that so important a subject was discussed in such a truly liberal spirit' where 'Babu Rabindra Nath Tagore read an admirable paper on the subject'.[33] Towards the end of his Shelidah stay, he married off his daughter Bela, who was nearly fifteen, and Rani (Renuka), aged twelve. Debendranath paid for both weddings and the dowries. Tagore had lost a lot of money in his endeavours to start indigenous businesses to help his countrymen on his estates. One can only speculate that it was a financial consideration and an exigency that made Tagore marry off his daughters at an early age, as his own financial situation was far from robust and he could depend on his father to approve of the wedding arrangements and finance them while Debendranath was still alive and able. In a letter to his wife, whom he intimately addressed as 'Bhai Chhuti', Tagore explained how they were fulfilling social expectations. Young girls were considered of marriageable age before they reached puberty, after which it was difficult to find a suitable groom for them. Tagore reminded Mrinalini how she had found it easier to adjust to the Tagore household because she had been brought there when she was young.[34] He reasoned that his daughters would find it easier to fit into their in-laws' house at their impressionable age. In the letters he wrote to Mrinalini and to his children, we see how close he was to them, how he shared his thoughts and misgivings with his wife – and spoke of their true partnership and companionship – and expressed his concern and deep affection for his children. He tells his wife in one letter, 'I have this constant worry in my heart about my children which I try to overcome.'[35] In another letter he says, 'Please do not work any harder for my happiness. Your love is enough . . . It is easier to move forward if we are united. I don't wish to leave you out of anything I do, but I hesitate to thrust my will on you.'[36] He asks, 'Why don't you write a letter to me every day?' and does not mind if it is 'long or short, good or bad'.[37] One incident exemplifies his attachment to his young family. On his way to England on a ship, just before they reached Aden, he had been seasick for three days. In a letter written on 29 August 1890 he wrote to his 'Chhoto Bou' how on Sunday night he felt that his spirit had left the ship and returned to their bedroom where Mrinalini slept with Bela and Rathi. He tells her to remember the date and know that he was with her then in spirit as he watched her, caressed her and kissed his children, before he left them sleeping peacefully.[38] Ten years later, after leaving Bela with her husband near Patna, where he practised as a lawyer, Tagore wrote to Mrinalini assuring her that he had left his Bela well and happy. Yet Tagore had witnessed the loneliness and fragility of little Kadambari when she entered the Tagore household. He paid for Renuka's husband to study medicine in the UK and had the consolation of having this frail, ailing daughter stay at home while her husband was away. Soon after both weddings, Tagore moved with Mrinalini and his children Rathindranath, Renuka, Samindranath and youngest daughter Mira to Shantiniketan. All his life he was propelled by a restlessness which accounted for the many journeys he made, in India and abroad.

5

The Abode of Peace

The silence that had impressed Tagore during his time in the land of the Padma would surround him at Shantiniketan, 'the abode of peace', where he moved with his family in 1901. In a letter to his niece Indira in October 1894, he wrote about waking up at dawn in his south room at Shantiniketan where he felt his 'lassitide' was 'dispelled'. He spoke about 'the mornings [which] are so deeply quiet and beautiful and bright', similar to what he experienced on the verandah of the house in Shimla, 'the same peace and beauty descends upon the mind'.[1] His intimate encounter with nature amid the rural Bengal landscape occurred at Shelidah and the surrounding estates. At Shantiniketan he felt close to nature, a bond which would always remain, which sustained him and which he sought when the world seemed too much. In another letter to Indira during the same trip he described a scene:

> The skies are blue, the plants and trees shimmer, the green rice fields in between seem wrapped in the soft, pale light of the sun . . . I'm sitting here overjoyed, submerged in a flood of ice-clean *hemanta* [autumn] light . . . there's no one to disturb me here . . . I feel like a proper *nabab*.[2]

The freedom that this unfettered landscape provided was the perfect setting for Tagore, who remained a strong advocate for freedom throughout his life.

Tagore moved to Shantiniketan with the purpose of setting up a school at the ashram his father had established with a Trust deed. He had travelled with several family members and friends to attend a formal celebration of the opening of the ashram in 1891. Before taking up the task of opening a school there, he sought and obtained his father's blessings, but he had very limited resources. The dry hot climate for many months in the year meant that this red-soil district was mostly covered with stubble and a few straggling bushes and trees. But soil, plants and saplings had been brought to replenish the land and to put a green mantle over these barren fields. The land was watered by the Kopai, a small river, a *chhoto nadi*, which is symbolic in Tagore's poetry, signifying the humble rural communities which thrive along its banks. The ashram was expanded and a house resembling the Shelidah estate was built. Imported painted glass was brought to build a prayer room, the *Upashana ghar* or Mandir (temple). Later Rathindranath, Tagore's son, who trained in agriculture at the University of Illinois, effectively brought about a green revolution at Shantiniketan, which is known today for its abundance of flowers and trees.

Tagore's encounters in Shelidah showed him the need for rural improvement and he was convinced this could be accomplished through education; education that was not disengaged from the regional and cultural reality of the country, but rather deeply embedded within it. His own desultory experiences at the leading schools of his time in Calcutta, with their mind-numbing mechanical methods and instruction in English, had deeply ingrained in him the need for school education to be conducted in the mother tongue. He had been the teacher of his children at Shelidah, but he realized that this was inadequate. All his life, Rabindranath looked for the good teacher as a role model imperative to a sound education; he sought teachers whom he could invite from across the nation and the world to teach at his institution. The school had a humble beginning with only five boys (including his son, Rathindranath).

Initially there were five teachers, of whom three were Christians. One was an Englishman named Lawrence who loved his caterpillars and slept with them crawling over him. Tagore had met him at Shelidah and invited him to teach at his school. A Bengali Catholic convert, Bramhabandhav Upadhyay, was a great admirer of the English theologian Cardinal Newman. However, Bramhabandhav's strict disciplinarian methods were not welcome at Shantiniketan. He left and later adopted orthodox Hindu ways and began an anti-British paper, which Rathindranath described as 'of a Hitlerian type'. Interestingly, it was Bramhabandhav who called Tagore 'Gurudev', an appellation that would be used by Gandhi (whom Tagore addressed as the Mahatma) and many others who came in close contact with him, including Leonard Elmhirst and Arthur Geddes.[3]

Just before he moved to Shantiniketan, Tagore had written an innovative volume of poems, *Kshanika* (Momentary, 1900), with short and pithy pieces remarkable for their use of conversational Bengali, which he had used with confidence in his short stories. This collection and his collection *Kalpana* (Imagination, 1900) were his parting gifts to a century. The following year marked a turning point, with his collection *Naivedya* (Offering, 1901), which was almost a premonition of the dark decade of loss that would mark his personal life at the start of the new century. The poems here were very different from his earlier volumes – they embodied Tagore's spiritual search as the artist in him communicated with the divine in the poems, marking the beginning of what the Tagore scholar and translator William Radice calls the *Gitanjali* phase.[4] This is shown in lines such as the following:

> When the heart is hard and parched, come upon me
> with a shower of mercy.
> When grace is lost from life, come with a burst of song.

My heart longs to join in thy song,
but vainly struggles for a voice. I would speak,
but speech breaks not into song, and I cry out baffled.

He it is, the innermost one,
who awakens my being with his deep hidden touches.[5]

The school at Shantiniketan began in December 1901 with meagre resources. The luxury that Tagore had known at Jorasanko was that of a rich cultural atmosphere of creative experiment seeped in a socio-political awareness of his Bengali/Indian heritage and consciousness. Financially the family had recovered from Dwarkanath's debts through Debendranath's sharp supervision of expenditure and astute control of the landed property. Life at Jorasanko was comfortable but not lavish. Jyotirindranath's well-meaning but hapless business ventures, especially his last debacle with his ill-fated steamer company, had gravely depleted his fortunes. Neither he nor Tagore had the business acumen of their grandfather. Tagore had lost much of his own resources in his modest attempts at setting up indigenous businesses for his tenants in his estates, most of which proved unsuccessful.

The school opened with a small ceremony where the boys were gifted with red silk *dhotis* and *chadors.* Satyendranath conducted the prayers and Tagore sang songs he had composed for the occasion, one of which was 'Mora satyer pare man' (We Dedicate Ourselves to Truth). This dedication to 'truth' remained at the core of Tagore's ideology through the vicissitudes of life. Apart from the guest house at Shantiniketan, there was a building with three rooms which became the school and a library that was built alongside. Tagore had asked his employee at Shalidah, Jagannath Roy, who was also a homeopath doctor, to come and help him at Shantiniketan. Roy became an all-round manager of the school, including supervising the dormitory that was built to provide shelter to both students and teachers. The school was named Bramhacharya Ashram following the Upanishadic tradition, but true to Tagore's own ideal of freedom it was imbued with what became known as the Rabindric spirit, free from orthodoxy and religious constraints. Tagore's imagination had been fired by the concept of the *tapovan* which he revived in this modern version of the forest hermitage. Initially he did not take fees from his students, a feature of the guru–shishya tradition, where the teacher took on full responsibility of providing for his disciples/pupils in a lived experience of holistic learning, which included daily chores like cleaning and cooking, as well as tasks which inculcated self-sufficiency, such as planting and cultivation, alongside reading and discussion of texts. In his essay 'A Poet's School' (1926), Tagore described how his students 'take great pleasure in cooking, weaving, gardening, improving their surroundings, and in rendering services to other boys, very often secretly, lest they should feel embarrassed'.[6] 'Their classwork has not been separated from their normal activities but forms a part of their daily current of life.'[7] Rathindranath spoke of the sense of camaraderie that existed: 'joys and sorrows' were shared by teachers and pupils – they were an 'essentially happy lot'. He speaks of his father's presence and participation when he was there, as he never tired of composing songs and poems and singing or reciting them; rehearsing and directing his plays; recounting stories from the *Mahabharata*; taking classes and playing indoor games with the boys.[8] Weather permitting, the classes were held under the trees where students and teacher could be close to nature. The love of nature, the close association with one's environment, was nurtured here, where simplicity (not the virtue of poverty) was adopted as a way of life for building character, without the appurtenances of modern living and equipment which Tagore felt cluttered education and where the role of the teacher and the importance of the student were minimized. He epitomized this later in his delightful story *Tota Kahini* (The Parrot's Training, 1918). He remembered his own schooldays which had 'tortured' him with 'the fact that they did not have the completeness of the world . . . But children are in love with life, and it is their first love'.[9]

The method of rote learning which prevailed at the time was replaced by creative and innovative education. For a long time his school was seen as an example of a poet's eccentric wish fulfilment; even when students were sent to him, they were considered the 'difficult' ones. Initially there were only boys, but slowly girls came to stay and study at his ashram.

The Shantiniketan experiment would prove a financial burden in the years to come. Initially Tagore sold his bungalow at the seafront in Puri and his wife willingly parted with most of her jewellery to meet the costs. An annual income of Rs 1,800 was realized from the ashram's Trust and Tagore utilized his own slim monthly income of around Rs 200 to keep the institution going. But it was never enough. As time went on, he sold the copyright to his publications to obtain money to sustain his institution. In a letter to his friend

A bookbinding class at Shantiniketan.

and close associate, the English missionary Charles Freer Andrews, he wrote 'I sold my books, my copyrights, everything I had, in order to carry on with the school. I cannot really tell you what a struggle it was, and what difficulties I had to go through.'[10] The meals at the school were vegetarian and Rathindranath recalls how his mother, always affectionate and motherly and an excellent cook, would prepare delectable dishes with simple ingredients that were available for the children to supplement the boys' simple fare. She also turned a blind eye when they invaded her larder. In fact, Mrinalini was like a mother to all the young boarders, planning their meals and looking after them. She was a close companion to Tagore in spite of the hardships of a pioneering life.

As mentioned, Mrinalini came to Jorasanko as a little girl with little education, making a huge transition from a humble background to an aristocratic household which was a beehive of literary activity. With her inherent practical nature and her quiet sincerity, she soon made herself proficient in English and Sanskrit, and joined Jorasanko's cultural life, acting with admirable skill in her husband's play *Raja o Rani*. She equipped herself to be Tagore's staunch supporter and dedicated partner and remained a meaningful presence on his estates and at his institution. He had entrusted her with the task of translating the *Ramayana* from Sanskrit to Bengali, which she did assiduously, but could not complete.

Rathindranath and his classmates experienced a kind of freedom that Tagore had longed for when he was growing up. There was a gifted teacher, the 21-year-old Satish Chandra Roy, who was with them for a year. He could recite Kalidasa, Virgil, Dante, Goethe, Shakespeare and Tagore by heart. During the summer holidays when all the other boys had gone home, Rathindranath spent most of his time with Satish, as they scoured Tagore's rich library, reading and discussing various books which Tagore had brought from Calcutta and which became the nucleus of the vast library that grew round it. They would go for long walks through the rolling countryside and lie under the stars on the bare ground at night as Satish recited Bengali poetry, sometimes until dawn. One evening as a spectacular storm gathered and burst upon them, Rathindranath was mesmerized to see how the beauty of the storm electrified Satish's poetic soul as he recited Tagore's poem 'Barsha-Shesh' (The Year's End), his voice matching the storm.[11] However, one moment Satish was there and another he was gone; he had disappeared into the storm and his injured body was found the next day. He died soon after of smallpox. This was a deep blow for the poet and Shantiniketan was thereafter marked by personal losses that followed in quick succession.

Earlier, in 1899 and 1902, Tagore had lost two nephews who were very close to him, one of whom was Balendranath, who had been close to Mrinalini and was Tagore's right hand at Shelidah. In the early days of the Shantiniketan experiment, Mrinalini fell ill. She had to be moved to Calcutta for treatment and her family went to visit her there. The last time the children, Bela (Madhurilata), Rathi, Rani (Renuka), Sami (Samindranath) and Mira, saw her, her tears rolled down her cheeks as she looked at them, unable to speak. She died in 1902. Her death was a great blow to all the inmates: the students, teachers and other workers of the ashram. Tagore maintained an outward calm on losing his life partner, but henceforth, he was truly alone. His bereavement found expression in a series of poems, *Smaran* (In Remembrance): 'Love came, and left, opening the door / Never to return.'[12]

On his return to Shantiniketan from Calcutta, Tagore tried to immerse himself in his work, but Rani, who had always been delicate, developed tuberculosis. He made a frantic effort to help her recover by taking her to the salubrious ambience of Hazaribagh, and when that failed, in order to bring back Rani's strength, he moved to Almora. He left Rathindranath in the care of teachers like Mohit Kumar Sen, who taught him Milton and Shakespeare, and

Bidhishekhar Bahttacharya, who taught him Sanskrit and Pali. He took little Sami and Mira with him. It was on this convalescent trip that he composed delightful and poignant poems for his children so as to entertain them. These were published in *Shishu* (The Child, 1903; *The Crescent Moon*, 1913).[13] While he nursed Rani, his creative output continued: he wrote his probing novel about the *andarmahal*, *Chokher Bali* (Eye Sore), and *Nauka Dubi* (Boat Wreck), with its eventful plot of mishaps and identity confusion. But Rani could not recover, so Tagore brought her back to Calcutta, where she died in 1903. Each time Tagore lost someone dear to him, he plunged himself into work. Shantiniketan, which had begun with five boys, had grown to accommodate fifty students. It was at this time that his father, Debendranath, died on 19 January 1905 at the grand age of 87. He had been Tagore's banyan tree and unwavering supporter. Debendranath had, through his various measures, entrusted the care of many of his projects to his youngest son, who would carry the legacy of the Tagore family and be the bastion of the Bengal Renaissance during its final years. He had made Tagore the sole executor of his will and the family estates had been divided up. The death of the Maharshi was a great blow to Tagore. He left Tagore with a monthly income of Rs 1,250–1,500, a handsome sum for a poet, but inadequate to run a school.

More tragedies were to follow. Sami and Mira were with Tagore, but Rathindranath had been sent to America to study. Sami was on holiday with his friends at Monghyr (now Mungar), where he contracted cholera. Tagore rushed to see him, but Sami could not be saved and died in 1907. Soon after, his eldest daughter, Bela, who was with her husband in Calcutta, developed tuberculosis like Rani. Tagore stayed with her and nursed her with fatherly devotion, but he could not hold death away.

This was a dark period for Tagore, especially with Rathi far away. But his pen and educational work flowed in a relentless tide of activity. From 1901 Tagore took on the editorship of *Bangadarshan*, the journal started by Bakimchandra Chatterjee, which Tagore continued for five years.

While personal tragedy buffeted Tagore like a relentless torrent, another storm had been rumbling in the political arena which would impact Tagore and call him from his abode of peace. Tagore's inherent love of freedom would characterize his ideals and imbue his multiple projects throughout his life. He sought freedom for his countrymen at all levels: freedom from superstition, orthodox religious practices, religious divisiveness, caste and class barriers, and political bondage. He expressed this longing through his various writings, addressing contemporary events and the current reality. His love for his country was for its society, its community of people and for their full emancipation. He was critical of those who governed India with an apparent lack of both sympathy and desire to establish improvement programmes for the struggling millions. The callousness of the pomp and splendour that marked the Delhi Durbar found a response in his poem read at the Hindu Mela in 1877.[14] We have seen how the Hindu Mela, with its focus on indigenous crafts, performances and products, had been given impetus by the Tagore family as a platform for patriotic endeavour. Among many other ventures and programmes, Balendranath, Tagore's nephew, had established the Swadeshi Store as an outlet for home-made products. Tagore was against the Congress policy of begging for favours from the foreigner. All his life, he inculcated a culture of self-sufficiency among his students, associates, tenants and his rural countrymen.

In January 1904, when the idea of the first Partition of the Bengal Province was mooted by Lord Curzon, the Swadeshi (of the homeland) Movement gathered support and momentum as foreign goods were boycotted and destroyed in bonfires and the protest against foreign domination gathered strength. In this year Tagore gave his lecture on 'Swadeshi Samaj' (Society and State, published in 1908) to a packed audience at the Minerva Theatre, where he pointed out that most of India's population lived in villages. He stressed the close relationship that existed between people as evident in the idea of the extended family, and people who retained contact with the familial home when they moved, from which tradition sprang the kinship bond where relationships were struck up as people addressed neighbours as 'auntie', 'father' and 'brother'. This was the *samaj* that signified India. In his lecture he laid out a comprehensive programme for the rural reconstruction of Bengal based on developing self-reliance, a proposal which was marked by his distinctive brand of constructive nationalism. In a letter written later to C. F. Andrews, Tagore pointed out that there is no word in Bengali for 'nation', and as it is a term borrowed 'from other people, it never fits us'.[15] What comprised India was *samaj*, an interlinked, interrelated community of social interchange. Tagore was not an advocate of narrow nationalism – a belief that would ultimately pull him back from the nationalist politics that galvanized the masses under Mahatma Gandhi's charismatic leadership from the 1920s onwards. However, when the official announcement of the imminent Partition of Bengal was made on 19 July 1905, which would become effective on 16 October 1905, he was vociferous in his protest. He gave lectures, and his poetry and other writing voiced his resistance to the idea of partition. It was during this period, in a surge of patriotism, that he composed 23 patriotic songs – some of which he sang himself as he led processions – which were sung with fervour by protestors against the division of Bengal. These moving songs, which evoked the fertile landscape, the many rivers and the spirit of Bengal, would prompt Ezra Pound to say that Tagore sang Bengal into a nation.

Ostensibly the aim of the 1905 Bengal Partition was to make the administration of an unwieldy province more manageable as the Bengal Province included Bengal, Bihar, Orissa and Assam, with Calcutta as the capital of the British Raj. The underlying reason was to curb the growing national consciousness of the Hindu Bengalis and their dominance in various spheres of life. Herbert Hope Risley, a colonial administrator with the ICS, had said that Bengal was a power, but a Bengal divided would pull in different directions, weakening the position of the Bengali *bhadralok* (well-educated, properous gentlemen), making them a minority in east and west Bengal. It was seen as a projection of the government's divide and rule policy and the protest on the ground of all communities was tremendous, including that of Henry John Stedman Cotton, former Chief Commissioner of Assam (1896–1902). As a sympathizer of Indian nationalism, he had been president of the Indian National Congress in 1904. On the day of the first Partition, a huge gathering started from Jorasanko with Tagore at its head, which proceeded to the Hooghly River. It was declared Rakhi-bandhan day (the tying of the knot of friendship and brotherhood). As the procession started, it passed the stables where Muslim ostlers were busy with their stable maintenance chores. Tagore walked in while others held back in apprehension. He tied rakhis (a band to mark friendship) on the wrists of the ostlers, who accepted his gesture amicably.

The procession continued, with rakhis being given to passers-by and bystanders. It stopped at the Chitpur Road Mosque, where Tagore tied rakhis on the mullahs as a gesture of Hindu–Muslim unity. The ostlers and the mullahs must have recognized the national poet, who was held in high esteem across the country, and accepted his intimation of friendship graciously. The procession proceeded through the streets of Calcutta with participants singing 'Bidhir bandhan katbe emon saktiman, tumi ki emon saktiman?' (Are you so strong that you can cut this fate-forged bond?), 'Jadi tor dak shune keo na aashe, tobe ekla chalo re' (If no one answers your call, then walk alone – a favourite of Gandhi's and of the firebrand militant political leader Netaji Subhas Chandra Bose), 'Banglar mati, Banglar jal / Banglar bayu, banglar phal, punyo hok' (Let the earth and water / the air and fruits of Bengal be blessed) and 'Aamar sonar Bangla, ami tomae bhalobashi' (My golden Bengal, I love you – the song would become the national anthem of the newly formed nation of Bangladesh in 1971).

In the afternoon, the procession entered the large courtyard of eminent physician and professor of anatomy Pashupati Bose's house in Baghbazar in north Calcutta, where Tagore appealed for a National Fund to be established to construct a People's Hall. The strength of nationalist emotions was such that the handsome sum of Rs 50,000 was collected on the spot.

In November that year, while Tagore was with Jatin Bose, his poet friend Akshay Chaudhuri's son-in-law, he floated the idea of a national university and found instant encouragement, which led to the establishment of the National Council of Education. He offered to draft the syllabus himself and draw up other details for the proposed institution. After attending the initial meetings, Tagore realized that some members wished to establish a rival of Calcutta University, which made him withdraw completely from the Council. (This idea of a national institution would be the nucleus for the establishment of Jadavpur University.) However, the seed for a national university would bear fruit in the realization of Tagore's vision at the beginning of the third decade of the twentieth century.

The Swadeshi Movement attracted enthusiastic youths, many of whom left their schools and colleges to join the activities of the nationalists. Some youths believed that they should boycott all government institutions. A group called Bichitra came to meet Tagore at his house in Shantiniketan. They told him that if he so desired, they would leave their studies to dedicate themselves to the cause of the freedom struggle. He not only refused to grant them permission to leave school, but told them to refrain from doing so. They went away angry at what they saw as his lack of patriotism. In a letter to C. F. Andrews in March 1921, Tagore recalled this incident and explained 'the anarchy of emptiness never tempts me, even when it is resorted to as a temporary measure. I am frightened at an abstraction which is ready to ignore living reality.'[16]

In the meantime, the Swadeshi Movement had turned to violence and generated divisiveness along religious lines. Tagore had come into contact with his Muslim tenants in his family estates and was acutely aware of the poor vendors' reliance on selling foreign goods, which, being factory made, were affordable for the general buyer; home-grown industries, with their lack of funds and technology, could not compete with the quality and quantity of available goods. The cult of the Mother Goddess, which gripped the nation in a bid to subvert the new border that saw vivisection as a threat to the image of Mother India, led to acts of sabotage, public bonfires and communal riots that spread like a conflagration across the province.

Rathindranath noted how in 1905 he and his friends were flattered to be called by the barrister P. Mitter to meet him at the Dak bungalow, where he told them about the Anushilan Samiti, which was secretly involved in organizing a movement to drive out the British. The violence that was adopted by some swadeshis horrified Tagore, as he always believed in dialogue and communication rather than violence to settle grievances and disputes. He had erupted on the nationalist scene in 1905 with his lectures, songs, poems and other writings as his beloved Bengal/India was being fragmented, but now his withdrawal from the political scene had a phenomenal effect on his countrymen as his absence was felt and criticized roundly by his detractors who found it difficult to comprehend Tagore's idea of the nation, of India's *samaj* and his dedication to the vision of it that he cherished. Yet earlier, in 1898, following the Seditions Act passed by the government to suppress the nationalist movement, the nationalist leader, Bal Gangadhar Tilak, had been arrested and jailed. Rabindranath had been involved in raising public funds for Tilak's defence trial and wrote and read 'Kantharodh' (The Throttle) as a protest against the Act at a public lecture in Calcutta. In a letter to C. F. Andrews written later, in January 1921, he noted, 'The complete man must never be sacrificed to the patriotic man, or even to the merely moral man.'[17]

In his own defence, he was to write his novel about nationalism, *Ghare Baire* (The Home and the World, 1916), where Nikhilesh, the liberal and gentle zamindar, who is involved in various swadeshi businesses in a programme of constructive regeneration on his estate (and understands the plight of his poor Muslim tenants), is a reflection of the poet himself. His friend, Sandip, is the swadeshi leader who travels first class, wins over Nikhilesh's wife Bimala, whom he puts on a pedestal as an iconic projection of the Mother Goddess, Mother India. Sandip is responsible for sparking Hindu–Muslim riots in a neighbouring zamindari estate. The novel alternates between the voices of the three narrators – Nikhil, Sandip and Bimala – whose different perspectives portray the microcosm of a reality; Nikhil's home and life are destroyed and a fire scourges the neighbourhood, suggestive of the fragmentation that is effected at the macro level of a nation.

On the crest of the surging violence of the Swadeshi Movement, Tagore had retreated to his rural corner, his abode of peace at Shantiniketan, immersing himself in many creative projects of writing, education and rural engagement. He had drawn up a plan and engaged some volunteers to work on improving the economy of the villages around Shantiniketan, in an effort to replenish them with new life and hope. It was at this stage that he felt that he needed trained agriculturalists to take his rural reconstruction programme forward. With this in mind he sent Rathindranath, Rathi's friend Santosh and his son-in-law (Mira's husband) Nagendranath Ganguly abroad to study – not at Oxford or Cambridge or Harvard, as was the norm with enlightened Indian families, but to the University of Illinois in Urbana, to train in agriculture and animal husbandry. Tagore had deliberately taken Rathindranath away from city life to 'allow him the freedom of primeval nature', and to feel the same kind of freedom his father had let him experience on his earlier visits to Shantiniketan as a child.[18] At Shantiniketan, Rathindranath was surrounded by trees, he could swim and row across the river, scour the sandbanks and return late for meals without being questioned. He did not have the material comforts of city life, but he had his teacher in nature. It was also, as already mentioned, in Shantiniketan where Tagore would have to brace himself for many disappointments and personal losses. In a letter to his friend Priyanath Sen on 30 May 1903, he wrote that he had set his boat afloat a stormy sea and had no idea where he would find anchor; with his children scattered, he had to somehow pull his life together and carry on.[19] But a mantle of peace would descend on him here, in this place where he discovered his inner life, a spiritual life that was not separate from the world, but to be found as an 'innermost truth'. The inner life as distinct from the outer life was like the lamp and the mirror – in one, light was shed from a spiritual understanding of the world, and in the other it was reflected. It was the discovery of the infinite in the finite that found expression in poems like 'Jete Nahi Dibo' (I Won't Let You Go), which he wrote while Mrinalini was alive.[20]

The manifestation of Bramha, the creative truth, could be realized through the creative principle which all human beings

Tagore teaching at Shantiniketan.

possess. For Tagore, 'the object of education is to give man the unity of truth'.[21] Of the school he says that it grew out of a creative spirit and 'not from any custom-made religion'. It was conceived with the aim of freeing the minds of his students 'from blind superstition, leading them to a state of creative unity', beyond the differences of 'caste or creed'.[22] Tagore would go on to identify his *Jiban Debata*, the Lord of his Being, which he would explore and describe at length in *The Religion of Man* (1931). He acknowledged in a letter to Sir Jagadish Chandra Bose's wife, Abala Bose, in October 1903, 'I now know, it does not help me to be away from it [his school] because I don't get any peace of mind while I am away.'[23] Henceforth Shantiniketan would always beckon the poet throughout his life, where he would return with relief after periods of restless travel. Shantiniketan was what he now considered his home, having moved physically and emotionally away from his Jorasanko birthplace.

6

From Shantiniketan to the World Stage

Tagore retreated to Shantiniketan to continue his programme of positive action in his institution. He believed this was the truest way he could contribute to freeing the minds of his people – through a liberal and holistic education and through rural regeneration. From this remote corner, Tagore still remained connected to the nation and the world. When plague broke out in Calcutta, he helped Sister Nivedita (Margaret Noble), the Irish disciple of Swami Vivekananda, in her relief work, organizing medical aid and providing succour to those suffering. In spite of the paucity of funds at Shantiniketan, Tagore was actively involved in fundraising to support the scientist Jagadish Chandra Bose to stay in England to continue his innovative research in botany and share his findings with the scientific community in the West.

At Shantiniketan he realized that there was a dearth of up-to-date learning material, primers and textbooks in Bengali, so he took on the task of writing them as part of a systematic programme of building educational tools. He encouraged his teaching team to do the same. The school had begun with the idea of the *tapovan*, the forest hermitage, and continued the Upanishadic mode of guru–shishya (teacher–disciple) education. However, he soon realized that for a holistic education, the school had to move away from any religious overtones; one of Tagore's greatest contributions to Indian secular thinking and policy was to slowly replace all religious festivals with folk festivals – *Sarodutsav* (celebration of autumn) and *Basanta*

Utsav (spring festival) – that were rooted in Indian culture and closely reflected the changing seasons and commemorated significant life-sustaining activities like *halakarshan* (ploughing the land) and *briksharopan* (tree planting).

A succession of plays, for example *Prayashchitta* (Atonement, 1909), mark this period. *Atonement* is an action-filled play about intrigue, based on his earlier novel *Bou Thakuranir Hat* but with the addition of a new character which anticipates Mahatma Gandhi and his nationalist policy of using non-violence as a tool of non-cooperation. *Raja* (1911) and *Dak Ghar* (The Post Office, 1912) each have a young boy as the central protagonist. The latter was translated by W. B. Yeats and performed in London by the Irish Players in 1913. Its lyricism, affirmation of life and nature, and its depiction of human dignity in the face of death have made it a masterpiece of international relevance. *The Post Office* was Tagore's own confrontation with the grim reality of his son Samindranath's death and in this play he shows his profound understanding of the significance and meaning of a young life.

Disturbed by the discriminations practised by Hindu orthodoxy, Tagore wrote his seminal novel *Gora* (1910), about an Irish boy who is orphaned when his parents are killed during the Indian Revolt of 1857. He is found and adopted by Anandamoyi, the childless Brahmin wife of a conservative Hindu patriarch, and grows up to be both a fiery defender of Indian nationalism and a rigid practitioner of the Hindu faith and its caste boundaries. Gora distances himself from Sucharita, the girl he loves, whose liberal Bramho upbringing finds her disturbed by Gora's initial inflexibility and contradictions. On a visit paid by Sister Nivedita to Tagore at Shelidah, he told her of the story of Gora on his houseboat, *Padma*. Nivedita was critical of the ending, in which Gora turns away from Sucharita as the country demands his attention. Nivedita accused Tagore of being restricted by the very society he was criticizing and giving Gora the 'safe' ending his readers would expect. Tagore relented and altered the ending of *Gora*. Gora's confrontation with the truth of his identity is a cathartic moment in the novel, a realization which makes him declare that he is now a true Indian as he feels no opposition between Hindu, Muslim and Christian in his being. This is the India that Tagore understood and wrote about in his essay on Indian history, *Bharatbarsher Itihasher Dhara* (The Course of Indian History, 1912), delivered as a public lecture in Calcutta. His insightful understanding of India's diversity led him to write the song 'Jana Gana Mana' the same year, which was sung on the 26th Indian National Congress session and later adopted as India's national anthem in 1950.

Undeterred by the criticism of a strong patriarchal society, Tagore went on to write a lively satire against religious orthodoxy in a play, *Achalayatan* (The Petrified Place, 1912), where the chief character is once again a young boy, Panchak, who is a novice monk at the Castle of Conformity (Achalayatan) and is criticized for his love of singing and his association with the inferior tribes. The Great Teacher appears and with Panchak leads the downtrodden tribes to bring down the high walls of the Castle of Conformity. Tagore's detractors had no difficulty in discerning the object of his sharp criticism. The response from his Bengali critics was furious.

In 1910 William Rothenstein, the English painter and one of London's Bloomsbury Group, had visited Jorasanko to meet Tagore's artist nephews, Abanindranath and Gaganendranath, who were leading exponents of the Bengal School of Modern Art. Rothenstein had heard about them from Sir John Woodroffe and Sir Harry Stephen while at Benares. Interestingly, the nephews had not spoken about their illustrious uncle. Rothenstein was struck by Tagore's quiet presence; he felt that his outward physical beauty was radiated by an 'inner charm' and wanted to draw him. It was later, when he came across the short story 'Kabuliwala', translated by Sister Nivedita in the *Modern Review*, that Rothenstein sought to read more of Tagore's work, and was sent some translations of his poems by Ajit Kumar Chakrabarty. Rothenstein was greatly moved by the quality of the verse.[1] According to Prabhatkumar Mukhopadhyay, on his return to London, Rothenstein had asked Pramatha Lal Sen of the Cooch Behar Maharaja's family and the philosopher Dr Brajendranath Seal to invite Tagore to visit London, where he would be able to interact with some leading minds of his time.[2] The desire to visit England took root now and Tagore started on 19 March 1912, but illness intervened, so the journey was postponed and his luggage had to be removed from the ship at Madras. He moved to Shelidah for his convalescence.

Earlier, between 1907 and 1910, when he felt buffeted by the successive deaths of loved ones, he had written his lyrical poems (which formed his Bengali *Gitanjali*). Tagore wrote to his niece, Indira Devi, about how the translations of the poems for the English *Gitanjali* came about while he was at Shelidah after his aborted journey to England in 1912. He described the atmosphere and ambience in the month of Chaitra (March–April), full of bird song and the fragrance of mango blossoms. Characteristically, he was unable to remain idle for long, and found it difficult to take up new writing, so he went back to his *Gitanjali* lyrics and translated them into prose poems, filling a small notebook with his distinctive artistic handwriting. He said he did this because he 'simply felt an urge to recapture through the medium of another language the feelings and sentiments which had caused such a feast of joy' in him 'in days gone by'.[3] He continued to translate a few more poems while on the ship. However, the poems which later became known as the *Gitanjali* in English were not all taken from the Bengali *Gitanjali*, but were selected by him from the earlier collections *Naibedya* (Offerings, 1901) and *Kheya* (The Ferry, 1906), as well as the Bengali *Gitanjali* (1910).[4] During these weeks of recovery, he also wrote many songs which would be later gathered and published in *Gitimalya* (Garland of Songs, 1914).

Once he had recovered, Tagore set sail for England on 27 May 1912 with Rathindranath and his daughter-in-law Pratima Devi on what would prove a life-changing journey for the poet. He took with him the notebook that was small enough to fit inside his coat pocket. However, once in England he entrusted the notebook to the care of Rathindranath, who, amidst the confusion of taking a tube from Charing Cross station to their Bloomsbury hotel, left the briefcase with the notebook behind. Once the loss was discovered, Rathindranath went back to the station and discovered that one kind traveller had found it and left it with the lost property office. One wonders what route the history of Tagore's reputation as a poet in the West and on the international stage would have taken if this notebook had been irretrievably lost. This anecdote could have been the subject of an Oscar Wilde play depicting the absurd ways in which fate works.

Soon after his arrival in London, Tagore met Rothenstein and handed over his notebook of translations 'with some diffidence'.[5] Rothenstein felt that the poems were 'of a new order . . . on a level with that of the great mystics', and Andrew Bradley, with whom he shared the poems, agreed.[6] This was the impression that would accompany Tagore and his poetry, and which would colour the West's response to him and account for the swings in reception, from enthusiastic praise, to caution and derision, to an even more damaging, stultifying indifference. The ambivalence evident in the Western response to the Eastern 'prophet' was abetted by Tagore's own ambivalence: on the one hand he went along with the 'sage' image that he epitomized, and on the other, he continued to write against religious, social and political oppression and remained steeped in his pragmatic enterprises of all-rounded education and rural regeneration.

In London Rothenstein found him a house near his own in Hampstead Heath and organized the introduction of Tagore to London's literati. Rothenstein would remain his steadfast friend and champion in spite of diverse and altering opinions of the chameleon-esque public. Bradley's recognition of having 'a great poet among us again' was shared by W. B. Yeats.[7] Rothenstein had given typed copies of the manuscript to Bradley and sent copies to Yeats (at the former's request) and Stopford Brooke. Rothenstein arranged a meeting between Tagore and Yeats on 27 June.[8] At a soirée at Rothenstein's Hampstead residence on 7 July, Yeats read some of the *Gitanjali* poems to select guests,[9] including Ernest Rhys, the poet editor of Everyman's Library, and Charles Freer Andrews (both Rhys and Andrews remained Tagore's close associates and supporters), May Sinclair, Alice Meynell, Ezra Pound, Charles Trevelyan, Henry Nevinson and Arthur Fox Strangways.[10] The impression Yeats's rendition of Tagore's poems made on his audience that night is evident in a letter written by May Sinclair to Tagore:

> May I now say that as long as I live . . . I shall never forget the impression that they made. It is not only that they have an absolute beauty, a perfection as poetry, but that they have made the present for me forever the divine thing that I can only find by flashes and with an agonizing uncertainty . . . You have put into English which is absolutely transparent in its perfection things it is despaired of ever seeing written in English at all or in any Western Language.[11]

On 10 July Rothenstein had organized a dinner at the Trocadero Restaurant for seventy people at which Yeats proposed the toast and read three poems from Tagore to a rapt audience, among whom were Yeats's friend Maud Gonne, H. G. Wells, Cecil Sharp and Ralph Vaughan Williams.[12] Yeats selected and arranged the poems and pencilled in his suggestions for Tagore to consider, and subsequently 103 poems were published in a limited edition (of 750 copies) of *Gitanjali* by the India Society of London in November 1912. The events that followed Rothenstein's introduction of Tagore and

Gitanjali, translated by Tagore in a notebook for William Rothenstein.

> 80
>
> I know not how thou singest, my master! I ever listen in silent amazement.
>
> The light of thy music illumines the world. The life breath of thy music runs from sky to sky. The holy stream of thy music breaks through all stony obstacles and rushes on.
>
> My heart longs to join in thy song but vainly struggles for a voice. I would speak but speech breaks not in song and I cry sorely baffled. Ah, thou hast made my heart captive in the endless meshes of thy music, my master!

Rabindranath at William Rothenstein's house. Sitting, L–R: Somendra Dev Varma, Rabindranath and Rathindranath; standing, L–R: Dr D. N. Maitra, William Rothenstein with son.

Yeats's reading of the *Gitanjali* poems cascaded in a breathless stream that led to the Nobel Prize. In March 1913 Macmillan published *Gitanjali* as the world would know it. Yeats had initially suggested a 'who's who' section on Tagore, with a timeline beginning with his birth and dates of his publications, but this was inexplicably left out. Yet the edition appeared with Yeats's ecstatic Introduction, part of which is worth quoting here:

> I have carried the manuscript of these translations about with me for days, reading it in railway trains, or on the top of omnibuses and in restaurants, and I have often had to close it lest some stranger would see how much it moved me . . . And yet we are not moved because of its strangeness, but because we have met our own image, as though we had walked in Rossetti's willow wood, or heard, perhaps, for the first time in literature, our voice as in a dream.[13]

Thomas Sturge Moore, the poet and artist and a member of the Royal Society of Literature, nominated Tagore for the Nobel Prize in 1913. Both Fox Strangways and Sturge Moore were responsible for seeing *Gitanjali* published in March 1913 and ten editions of it were printed before the declaration of the Nobel Prize. Later, Sturge Moore's wife, Marie, translated Tagore's collection *The Crescent Moon* into French (*La Jeune lune*, 1924).

Much has been written and recorded about Tagore's meetings with leading intellects of his time and their reaction to and estimation of his persona and work, which many found difficult to separate. His strikingly handsome appearance, his piercing eyes, his tall presence and calm demeanour could hardly be ignored and were commented on by those who met him and heard him speak, some of whom described him as Christ-like. Frances Cornford, Darwin's granddaughter, after meeting him at Cambridge, said, 'I can now imagine a powerful and gentle Christ, which I never could before.'[14] Clad in

Tagore's original Bengali text for *Gitanjali*, from which the handwritten excerpt pictured on p. 123 was translated.

his self-designed flowing robes and his distinctive beard, he looked the part of the Eastern mystic that the West was willing to accept, an orientalist view that was responsible for the conflicting estimations of Tagore's standing as a writer in the West.

Interestingly, the Nobel Prize was given to Tagore for Literature in English. The response in the British press was by and large complimentary. The *Times Literary Supplement* said of the poems on 7 November 1912, 'they are prophetic of the poetry that might be written in England if our poets could attain the same harmony of emotion and idea.'[15] The *Manchester Guardian* noted how for Bengalis this was 'the epoch of Rabindra Nath',[16] and commented that 'in fact, there is not a radical difference between his lyrical art and that of Europe'.[17] In an article in the *Daily Mail*, 'A Great Man from Bengal', F. Ashworth Briggs said, 'I remember no one whose work has given me more delight, refreshment, and surprise.'[18]

As mentioned earlier, there were ten editions of *Gitanjali* published before Tagore won the Nobel Prize. It is one of the world's most translated books, translated into several languages in India and in the West and East and it has never gone out of print. The conflicting responses ranged from a sense of solace *Gitanjali* provided, the appeal of the beauty of its language, the simplicity of its imagery and the purity of its thought, to outrage that someone who was not white, not from Europe – moreover, someone with an unpronounceable name – could win the Prize that had bypassed all the 38 other nominations. Though the anger at Tagore's name bypassing that of European and American contenders was expressed by many, the top British contender for the Prize, Thomas Hardy, remained silent, neither dismissive nor appreciative of the recipient of the Prize.

One of those who found the poems moving was the war poet Wilfred Owen, whose notebook had lines from a *Gitanjali* poem, 'Parting Words', written in it: 'When I go from hence / let this be my parting word, / that what I have seen is unsurpassable.' His mother, Susan Owen, mentioned this poem in a letter to Tagore after her son's death, asking where she could find the book which had the poem.[19]

Like Yeats, Ezra Pound was moved deeply by the *Gitanjali* poems. He wrote profusely on Tagore. He found a Hellenic purity in the songs:

> But beneath and above it all is the spirit of curious quiet. We have found our new Greece suddenly. As the sense of balance came back from Europe in the days of the Renaissance, so it seems to me this sense of a saner stillness comes now to us in the midst of our clamour for mechanisms.
>
> I am not saying this hastily, nor in an emotional flurry, nor from a love of brandishing statement. I have had a month to think it over . . . Here is in him the stillness of nature . . . Briefly, I find in these poems a sort of ultimate common sense, a reminder of one thing and of forty different things of which we are ever likely to lose sight of in the confusion of our Western life.[20]

After spending four months in Britain, Tagore, with his son and daughter-in-law, travelled to America, where he settled in Urbana, near the university. Here in these quiet backwaters of a university campus in the Midwest, Professor Arthur Seymour and his wife Mayce were his warm hosts, and it was here that Tagore met several academic staff and church ministers. He settled down to enjoy the winter sunshine on crisp cold days at Urbana with the intention of providing Rathindranath with the opportunity to pursue his doctoral studies. But this was not to be. Far from having a quiet holiday, an invitation from the Unitarian Club to speak sparked off a series of lectures. He gleaned these from his sermons which he had read every Wednesday at the Mandir at Shantiniketan. He also used these themes for the lectures which he was invited to give at Harvard University by the philosopher James Houghton Woods to his philosophy class and at the Philosophy Club. Woods invited him at the suggestion of the director, A. Lawrence Lowell, who had a recommendation from Goldsworthy Lowes Dickinson at Cambridge (author of *Letters from John Chinaman*, 1913), a philosopher who was close to the Bloomsbury Group, and had earlier sent an invitation to Tagore from Kings College, Cambridge, where Rathindranath had spent two days with the political scientist and philosopher.

Tagore used these lectures in May–June the following year for his talks in London, which were later edited by Ernest Rhys and published in a collection of essays titled *Sadhana: The Realisation of Life* (1915). These essays had such poetic moments as to mesmerize Tagore's audience by their ability to see beauty and lessons in nature, but they were imbued with moral reflectiveness and marked by philosophical elaborations. This contrast and the essays' Upanishadic discourse on the presence and meaning of Bramha would baffle many.

T. S. Eliot was one of Wood's students. He attended one of Tagore's lectures at Harvard. He remained silent on Tagore then and later, and one wonders whether this was because of Tagore's acceptance of the invitation from the Unitarians whom Eliot had left behind. His classmate R. F. Rattray later wrote to Tagore saying that his Harvard lectures could have been the reason for the final words in Eliot's poem *The Waste Land* (1922), 'Shantih shantih shantih'. One finds a similarity between Tagore's concerns and the warnings of the repercussions of Western materialism and mechanization in Eliot's poem.

In the meantime, an excited Pound was preparing to publish some of Tagore's poems in *Poetry*, knowing 'for weeks that he [Tagore] was the event of the winter'. Six poems were published in the third issue of *Poetry* with a note of appreciation by Pound. Harriet Monroe, on getting a note from Tagore requesting two copies of *Poetry*, was alerted to his presence in the U.S. and promptly sent him an invitation to come and stay in Chicago. After some hesitation, Tagore accepted and spent around three weeks there. Monroe introduced him to Harriet Moody, the widow of the poet and playwright William Vaughan Moody, who accompanied them to New York and Harvard, and opened her flats on Washington Square in New York and on Cheyne Walk in London to them. Henceforth, Harriet Moody would provide a home away from home in America to Tagore and his family, and her warm hospitality to writers and artists enabled him to meet several great minds of his time.

Toronto's *Globe* reported on the recipient as 'not what we call "white"' and commented that his 'name has a curious sound. The first time we saw it in print, it did not seem real.'[21] The *Los Angeles Times* said how European and American writers were discouraged by this conferring of the Nobel on 'a Hindu poet whose name few people can pronounce'. The *Globe* article asked a parenthetical question, '(Have we not been told that the East and the West shall never meet?)'[22] Yet it would be Tagore who would take on the self-imposed role of an ambassador for bringing the East and West closer as he met leading intellectuals, artists and leaders of his time and spoke on invitation at public gatherings, endorsing Kipling's final lines that clinch his poem 'The Ballad of East and West' (1889), that 'there is neither East nor West, Border, nor Breed nor Birth, / When two strong men stand face to face, though they come from the ends of the earth.' There was a general opinion that Tagore had not acknowledged his debt to Christianity, believing that his philosophy could not have owed anything to the Vedas and the Upanishads as he claimed, but to Western Christian ideals, since the East, being a moribund society, had nothing to offer to the West. However, the Nobel Prize committee recognized Tagore's spiritual philosophy as emanating from his Eastern heritage and the role and influence of his father, Debendranath, as a religious reformer in Bengal and the leader of the Bramho movement.[23]

George Bernard Shaw, who, like Bertrand Russell, blew hot and cold about Tagore, had an off-stage character, named Stupendranath

Begorr, in a short play. However, later in 1931, after a long talk with Tagore in London, he was appreciative of Tagore's bridge-building efforts between Britain and India and after Tagore's death in 1941, he recommended that Tagore's portraits, including one by Rothenstein, be hung in Britain's National Gallery.[24]

There has been a misconception prevalent in the literary history of the reception of *Gitanjali* that the translations were mainly the work of Yeats. One British correspondent of *The Times*, Sir Valentine Chirol, publicly made the accusation that Tagore was guilty of taking credit for what had been Yeats's work. Rothenstein has corrected this illusion in his autobiography *Men and Memories*:

> I knew that it was said in India that the success of *Gitanjali* was largely due to Yeats' re-writing of Tagore's English. That this is false can easily be proved. The original MS of *Gitanjali* in English and in Bengali is in my possession. Yeats did here and there suggest small changes, but the main text was printed as it came from Tagore's hands. And even for those who were not intimate with the facts of the case but judged *Gitanjali* on its literary merit alone, it was felt that 'no amount of correction – short of absolute re-writing – could make it what it is.'[25]

One lady, believing like many that C. F. Andrews had translated the poems in the English *Gitanjali*, even wrote to Tagore for his signature and asked for Andrews's address so that she might obtain his autograph as well and thus have 'both authors' in her copy of the *Gitanjali*.[26]

There is a general assumption that the Nobel Prize was awarded on the basis of *Gitanjali* alone, but other books by Tagore, namely *The Gardener* (1913), *Lyrics of Love and Life* (1913) and *Glimpses of Bengal Life* (1913), were received by the Nobel Library before the decision of the Nobel Prize was made by the committee. It had also received the Bengali collections of *Naivedya*, *Kheya* and *Gitanjali* on

18 July 1913, which were the sources of the poems in the English *Gitanjali*. Moreover, one of the members of the Swedish Academy was Esaias Tegnér Jr, who had some knowledge of Bengali and had issued all three of the Bengali books in August that year, which diminishes the claim that *Gitanjali* was the sole book on which the Nobel Prize was predicated. In a statement issued by the Swedish Academy to the committee on 24 October, it was recommended that the award should go to the French writer and critic Émile Faguet. So the annoyance of a section of the public at the choice of Rabindranath Tagore replacing Thomas Hardy seems misplaced. The borrowing register of the Nobel Library records that *The Gardener* and *Glimpses of Bengal Life* were borrowed several times between late October and early November and one member took out *Glimpses of Bengal Life* on 13 November, which means that between 24 October and 13 November, the reading of Tagore's works swung the pendulum of the committee in favour of Tagore as they had read beyond his English *Gitanjali*. Gustaf Verner von Heidenstam, a renowned Orientalist who was a member the Swedish Academy, wrote a letter on 18 October 1913 to Erik Axel Karlfeldt, permanent secretary of the Academy, who was on the Nobel committee, which was mentioned at a committee meeting on 23 October. In it Heidenstam said that 'Tagore's thought and poetry was "united in a depth of rare spiritual beauty," were indicative of a "purity of heart" and "natural sublimity" such that no contemporary writer on the world stage matches him.'[27] The flurry of borrowing of Tagore's books from the Nobel Library might have been prompted by this recommendation, after which the decision of the recipient of the Nobel Award was made. In the award ceremony speech by Harald Hjärne, chairman of the Nobel Committee of the Swedish Academy, delivered on 10 December 1913, he mentioned the committee's consideration of works beyond *Gitanjali*:

> *Song Offerings* (1912), a collection of religious poems ... the second cycle of poems that came before us, *The Gardener, Lyrics of Love and Life* (1913) ... prose stories ... *Glimpses of Bengal Life* (1913) ... both a collection of poems, poetic pictures of childhood and home life, symbolically entitled *The Crescent Moon* (1913), and a number of lectures given before American and English university audiences, which in book form he calls *Sâdhanâ: The Realisation of Life* (1913) ... [which] embody his views of the ways in which man can arrive at a faith in the light of which it may be possible to live.

The speech also shows a full awareness of Tagore's rich cultural familial background, the contribution of his family to the socio-religious fabric of Bengal, Tagore's contribution to education at his 'open air school' and the high respect in which he was held as a creative artist and intellectual at home, as well as his reception as 'an honoured guest' in England, America and Paris. It is an informed and in-depth estimation of his life and work up to November 1913.

After the news of the Nobel Prize reached Tagore, he would not be able to retreat at will to the land of the Padma at Shelidah or to Shantiniketan. The applause and incredulity, the glowing tributes and damning critiques, the appreciation and vituperation that followed would keep the poet forever in the public eye. When the news of the Nobel award reached Tagore he was in Shantiniketan; Edward Thompson, principal of the Wesleyan College at Bankura, was with him. Tagore told him, 'I shall never have any peace again.' Thompson recalls, 'It was a night of wild excitement without, the Santiniketan boys parading the grounds singing, the masters as excited as they. But within, the poet was troubled with misgiving for the future', and Thompson goes on to say that though the 'fears' faded in the clear light of the next morning, 'they remained, and were quickly realised', as requests for introduction to books, letters and reporters poured in.[28]

To his close friend Rothenstein, Tagore wrote, 'The very first moment I received the message of the great honour conferred on me by the award of the Nobel Prize my heart turned towards you with love and gratitude. I felt certain that of all my friends none would be more glad at this news than you.'[29] The expression of affection between men in Tagore's time was not uncommon as it had none of the connotations of same-sex love.[30] Rothenstein attached great importance to his friendship with Tagore, noting, 'No man's company gives me more pleasure than Tagore's, but amongst his disciples I am uncomfortable'; he was wary of their 'easy idealism'.[31]

Earlier, it was Tagore's father who had rewarded him for his poetry – his father who, when told that young Rabi had composed Bramho songs, called him and asked him to sing them to him. On hearing Tagore sing his compositions in his engaging voice, Debendranath was both surprised and moved. He said that such a poet would have been rewarded earlier by kings who would have understood the beauty of the language of the songs, but since this was not to be, he himself gave him a generous monetary award. Later when Tagore dedicated his collection of poems *Naivedya* to his father and read them out to him, Debendranath rewarded the mature poet with a sum to cover the expenses of the publication of the volume.[32] The Nobel Prize money was invested in the bank Tagore had set up, and its interest would help to keep his institution afloat in subsequent years, though the lack of funds remained a constant source of anxiety for the poet.

Conflicting attitudes of the public to the award were also prevalent at home. In October the Viceroy of India, Lord Hardinge, ordered that an honorary degree be conferred on Tagore by Calcutta University, in spite of rumblings lower down about Tagore being a 'bad character'. Lord Carmichael, governor of Bengal, complied with the viceroy's directive and honoured Tagore alongside the prominent French orientalist scholar Sylvain Lévi on 26 December

1913. Lévi would be the first foreign scholar to come and teach at Shantiniketan. One section in Calcutta University dismissed Tagore as writing 'bad Bengali'. In fact, students appearing for the matriculation examination at Calcutta University in 1914 were set a passage from Tagore and were asked to rewrite it in 'chaste Bengali'.[33]

Many among the Calcutta literati had been bitter critics of Tagore, so when they were part of the five hundred Calcutta citizens who came to Shantiniketan to pay their respects on 23 November 1914, Tagore was furious and did not mince his words. He found their sudden recognition of his genius galling, as they had had to wait for him to be recognized in the West in order to accept his greatness as a writer in his homeland. He was outspoken in pointing out their insincerity.[34] His long-standing detractors were understandably angry. But Bipinchandra Pal, a respected political leader, was both sympathetic and understanding: 'Tagore would not have been what he is if he had failed to administer this salutary rebuke to those who evidently looked up still to European appraisers for the determination of the intellectual or moral values of their national efforts and achievements.'[35]

The writing of the prose poems which translated the thought, imagery and rhythm of his original lyrics into English and the writing of essays for the lectures given in England and America, gave Tagore a new insight into the use of English and his own facility with it. In a letter to James Drummond Anderson on 14 April 1918, he wrote:

> I have come to know the wonderful power of English prose. The clearness, strength and the suggestive music of well-balanced English sentences make it a delightful task for me to mould my Bengali poems into English prose form . . . In English prose there is a magic which seems to transmute my Bengali verses into something which is original again and in a different manner.[36]

This confrontation with the truth about his own facility with the English language after he had met and communicated with various members of the Bloomsbury Group, talked at public gatherings and interacted with many individuals in England and America, was the beginning of a new phase in Tagore's life. He was now not just Bengal's poet, but a poet of national importance in India and of international esteem abroad. Henceforth, he knew and practised with ease the freedom and joy that the English language gave him, letting his ideas and message spill over Bengal's border across India and into the world, both in the East and the West. His own Bengali creativity continued. As political events unfolded at home and materialism and militarization gained ground abroad, Tagore felt disturbed into action to protest, to write and speak out. The rest which he needed and sought would not come easily to the poet-ambassador dedicated to East–West understanding and interchange in his post-Nobel Prize years.

7
The Renunciation of Knighthood

Tagore had been away from his institution and his estates for a long period and he was disturbed by the unavoidable neglect of his projects in his absence. This would be a constant worry from now on as he was pulled in different directions – the inherent requirement to write, the commitment to his educational and socio-economic projects, the urgency of raising funds for the latter, his involvement in public matters in India and his self-imposed bridge-building role in the world.

The Nobel Prize was a test to highlight those who would retain their faith in his artistry, ideas, opinions and his integrity, and those who were angry or scornful that he had been awarded the limelight by the prize. The scathing, contemptuous and persistent detractors at home and abroad accounted for a deep depression in Tagore as he moved around restlessly after his return in 1914 to India.

In these initial years, there was a general belief among many Indians that Shantiniketan was a kind of reformatory for difficult children. Some thought of it as a poet's whim. The Indian government clandestinely sent around circulars to government employees and those loyal to the government, directing them not to send their wards to Tagore's school.[1] It was a grim warning of the suspicion with which he would be held in some corridors of power.

Just as Debendranath had been a veteran itinerant, escaping every so often on trips to Shantiniketan and across India, Tagore was hit by this urge to be on the move at various intervals. From Shantiniketan he sought the seclusion of the riverine terrain at Shelidah, spending time on the *Padma*. He returned to Calcutta from time to time, but remained in touch with his school and estate. When he returned to Shantiniketan, he retreated to the house at Surul, where Rathindranath and Pratima had been urged to take up residence to oversee the rural resuscitation programme in practice. He seemed to be in search of an elusive peace. He journeyed to the Himalayas; to Nainital; Bodh Gaya on the Ganga where the Buddha had gained enlightenment; Darjeeling; Allahabad; the confluence of Ganga and Jamuna, and Agra, where the sight of the Taj Mahal led him to write his famous poem 'Shah Jahan', a powerful analysis of death and love, a paean to beauty and its significance in the annals of time. An English version of *Chitrangada* (1892) called *Chitra* (1913) had been published by the India Society of London during this period, to critical acclaim. However, between 1914 and 1916, Tagore had written two books, his collection of poems, *Balaka* (Wild Geese) and his novel *Ghare Baire* (The Home and the World), both published in 1916. We see a distinctive development in the poems of *Balaka*, which Edward Thompson describes as 'far stronger and deeper' than his earlier work as they take on a new intensity, while his novel, as discussed in a previous chapter, engages directly with nationalist debates.[2]

In the meantime, C. F. Andrews, who had visited Mahatma Gandhi in South Africa, suggested that since Gandhi's Phoenix Ashram was being wound up there, the boys of the ashram should come and stay at Shantiniketan, which Tagore readily agreed to. The Phoenix boys arrived in November 1914. After his initial 'misgivings' about the boys and their system of training, he conceded to Andrews that they were actually quite 'lovable'.[3] He would always retain an affection for his wards and just as he was willing to revise his opinion on further evidence in this case, he would continue to do so in graver matters. Gandhi arrived in February the following year when

Rabindranath was away. They met in March 1915 on Rabindranath's return to Shantiniketan in what would be the beginning of an association of mutual respect in spite of some fundamental differences in their approaches to political strategies and social reform. Andrews would remain a conduit between the two when they were too busy to communicate directly with each other. Gandhi approved of the idea of simplicity in the ashram and proposed that in order to achieve simplicity in its fullness, the boys should practise self-sufficiency. With Tagore's approval, the experiment was launched on 10 March. The difference between the Shantiniketan and the Phoenix boys soon became evident. While the latter were eager to help with all sorts of menial tasks in the running of the ashram as per Gandhi's ideology, the Shantiniketan boys held back after the initial excitement of the new approach wore off. Gandhi's example of self-dependency petered out once the Phoenix boys had left, but the tradition has continued, with 10 March being observed as Gandhi Day, when the servants are given a day off and the students and teachers take on the role of cooking and cleaning at the school. During his stay at Shantiniketan, Gandhi was openly critical of the Brahmin snobbery of the Shantiniketan boys in his conversation with Tagore, something that the poet had overlooked. Tagore set about doing away with the caste-based distinctions at Shantiniketan, where all differences – of gender, caste, class and race – are unacceptable. Dwijendranath, Tagore's eldest brother, had warmly welcomed Gandhi at Jorasanko in Calcutta. Subsequently, this mathematician, who was a dreaming, creative, simple man, would prove prescient and perceptive when he predicted to Rabi, 'This man will deliver India.'[4]

Following the announcement of the Nobel Prize, Lord Carmichael, the governor of Bengal, who was predisposed in favour of Tagore, handed over the diploma and medal on behalf of the Swedish Academy early in 1914. He paid a visit to Tagore's school on 20 March 1915, signalling the government's approval of the poet's institution. Tagore's detractors in Calcutta were quick in their criticism, taking his courtesy to his guest as a sign of toeing the government line. Following this visit, a knighthood was conferred on Tagore, which he accepted with grace. However, this honeymoon with the authorities would not last long.

As the First World War broke out, the Europe Tagore admired was drawn into a bloody conflict which destroyed the very institutions that had been the bedrock of Western civilization. It was announced that India was at war, even though no Indian had been consulted. Tagore had been to the West. The call to the East had now come. Japan beckoned. Okakura Kakuzo, who had initiated the idea that 'Asia is one' and advocated a powerful united East, had made a lasting impression on Tagore; the Japanese scholar's request to the Bengali poet to travel to Japan inspired an urge in Tagore which remained with him after Okakura's death in 1915. A deputation of Japanese gentlemen paid him a visit and extended an invitation. He decided to keep his promise to Okakura, but plans to visit Japan were aborted twice in 1915 (in January and June) owing to the paucity of funds. Japan's changing economic and political strategy had been witnessed by C. F. Andrews, who wrote to Tagore about this reality. Her rapid militarization, imperialistic expansion and ambition, as well as her relentless embracing of modernity, disturbed Tagore.

Before Lord Carmichael left office, he gave Tagore a letter of introduction to the British ambassador in Tokyo. Tagore was finally able to set sail on a cargo boat in May 1916, accompanied by Andrews, W. W. Pearson and a Bengali art student. They stopped at Rangoon, Penang, Singapore and Hong Kong before reaching Kobe. In Kobe Tagore visited a college for women. There is a charming photograph of him with immaculately coiffured Japanese female students seated on the ground with Tagore sitting in a Buddha-like position on a platform, facing them.[5] His prophet-like appearance made an impression on his audience. The prime minister, Count Okuma, welcomed him in Japanese and when Tagore answered in Bengali, the Count apologized for not knowing English, which brought smiles to his audience. However, the smiles would soon be replaced by resentment at Tagore's words of warning against Japan's galloping technological progress at the cost of her traditionalism; he believed her embracing of Western-style modernity was at odds with her particular sense of beauty. The artistry of simplicity cultivated in Japanese life appealed to Tagore. The minimalism expressed in brush strokes, calligraphy and in the poetic forms of haiku and tanka found their way into the pithy and short reflective lines Tagore inscribed on ladies' fans and other artefacts during this trip. This trip inspired the sharp imagist suggestiveness that found expression in aphorisms and epigrams in *Stray Birds* (1916).[6] His lectures in Japan have been published in his essay 'Nationalism and Japan'.

The tide against Tagore's magic was turning. Japan's successful intrusions into Korea and China were the source of nationalist pride in Japan, so his words did not resonate with his Japanese audience. On subsequent visits to Japan in the interwar years in 1924 and 1929, Tagore remained trenchant in his criticism of Japan's militarism and modernization, and his warning of the grave consequences proved

Tagore in Japan.

all too prescient when Japan joined the Axis powers during the Second World War. There were those who would continue to revere the poet, however. Yasunari Kawabata, the 1968 Nobel Laureate, saw his photographs at seventeen years old and remembered him as a 'sage-like poet . . . with deep, piercing eyes'.[7]

Meanwhile, James Pond, Tagore's agent in America, had been busy organizing an extensive lecture tour for him which became, as Pond had predicted to Macmillan in New York 'the biggest [event] in lecture history', with Tagore justifying his 'top billing' in 1916. The idea was that he would read largely from his poetry, plays and short stories, interspersed with philosophical talks on religion and art. Instead he spoke against nationalism and capitalism, with occasional readings. The *Minneapolis Tribune* reported that Tagore charged Americans '$700 per plead'.[8] He was acutely conscious of the irony of lecturing in order to raise funds for his school, while he spoke against the ills of materialism. However, the lectures were crowded, as Pond's publicity had been effective. Tagore travelled to 25 towns and cities, including Seattle (where his sponsors were the Sunset Club), New York (at Carnegie Hall), Denver, Salt Lake City and San Francisco. As a follow up to his last visit, he was invited by Unitarian churches as well as colleges and universities. At Yale he was awarded the Yale Bicentennial Medal. In San Francisco his success roused the apprehension of resident Indian Sikh revolutionaries, who believed Tagore was anti-nationalist and an agent of the British Empire. A plot to assassinate the unsuspecting poet in his hotel was averted when one would-be assassin shot another in an altercation in the hotel lobby. Tagore had no inkling of the danger to his person or the significance of the police protection to escort him as he left for Santa Barbara. Through this hectic tour, he kept up his correspondence with his old friends Harriet Monroe and Harriet Moody.

But this hotel incident was soon followed by a far more serious one. Tagore had requested that his publisher, Macmillan, approach

President Woodrow Wilson to seek his permission to dedicate his book on nationalism to him. The President expressed his 'warm appreciation of the motives' behind 'Sir R. Tagore's "request"' but declined since he 'had to take all sorts of international considerations into my thought and must err if I err at all on the side of tact and prudence'.[9] The investigation of the revolutionaries found papers which implicated Tagore in a far-fetched intercontinental plot stretching from Count Okumo in Japan to German officials in America and Indian revolutionaries in the USA. William Wiseman, chief of British intelligence in America, had advised President Wilson's chief personal adviser that the president of America should not accept Tagore's dedication. When Tagore learned of the true reason for the president's refusal, he was angry and sent a cable to the president and a volley of letters to President Wilson, Count Okuma, Macmillan and Lord Chelmsford, who succeeded Lord Carmichael as governor of Bengal. The former, unlike his predecessor, held Tagore in high suspicion. Tagore denounced the 'audacious piece of fabrication' and the 'indignity' of having his name 'dragged into this mire of calumny'.[10] In the letter he praised American hospitality and kindness and sent an assurance to Americans that he had accepted their warmth with no intention of committing treason against their nation. In a subsequent visit to America, he would not experience the same welcome. The unfounded allegations against Tagore, even when shown to be false, affected the sales of his books there. As the war waged on and America decided to join the conflict, Pond faced bankruptcy.

At home, Tagore was a public figure and his voice mattered – sometimes heeded, sometimes not – but it did have an impact, negative or positive as the case may be. When in 1916 some previously expelled students assaulted a teacher, E. F. Oaten, who had made derogatory remarks about Indians at Presidency College, an enquiry was started. Tagore wrote to Lord Hardinge and Lord Carmichael, weighing both sides of the matter, trying to maintain a just stand, suggesting that war service could be a leveller as Englishmen could welcome Bengali volunteer soldiers on a more equal footing, fighting shoulder to the shoulder for the same cause. His intervention was received coolly by both parties.

Matters came to a head when the theosophist leader Annie Besant, an advocate for India's political freedom, Home Rule, was arrested and jailed in 1917. Tagore, who understandably kept a distance from the Theosophists, spoke out against her detention. More and more nationalist activists were being sent to prison and held without trial, many of whom he knew personally. Tagore was disturbed and worried about the tabs kept by the police on his students, knowing how their careers could be marred by these police records. His letter to the secretary of state, Edwin Montagu, in 1982 voiced his concerns about the harassment of young men in Bengal by the government and the constant strain of being held under suspicion, which affected their employment prospects in their country. In this context, he had told his editor that the only European who had 'shared our sorrow' was Annie Besant, who had thus incurred the 'anger and derision of her countrymen'.[11]

The repressive Rowlatt Acts, which introduced imprisonment without trial and indefinite detention, was met with stiff resistance from Gandhi and his followers. On Gandhi's request, Tagore sent a letter of support for Gandhi's agitation but added a strong note of warning against the repercussions of non-violence which was for 'heroes and not for men led by impulses and emotions'. He pointed out that 'evil' begets evil, and 'violence and insult' from one side results in 'vengefulness' on the other.[12] Once again, Tagore was prescient. The clamp-down on protesters was harsh and the retaliation from the people was violent. On 13 April 1919 a meeting was held in Jallianwala Bagh in the Punjab on Baisakhi, the Punjab spring festival, in a walled garden. Fearing insurgency, General Dyer surrounded the unarmed gathering and ordered his troops to fire. They fired into this walled space from which there was no escape, and stopped once they had emptied their ammunition, killing 379 unarmed citizens and injuring 2,000. The news of the massacre did not reach the public immediately. As it leaked through the press, Tagore was deeply shaken, not just by the atrocity, but by the silence from Gandhi and the Indian national leaders and the government itself, none of whom condemned the killing. When no protest was forthcoming from his countrymen, Tagore took it on himself to write a letter on 30 May 1919 to Lord Chelmsford, confronting the truth of what this massacre meant for Indians and British policy in India; he relinquished his knighthood as his solitary mark of protest.

His earlier song 'Jadi tor dak shune keo na ashe, tobe ekla chalo re' (If no one answers your call, then walk alone) evoked the mood of the moment. Henceforth, many a time Tagore would be an isolated voice, standing apart from public and popular thought and opinion. To Lord Chelmsford, he wrote, 'The enormity of the measures taken by the government in the Punjab for quelling some local disturbances has, with a rude shock, revealed to our minds the helplessness of our position as British subjects of India . . . The time has come when badges of honour make our shame glaring in the incongruous context of humiliation.' He wished to be 'shorn of all special distinctions' and stand by his countrymen, taking a humanist stand. This incident formed the watershed in Tagore's life as it marked his disillusion with the government in India, and its claims to justice and fair play. In the eyes of the government it confirmed the poet's resistance to imperialism. His letter, like the one to President Wilson, remained unanswered, and his renunciation of his knighthood was never formally accepted. In official records Tagore remained 'Sir Rabindranath'.

8

Where the World Meets in a Nest

It was probably during his first visit to America, while he was residing near the university campus in Urbana, Illinois, that the idea of a campus university in India took root in Tagore. As early as 1916 he had written to Rathindranath from Japan:

> The Santiniketan School must be the thread linking India with the world. We must establish there a centre for humanistic research concerned with all the world's peoples. The age of narrow chauvinism is coming to an end. For the sake of the future the first step towards this great meeting of world humanity will take place in these very fields of Bolpur. The task of my last years is to free the world from the coils of national chauvinism.[1]

This reference to national chauvinism can be interpreted as the narrow nationalism that Tagore actively resisted right through his life in his work and writing. Tagore set up his campus university in the fields of Bolpur. On 22 December 1918, at a special meeting at Shantiniketan, he explained his idea of the university to his students, teachers and invited guests. It was to be an institution where differences of religion, caste, race and class would be levelled by people coming from all backgrounds to study together and teach. It would be a cultural learning centre promoting cooperation and coordination between the East and the West and engaging in collaborative research. Its motto, *yatra visham bhavati ekanidam* (where the world meets in one nest), embodies Tagore's ideal of social inclusion, universal understanding and acceptance. It was formally established three years later on the same date, 22 December (8 Poush according to the Bengali calendar) 1921.

Tagore toured south India in 1919 and later western India, describing his concept for his Indian university in his lecture 'The Centre of Indian Culture'. In 1920–21 he travelled to Europe and the USA, seeking funds and support for his international university. He wrote to Rothenstein in 1921 about how the British Consul in an American town was trying to prevent an American supporter of his project from fundraising for his institution. Obstacles would be many, but there would be those who gave the institution their financial, moral and intellectual support: for example, both the Raja of Mahmudabad and the Raja of Benares, Madho Lal, who endowed the Sanskrit Chair to Visva-Bharati, lent their support, and many international scholars came to teach at the university.

Tagore explained that whenever the word 'university' was used, it signified a Western institution, a model that was associated with Oxford or Cambridge. In naming his institution Visva-Bharati – *visva* (universe) + *bharati* (knowledge) – he conveyed the objective of his institution. Just as he had done with his school, Tagore sought to create a seat of learning that was not an imitation of European institutions, but an Indian one which maintained a continuity with India's rich heritage, finding its impetus in Indian philosophy, culture and knowledge, while being rooted in the contemporary world. It would be 'genuinely and creatively Indian'.[2]

On a visit to the Sylhet district in eastern Bengal in 1920, Tagore witnessed the grace and expressive beauty of the Manipuri dance form. He invited two Manipuri dancers to his institution and they transformed the choreography of *Rabindra Nritya Natya* (Tagore's dance drama) and the subsequent production of *Chitrangada*, the dance drama using the Manipuri style. It was staged in Calcutta and across north India in cities like Delhi and Lahore to raise funds for his school. Tagore restored the dignity of Indian classical dance from the morass of British Victorian perspectives which had viewed it as a form practised by prostitutes, a view that was imbibed and internalized by the Bengali *bhadralok* culture until Tagore broke the taboo with the dance drama *Natir Puja* (The Dancer's Prayer), performed by girls from respectable families, reinstating the respectability of dance in the heart of middle-class Bengali society.[3] Sangit Bhavana, the institute of dance, drama and music, was founded in 1919 at Shantiniketan and remains an integral part of Visva-Bharati, like Kala Bhavana, the institute of fine arts (founded in 1919). Both thrived under the patronage and contribution of expert music exponents like Indira Devi and Dinendranath and leading artists like Nandalal Bose, Benodebehari Mukherjee and Ramkinkar Baij, respectively.

In 1917 several English translations were published, such as *My Reminiscences*, *Nationalism*, *Personality*, *The Cycle of Spring* and *Sacrifice and Other Plays*, but Tagore's output in Bengali was a slow process. *Palataka* (The Fugitive), a collection of narrative prose poems using conversational Bengali, with stories of human tragedy imbued with sadness and sympathy, which have an enduring appeal, did not come out until 1918. The mood of this collection reflected the personal tragedy of his daughter Bela's illness and death. The next collection, *Lipika* (1919; *Sketches*, 1922), has short poetic prose pieces in a mixture of styles, using allegory, irony, description and reflection, such as:

> Today I see that restless girl standing silently against the balustrade on the balcony, like the rainbow after a storm. Her large dark eyes are now calm, like a bird with dripping wings on the branch of a tree on a rainy day. I have never seen her so still. She seems like a river which has suddenly stopped in its tracks and become a lake.[4]

Tagore was precoccupied with setting up the university, but despite his time and energy being taken up with that project he continued to write and reply to letters and compose his inimitable songs, evoking the seasons and every mood that moved him.

In the meantime, another votary of truth, Romain Rolland of France, dedicated himself to promoting understanding between nations. He approached leading artists, writers and savants from various countries to sign the 'Declaration of Independence of the Human Spirit' (1919) after the devastation caused by the First World War. Tagore's lectures on 'Nationalism in Japan' had resonated with Rolland and he sought Tagore's signature for the document, which the poet gave willingly. Rolland would remain a friend to both Tagore and Gandhi, and was the latter's biographer.

Before the formal establishment of Visva-Bharati, Tagore was assailed by his characteristic wanderlust. He started for England again on 20 May 1920. Rathindranath noted in his biography how the devastation of the war in Europe had shaken the continent and the 'very foundations of their civilization had received a rude shock'.[5] The sale of Tagore's books had accumulated large royalties in Germany, but the bank with whom the money was held kept asking Tagore to encash it as the rising inflation was diminishing the sum rapidly. The delay in encashing meant that it dwindled to only a few annas and, as Rathindranath noted, 'Thus Father was saved the disaster of becoming a millionaire!'[6]

Tagore met some leading personalities of the time, including Lawrence of Arabia and Sybil Thorndike at the East and West Society at Caxton Hall, Lord Roberts, Lowes Dickinson and the economist John Maynard Keynes. The suspicion of the British Indian government continued to hound him. He had an invitation from Scandinavia and was preparing a visit when a lady, introduced by a renowned Orientalist and purporting to be interested in Eastern philosophy, proposed to accompany him on this trip as his secretary, which Tagore agreed to. However, it was soon revealed that she was a British spy – a deception that made an angry Tagore cancel his trip to Norway and Sweden. Instead, he proceeded to Paris, where he met leading figures of the day including Le Brun, the translator of Tagore's *The Gardener*,[7] and the renowned Sorbonne Indologist Sylvain Lévi at a reception at the Musée Guimet. He was deeply agitated when he visited the battlefields near Rheims and witnessed the deliberate devastation of France. Tagore, with his son and daughter-in-law, were the guests of the congenial, philanthropic banker Albert Kahn at Autour du Monde, Cap Martin, where they met a French artist who recounted how, in a small fishing village on the Italian Riviera, she had encountered a fisherman reading a book on the sand as he waited for his fishing nets to dry. When approached and asked what he was reading, the indignant answer was, 'Don't you see it is Tagore's *The Post Office*?'[8] In his reminiscences, Rathindranath tells a story he heard from an Indian army officer: once on a journey through the continent, the officer's train was stopped by a group of girls at a small station; the train was loaded with flowers and fruit, and the girls began shouting 'To the countrymen of Tagore!' The Tagores met the Karpeles sisters, Andree who was an artist and Suzanne who was studying Sanskrit, both of whom remained in touch with the poet and Rathindranath. They met the poets Comtesse de Brimont and Comtesse de Noailles and the latter spoke of the occasion when Clemenceau called her the day war was declared and together they read poems from André Gide's translation of *Gitanjali*.[9] After her meeting with Tagore, the Comtesse de Noailles told the poet that she had come to conquer, but was going away 'a devotee and worshipper'.[10]

From France he proceeded to Holland, where he was welcomed by his Dutch translator, Frederik van Eeden, who remained a good friend. Tagore was beset by a dilemma that would haunt him all his life. While he detected the ravages that materialism was causing contemporary society, the pressing necessity of the paucity of funds at Shantiniketan made it essential for him to raise money through his lectures – in which he could not avoid his warning against the aggression of capitalism, which in his view had led to narrow nationalism, militarization and a devastating war. However, his request to his agent James Pond to organize a second lecture tour in America on his proposed third visit to the country met with a negative response as Pond pointed out in a cable that post-war America would not welcome Tagore's message. After visiting Belgium, where he was welcomed by the king, he went back to Paris to see his daughter-in-law, Pratima Devi, who had had surgery. He returned to London, from where he decided he would travel to America.

Here his general reception was lukewarm. Of the five months spent there, four were spent in New York City. The *New York Times* published a fairly kind report of the purpose of his visit and announced the performance of the staging of two of his plays.[11] He could still gather crowds unaffected by political rumours. On 22 November 1920, his lecture on 'A Poet's Religion' at the Brooklyn Civic Forum gathered a vast crowd – so many, in fact, that some were turned away. There were many receptions and dinners for the Nobel Laureate where he met several leading figures of the day, including Lady Benson, who had been informed that Tagore was a yogi. When she found herself seated next to Tagore in her sleeveless dress, she carefully covered the arm next to him with a napkin, an act that went unnoticed by the poet. On this visit he did meet old friends like Harriet Moody, through whom he met the American heiress Dorothy Straight. He also renewed his acquaintence with Helen Keller and Jane Addams.

The one great success of his American visit was his meeting with the idealistic Englishman Leonard Knight Elmhirst, who was finishing his degree in agricultural science at Cornell. Tagore had heard from friends that Elmhirst wanted to work in the villages in India. He cabled him to come and see him, and thus began a friendship and collaboration that would bear fruit in India and in

Tagore and Leonard Elmhirst at Dartington Hall, 1926, England.

England. In fact, Elmhirst had wanted to meet Tagore and work at his institution, so when Tagore asked Elmhirst to come and set up and run his dream project, the Rural Reconstruction Centre at Surul, it was a fulfilment of his wish.

By this time, Tagore was tired, so he cut short his American trip, returning to London for three weeks in March 1921, from where he boarded a plane for the first time and flew to Paris. When he arrived in Paris he wanted to meet Romain Rolland, whose writing he admired, but no one would tell him where Rolland lived. He soon realized that this great votary of world peace and collaboration had become a *persona non grata*. After much difficulty he did find Romain Rolland's address and met him. He would have another opportunity to get better acquainted with the writer in the more neutral atmosphere of Switzerland, where Rolland later moved. While Tagore was in Paris he met the Argentinian poet and patron of art Victoria Ocampo, who became a devoted friend and admirer of Rabindranath's person and work. In Paris, the poet met up with his old friend Patrick Geddes, who was also a friend of Rolland. He was then invited to deliver his lecture on 'Message of the Forest' at the French University at Strasbourg where Sylvain Lévi was a professor. His next lecture was in Switzerland at the Rousseau Institute at Geneva, after which he went to Lucerne, where he celebrated his 61st birthday. It was here that he was sent the touching message that in Germany, leading writers and intellectuals like Thomas Mann, Count Hermann Keyserling, Hermann Jacobi, Gerhart Hauptmann and Rudolf Eucken had gathered to celebrate his birthday and had made a collection of German classics for Visva-Bharati's library.[12] Tagore's lecture trajectory made him weave in and out of Europe's cities, visiting Hamburg and Copenhagen, and speaking to a large audience at the University in Berlin on the idea of freedom through the realization of spiritual unity, a recurrent theme in his writing and various talks. He found India's true voice in spiritual leaders like Buddha and Guru Nanak and the poet Kabir, whose message would unite India's Hindus, Muslims, Christians and Buddhists. Elsewhere, he mentions India's Sikhs and Jains, all of whom can be brought together through cooperation, bringing unity which recognizes and celebrates India's diversity. This Berlin lecture was recorded and kept at the university's archives, where a section of it was retrieved after the university was bombed during the Second World War. It was sent in 1961 to Sahitya Akademi in Delhi, where it is still available.[13]

Tagore went on to accept an invitation instigated by Count Keyserling to meet and stay with the Grand Duke of Hesse at Darmstadt, where they had a thoughtful exchange on philosophy and metaphysics. There were no lectures and receptions here, but every day, as crowds gathered in the grounds, Tagore went out to meet and talk to the people with Count Keyserling as his interpreter, discoursing on philosophical subjects. One day, as Rathindranath reported, Tagore was driven with the Grand Duke to a park and sat on a hillock. The holiday crowd soon drifted to where he was seated and some 2,000 people spontaneously burst into song, singing for an hour as an unprompted ovation to the poet.[14] It was also at Darmstadt that Tagore received an invitation from an artists' club – the members of which were unhappy with Rabindranath being feted by dignitaries and said he should come instead to meet them. Tagore readily agreed and walked into a bohemian atmosphere, where beer mugs adorned the tables and cigar smoke hung heavy in the air – and where his audience did not get up to welcome him. He took it all in his stride and started speaking. Slowly the beer mugs disappeared from the tables and the cigars were put out as his audience listened with rapt attention. The 'frenzied hero-worship' in Berlin and the heady success of Tagore's trip to Germany were perhaps because of the boost his visit gave to a recently defeated nation whose morale and prestige were at a remarkably low ebb.[15] However, Tagore's interactions in Germany were viewed with suspicion and coolness in Britain and France and *The Telegraph* and *L'Eclair* branded them as propagandist.

In Sweden, at an official banquet hosted by Selma Lagerlöf and presided over by the King of Sweden, Tagore met some of the famous authors he had read in translation, including Knut Hamsun, Bjørnstjerne Bjørnson, Johan Bojer and Sven Hedin the travel writer, who 'had made the whole wide world his home'.[16] At Stockholm, he witnessed a performance of *The Post Office*.

Tagore returned to Germany to fulfil his lecture engagements. In Munich he heard from Thomas Mann and Kurt Wolff, his German publisher (who sold 'more than one million' copies of his books 'by the end of 1923'[17]), of the deprivation suffered by the people after the First World War. He was so distressed by the accounts that he donated the proceeds of his lecture to the 'famished children' of the city. Here he was met by a persistent Austrian lady who persuaded Tagore to accept the invitation of the people of Vienna who were waiting to hear him, which he ultimately did. In Vienna, he handed over his handsome honorarium to the people of the deprived city.[18]

During his intercontinental travels, Rathindranath recalls one incident when Tagore's German translators, Professor Meyer Benfey and his wife, were invited from Hamburg to the village where he was the guest of Mrs Van Eeghen. When the couple came down to breakfast, having arrived the previous night to meet Tagore, they shed silent tears at the sight of a table laden 'with all kinds of rich fare' – an abundance of food they had neither seen nor eaten in the past five years in Germany.[19]

Tagore travelled on to Czechoslovakia, where the joy of a people who had suddenly become free after years of foreign domination was visible. In Prague he lectured both at the German University and at Charles University, meeting two leading Indologists, Professor Moriz Winternitz and Vincenc Lesný, a Bengali scholar and the first European translator to translate Tagore from his original Bengali. He was also Tagore's biographer. Both scholars were invited to Visva-Bharati and remained close friends of Tagore. Today, Metropolitan University Prague and Charles University have strong linguistics departments where Bengali, Hindi and Sanskrit are taught. In Czechoslovakia, Tagore met the writer Karel Čapek and the composer Leoš Janáček.

The difference between the two countries was stark: the sense of abandon that came with unexpected liberation in Czechoslavakia was visible against the post-war suffering of the Viennese people, evident in their attire and emaciation; yet their love of theatre, opera and art was evident to Rathindranath on this visit.[20] Tagore's lectures were well attended and his handing back of his honorarium created a deep impression on the citizens of Vienna.

Apart from meeting many interesting writers, artists and intellectuals, Tagore had some significant cultural experiences in Europe. He saw *The Beggar's Opera* (which he did not enjoy) in London and *Faust* at the Grand Opera in Paris, which impressed him greatly. In Paris, Victor Goloubew invited Tagore to see his own collection of slides on Indian archaeology at the Musée Guimet.

Here he also encountered the Post-Impressionists who were considered controversial in art circles. Rathindranath writes about the remarkable paintings by Cézanne, Manet, Renoir, Gauguin and Van Gogh, the latter making the strongest impression on him.[21] In Vienna, Professor Winternitz, who had accompanied the Tagores there, persuaded Tagore to attend a performance of Wagner's *Die Meistersinger* at the Opera House, explaining the story and interpreting the music, ensuring the enjoyment of his guests of this difficult foreign composition.

For some time, Tagore had been missing Shantiniketan, and the call of the homeland finally prevailed. He returned in July 1921 when Gandhi's non-cooperation movement was in full swing.

In December 1921 Tagore opened his international university, Visva-Bharati. Intended to be not only in touch with its surroundings, but a continuation of it, its activities included agriculture, gardening, weaving and dairy keeping, with students and teachers working with and learning from ordinary people in the neighbouring villages in an atmosphere of mutual appreciation, learning and exchange. Indeed, 'exchange' could be the keyword for Tagore's 'nest'. He wanted his university to be, in the Indian tradition, a place which offered hospitality to guests and cultures from elsewhere, making it clear that, 'my guests from the West must be made welcome here'.[22] His university would 'invite students from the West and the Far East to study the systems of Indian philosophy, literature, art and music in their proper environment'. He felt that India, who had given much in the past and had become isolated through recurrent conquests and through her own internal constructs of social exclusion, could now, in the 'New Age', offer something to the world, from the depths of her forest abodes, a message of peace through cooperation in the aftermath of the 'wreckage' wrought by the First World War.

The first foreign scholars who came and taught at Visva-Bharati were Sylvain Lévi, who had been given an honorary doctorate with Tagore by Calcutta University in 1913. Lévi founded the Tibetan and

China Institute at Visva-Bharati and taught Chinese and Tibetan languages and the cultural links between the West and India. China Bhavana, a dedicated Institute for Chinese Studies, was later founded in 1937 with the help of the Chinese scholar Tan Yun Shan. The orientalist Winternitz of the Oriental Institute of Prague came to Visva-Bharati. Other foreign scholars followed, such as Patrick Geddes, the Scottish conservation architect, town planner, botanist, sociologist and educationist, who became a close friend of Tagore's and maintained a long correspondence with him between 1918 and 1930; Tagore also invited Geddes to submit plans for Visva-Bharati.[23]

Other visitors included the Viennese art historian and critic Stella Kramrisch; the French-Swiss linguist Fernand Benoit; the Russian scholar Igor Bogdanov, a specialist in Persian; the French artist Andree Karpeles; the Dutch musician Mary van Eeghen and musicologist Arnold Bake; the American nurse Gretchen Green; the Norwegian archaeologist Sten Konow; the writer James Cousins and linguist Mark Collins from Ireland; Miss S. Flaun, a recent graduate of the University of Columbia;[24] and the American theologian Stanley Jones. Others who were in close touch with Tagore and his institution were the Italian Sanskrit and religion scholars Carlo Formichi and Giuseppe Tucci from the University of Rome and the Japanese poet Yone Noguchi;[25] the Austrian industrial chemist Dr Bay; the painter Tan Seyn from Burma; and the Chinese artist Zhu Peong, who visited Tagore as late as December 1939.

Themes that were covered at Shantiniketan included the Vedic age, Buddhism, poetics and the culture of Asia, Indochinese contacts, Christian theology, Indo-Iranian philology, art and the history of Europe. 'The Dynamic Development of the Indian Religions from the Rig Veda to Buddhism' was taught by Formichi and 'Contacts between Ancient India and the West' by Lévi.[26] Uma Das Gupta points out that the cosmopolitan atmosphere at Jorasanko, where Goethe was read in German, Maupassant in French, *Shakuntala* in

Sanskrit and, one can add, Hafiz in Pharsi, influenced Tagore profoundly. It was this 'nest' at Jorasanko, where world literature met, that would lay the foundation for the belief in the validity of a cultural interchange for Tagore, which he put into practice at Visva-Bharati. At Visva-Bharati he wanted his students to reach out to the world and for the world to conglomerate at Visva-Bharati. Here guests would be realized as divine visitors, *atithi devo bhava*, and India's traditional spirit of hospitality would be practised.

When Tagore met Elmhirst in America in 1921, he told him of his 'educational enterprise' which was situated in a remote rural part of west Bengal, surrounded by villages of Hindus, Muslims and Santhals, who, apart from doing some menial work for the school, were quite cut off from the educational community. These villages were in 'steady decline'. Tagore had bought a farm with a building from the Sinha family at Surul. Malaria was rampant in this region. The area round the property was in 'decay'.[27] Would Elmhirst come to find out the cause for this and help with reviving and restoring village life in the hinterland of his institution?

Elmhirst said he would after he had finished his degree at Cornell, so that he might prove more helpful with his educational training. Elmhirst came to Shantiniketan in November 1921, along with a generous sum donated by Dorothy Straight, and set to work at Surul. He later married Dorothy, whose funds were permanently invested in a trust which kept the Surul project alive. Elmhirst would work closely with Rathindranath and in his absence, Arthur Geddes, the Scottish geographer son of Patrick Geddes, would continue the rural resuscitation programme. Many of Rathi's father's ideas and plans were implemented on the ground by Arthur Geddes between 1922 and 1924, when the latter taught at Surul. The 'nest' where East and West met was slowly fulfilling its mission.

After Elmhirst's arrival, Tagore put him in a team with Rathi, Santosh Majumdar (who had also trained in agricultural science and husbandry like Rathi) and two staff members, Kalimohan Ghosh and Gour Gopal Ghosh, and asked them to draw up well-considered plans to start the rural reconstruction programme. Elmhirst began his Bengali lessons at the same time. In January 1922 ten college students were eager to start work with Elmhirst in the villages. Thus on 17 February Elmhirst left for Surul with pots, pans and tools in a truck. Tagore took an active interest in his work, writing from Shelidah, 'Please take it seriously when I say that my whole heart is with you in the work you have started' when he learned of his methods of entrenching rubbish and night soil in the villagers' back gardens.[28] At Shantiniketan, when Elmhirst cycled early in the morning past Rabi's thatched mudhouse (this was before *pucca* buildings began being built in the north), the poet hailed him and asked him for news of his progress, and urged him to stay to sample newly arrived gifts of Bengali sweets and mangoes as Andrews 'won't risk them'.[29] Elmhirst wrote, 'As the months went by I found him [Tagore] more and more eager to come and visit the farm at Surul or to find time to discuss the puzzles that arose.'[30]

So from 1922 work began in earnest at the rural reconstruction centre at Surul that Tagore named Sriniketan (Abode of Well-being). Its objective was to bring hope and self-dependency to locals through participation in a revitalization programme that encouraged and thrived on interdependency and interchange between the institution and the surrounding villages.

Tagore described his institution as a place of pilgrimage in the new age, where there would be a confluence, 'a meeting of truths'. Today Shantiniketan, the school, the university and Sriniketan remain a place of cultural pilgrimage in India where many Indians and foreigners make it their sought-out destination, some drawn to it from curiosity and many with the sense of paying homage to India's myriad-minded man.

In early 1940, the year before Tagore's death, when Gandhi met the ailing poet, Rabindranath gave the politician a handwritten note saying, 'Accept this institution under your protection . . .

Visva-Bharati is like a vessel, which is carrying the the cargo of my life's best treasure and I hope it may claim special care from my countrymen for its preservation.'[31] Gandhi said that 'Gurudev' was truly international because he was national, so his institution was of international importance. Today Visva-Bharati, India's first central university, has the president of India as its *paridarsaka* (visitor). The governor of West Bengal is the *pradhana* (rector) and the prime minister of India is the *acharya* (chancellor). It is the task of the president of India to appoint the *Upacharya* (vice-chancellor) of the university. Tagore's ideal was to offer the best of India's hospitality to the world at Visva-Bharati and share her culture with others, while welcoming the best from other cultures – in a 'nest where the world meets'.

9

'The Call of Truth' and 'The Great Sentinel'

During the years Tagore was building up his twin institutions of Visva-Bharati at Shantiniketan and Sriniketan at Surul, his writing continued in its usual urgent flow. On his tours of Europe and America, he was fully aware of the irony of his self-imposed mission of calling for international cooperation between nations and promoting the East as relevant to a world fragmented and devastated by war, while boycotts, pickets and non-cooperation marked Gandhi's campaign for *swaraj* (home rule). Tagore had written to C. F. Andrews in May 1921, 'I am a poet, not a fighter . . . What irony of fate is this that I should be preaching cooperation of cultures between East and West on this side of the sea just at the moment when the doctrine of non-cooperation is preached on the other?'[1]

W. W. Pearson and Andrews had gone to South Africa to meet Gandhi and support his campaign for protecting Indian workers' human rights. They sought Tagore's blessings before they left India and on 5 December 1913, Tagore was one of the organizers of a meeting at the Calcutta Town Hall to discuss the plight of Indians in South Africa. Andrews wrote back to Tagore about his estimation of Gandhi in January 1914:

> I had no difficulty in seeing from the first Mr Gandhi's position and accepting it; for in principle, it is essentially yours and Mahatmaji's – a true independence, a reliance upon spiritual

force, a fearless courage in the face of temporal power, and withal a deep and burning charity for all men.[2]

It was Andrews who suggested that the Phoenix Ashram boys should come to Shantiniketan after their ashram had closed down. After their first meeting at Shantiniketan in March 1915, the bond between Tagore and Gandhi remained strong. In spite of their ideological differences, they held each other in high regard, Tagore addressing Gandhi as the Mahatma and Gandhi calling him Gurudev. Over the years they met several times in Calcutta, Ahmedabad, at Shantiniketan and at Yervada Jail when Tagore went to see the incarcerated Mahatma.

Gandhi launched onto the national scene of India with the Champaran Satyagraha (passive resistance) and his backing of the mill-workers' strike at Ahmedabad in 1917–18. Then came the infamous sedition bill, the Rowlatt Acts suppressing political agitation which was resisted by Gandhi's *satyagraha*, drawing a tremendous nationwide response. Henceforth, Gandhi was the indisputable leader of the nationalist movement. Gandhi requested Tagore send a message just before the countrywide *hartal* (strike) on 6 April 1919. The protests in the Punjab led to the declaration of martial law in the province, resulting in Rabindranath writing a letter to Gandhi on 12 April 1919 praising his leadership and mode of opposition, as he had shown how one could put into practice Buddha's saying, 'conquer anger by the power of non-anger, and evil by the power of good', though he remained deeply disturbed by the forces of evil and violence.[3] The very next day, the firing under General Dyer's orders at Jallianwalla Bagh happened. The silence from Gandhi and the Indian National Congress against this great human tragedy prompted a desperate Tagore to write to Lord Chelmsford, renouncing his knighthood.

In March 1920 Gandhi wrote to Tagore on behalf of the Gujarat Literary Conference asking him to visit Ahmedabad and his ashram.

It was a grand occasion and a memorable visit when Tagore gave a lecture on 'Construction versus Creation' at Anand Bhavan theatre, and the two great public figures of India conversed in the presence of a devoted audience at the ashram. Gandhi invited Tagore to his ashram again and assured him that he would always find a home there. Tagore would return to Ahmedabad several times after that. Of Shantiniketan Gandhi said it was his 'second home'. At Tagore's request, Gandhi was an adviser to the Village Industries Association at Birbhum and became a life trustee of Visva-Bharati.

After almost two years of apparent inactivity, Gandhi made a comeback on the national political front with the launch of his non-cooperation movement in 1921. On 23 February, in *Young India*, Gandhi published his six conditions for the campaign to obtain *swaraj*; (1) the adoption of non-violence as a resistance strategy, (2) establishing Congress organizations in all Indian villages, (3) (re)instating the spinning wheel in every home and the compulsory spinning of cloth, (4) collecting donations, (5) encouraging Hindu–Muslim unity and (6) abolishing untouchability.

Tagore had pointed out to C. F. Andrews that there is 'no word for nation in our language', so when we 'borrow' it from elsewhere, 'it never fits us'.[4] The nearest to 'nation' in India was *samaj*, civic society, standing for the Indian community. There were several principles of the non-cooperation movement on which Tagore and Gandhi differed. After the First World War, Tagore felt that cooperation and coordination between nations for universal unity and mutual respect were more urgent than ever. He felt that the West now needed the message of peace and hospitality from the East which India could offer. He was anxious about the hostility the foreigner could experience. Gandhi's call for non-cooperation was counterpoised against Tagore's dedication to internationalism on the world stage. Yet Gandhi saw no contradiction in his strategy when he said to the English 'Come and co-operate with us on our

own terms, and it will be well for us, for you and the world.'[5]
For Gandhi Indian nationalism was 'health giving, religious and therefore humanitarian'.[6] While Tagore was extremely critical of the strategy of the Indian National Congress to beg for small benefits from the foreigner, he was in favour of reaching resolutions through dialogue that promoted understanding. He took pains to cultivate relationships through letters he wrote to administrative heads on critical issues and in the lectures he gave on nationalism in the West and East about the disjuncture of the governance engineered by the state machine – which had no consciousness of the welfare of the *samaj*, the greater society, and the need to bring about moral and social upliftment through small projects in the apathetic villages of India. He conceded that this would be a long, drawn-out process, which he had started in his family estates and at Sriniketan, yet such projects could set an example and provide an impetus to other villages across the country. Yet Gandhi had promised *swaraj* in one year, a popular aim which had a heady effect on his followers. Allied to non-cooperation was the boycott of government educational institutions, which demanded activists leave their schools and colleges to join the movement. Tagore was utterly opposed to this as he felt that this would create a void in society leading to utter anarchy.

Tagore was not convinced that *satyagraha* would effectively remain non-violent, as it could lead to brutality on the one hand and prove a harsh test of the fortitude and patience of a defenceless nation on the other, and trying to keep in check the diverse strands of the agitating masses could prove a challenge. Tagore would be proved sadly right by the violence unleashed at Chauri Chaura in 1922, which compelled a shocked Gandhi to stall his call for non-cooperation. Tagore was also against the burning of foreign cloth as he believed that 'the question of using or refusing cloth of a particular manufacture belongs mainly to economic choice'.[7] Gandhi confessed that he did not 'draw any sharp distinction between economics and ethics'.[8] Tagore felt that 'the clothes to be burnt are not mine, but belong to those who most sorely need them'.[9] Gandhi's answer was, 'I venture to suggest to the Poet that the clothes I ask him to burn must be and are his.'[10] In *The Home and the World*, Nikhil raises the same question with Sandip as they watch the jubilation of swadeshis surrounding a bonfire that rages upon foreign clothes, for here is another kind of violence that is unleashed in a gleeful dance of destruction.

Rathindranath loved and respected his father and held Gandhi in high regard. Of the two men he notes how they could not look more different, one small and nondescript and the other tall, fair and handsome. Gandhi in his loincloth, clothed in the bare minimum in sympathy with India's impoverished millions, could not have presented a sharper contrast to Tagore in his double *djibba* (long coat), his trousers and his recognizable *pugree* (turban), his elegant sartorial style fashioned by himself as a reflection of his aesthetic standards. 'He had the peculiar knack of making the simplest thing look beautiful and the most expensive things look simple'.[11] While Tagore admired and respected Gandhi's courage in donning the garb of the poorest man in India, he would have been deeply uncomfortable to appear in anything that went against his 'artistic sensibilities'.[12] Moreover, Tagore was not a believer in the rigorous self-denial of austerity, especially in a country where deprivation was the lot of the majority and he believed that people should be 'encouraged to taste the good things in life'.[13] While Winston Churchill called Gandhi the 'fakir', many people in Europe, on seeing Tagore, exclaimed, 'How like our Prophet!'[14]

It was Gandhi's 'cult of the charkha', as Tagore referred to it in an essay of 1925, that brought the politician and the poet into the public arena in a debate which voiced their difference of opinion on the *charkha* – the spinning wheel – as the practical symbol of the nationalist movement. For Gandhi, the adoption of the humble spinning wheel in every Indian home would bring a means of self-reliance and activity back to the nation. It would address the prevailing sense of listlessness and hopelessness by inculcating self-help, and thus restore the dignity of a subject people. Tagore's espousal of modernity made him resist the *charkha* as the implement to free India's millions. He was in favour of science and technology that could help India to progress; he believed that going back to the *charkha* would prove regressive for the nation. Allied to the imperative of the *charkha* was Gandhi's directive to spin. At every Congress meeting, in all assemblies presided over by Gandhi, all nationalist Indians were advised to spin, to produce their own cloth, to hide their 'shame' and become self-sufficient and thus contribute to the national economy. Tagore encouraged creation over construction, of organic growth rather than rigidly monitored actions. He pointed out that this compulsion to spin at all costs was restrictive and stifling and thus harmful to the freedom that Gandhi was striving towards. Somehow, *swaraj* became a mantra and the people were deluded by the simple equation that spinning for a certain time every day would bring freedom to the nation. Gandhi tried to impress upon Tagore to spin and asked his students to do so to thus set an example to the nation. Tagore replied with his characteristic humour: 'Poems I can spin, Gandhiji, songs and plays I can spin, but of your precious cotton, what a mess I would make!'[15] Tagore decided to clarify his position in 'Satyer Ahaban' (The Call of Truth).[16] This was answered by Gandhi in 'The Great Sentinel', where he conceded that Tagore stood up against authority, a slave mentality and was a 'sentinel warning us against . . . Bigotry, Lethargy, Intolerance Ignorance, Inertia'.[17] But he dismissed Tagore's arguments as impractical, which could be excused as 'poetic license and he who takes it literally is in danger of finding himself in an awkward corner'.[18] Gandhi believed, 'True to the poetical instinct the Poet lives for the morrow' and was thus irrelevant for the times.[19] Spinning the *charkha* was a 'sacrament' that Gandhi wanted all Indians to accept in his bid for self-determination. Tagore was staunchly resistant to a repetitive action that would stifle the intellect and not allow man's reason to function. For Tagore, man's creative power is dependent on his inner life, acting on the tenets of Truth and Love, which Gandhi embodied in his person. Gandhi could stir the millions to action, but the spinning of the *charkha*, non-cooperation and boycott would not provide the assured path to the moral and intellectual freedom that Indians needed to be freed from within themselves.

The national debate isolated Tagore as a lonely voice against Gandhi's increasing popularity. The response to Tagore in the press could be openly belittling – the *Ananda Bazar Patrika* referred to 'the ludicrous opinion of the Poet' that 'appeal[ed] to those who live in a dream-world'.[20] During the months between March 1922, when Gandhi was arrested, and his release from prison in February 1924, Tagore retreated from public debate. This would be a pattern, where the poet would withdraw completely from criticizing Gandhi's political strategies every time the Mahatma was imprisoned. In 1925 Tagore's essay 'The Cult of the Charkha' was answered by Gandhi's 'The Poet and the Charkha'. Tagore's 'Striving for Swaraj' was published in 1925 and Gandhi's 'The Poet and the Wheel' in 1926, in the *Modern Review* and *Young India* respectively. In May 1925 Gandhi visited Tagore at Shantiniketan to discuss the pairs' differences on Gandhi's political programme. After a lengthy exchange, they agreed to disagree.

However, the mutual regard remained as Gandhi sought Tagore's blessings before each of his *satyagraha* campaigns and Tagore was always quick to respond with his support, respect and concern. Tagore paid a visit to Gandhi's ashram to boost the morale of the inmates when their leader was in prison and he visited Gandhi in Yervada Jail in Poona in 1932 when Gandhi was fighting against the government proposition of separate electorates. Tagore was with him when he broke his fast. To Tagore, Gandhi's self-inflicted penance was unacceptable, since Gandhi's person and life were more important to him and the nation than India's nationalist struggle. As late as 24 November 1932 Gandhi wrote to Tagore, 'Your precious letter comforts me. It is enough to know you are watching and praying.'[21] After Gandhi broke his fast on 20 September 1932, Tagore published 'An Appeal to My Countrymen: After Mahatma Gandhi's Epic Fast' in which he set out three resolutions to address social discrimination: (1) to refrain from looking down on anyone due to caste or community differences; (2) to open up all public places like temples, schools, gatherings, water tanks and so on, to all people, irrespective of caste or creed; and (3) to adopt a zero-tolerance policy in Indian society to resist all kinds of intolerance.[22]

There was one occasion when Rabindranath's anger against Gandhi's opinion was voiced in a fiery exchange. This was after the Bihar earthquake in 1934 when Gandhi said that for him this was a sign of 'divine chastisement sent by God for our sins . . . For me there is a vital connection between the Bihar calamity and the untouchability campaign.'[23] A visibly upset Tagore reacted instantly in a public statement. He said that in a country where such an 'unscientific view' would be 'readily accepted' by many people, it was unacceptable: 'We who are immensely grateful to Mahatmaji for inducing, by his wonder-working inspiration, freedom from fear and feebleness in the minds of his countrymen, feel profoundly hurt when any words from his mouth may emphasise the elements of unreason in those very minds.'[24]

Yet there were grave points on which both men agreed as they worked and called for Hindu–Muslim unity: the eradication of untouchability, the need for rural uplift through a constructive programme, the necessity of building self-reliance and self-help in Indian villages, the need for education to free the mind and education in the mother tongue. Gandhi sought Tagore's opinion for the adoption of Hindi as the national language of India, which Tagore agreed was the 'only possible national language' and advised on a period of preparation to 'pave the way towards its general use of constant practice as a voluntary acceptance of a national obligation'.[25] Years later, in 1944, three years after Tagore's death, Gandhi conceded that he had 'deceived' himself, the non-cooperation movement had not succeeded. At a conference of the Charkha Sangh he said, 'What I gave to the people was money and not the real substance – self-reliance.'[26] Gandhi valued Tagore as an honest and 'candid' friend. On 1 October 1940 Gandhi wrote to Tagore, 'You must stay awhile. Humanity needs you.' In his birthday message on 13 April 1941, Gandhi wrote, 'Four score not enough may you finish five', which received a rejoinder from Tagore, 'Thanks message but four score is impertinence, five score intolerable.' Even when Tagore was ailing and on the verge of death in 1941, he sent a song at Gandhi's request to Wardha Ganj in Maharashtra. In a message to the poet, Gandhi praised Tagore's vigorous mind which was still capable of composing songs in spite of his frail health.

The irony was that Tagore, who was an advocate for cooperation, had, in government records, become 'to all intents and purposes a non-cooperator' after he returned his knighthood.[27] He remained under government suspicion, as were his associates. Sylvain Lévi was suspected of having 'anarchical leanings', while the archaeologist Sten Konow wrote freely against British rule in India and Pearson and Andrews were both known for their pro-India stances. In Japan, Tagore met Rashbehari Bose, a wanted revolutionary, who continued to correspond with him even after his return from Japan. Tagore was a sympathizer of Subhas Chandra Bose, whom he had met on a ship journey back to India, and been impressed by the young man's leadership qualities. However, Lord Lytton (Governor of Bengal, 1922–7), who had visited Shantiniketan and knew Tagore, and was familiar with the poet's 'aim and ideas', was unwilling to draw conclusions about him 'solely upon police reports'.[28] Nevertheless, Tagore's letters continued to be opened by the police – a practice legalized with regard to all inmates of Shantiniketan in March 1931 – and, as mentioned earlier, secret circulars were sent to government officials warning them against sending their wards to his institutions (which were seen as founts of seditious ideas). Tagore's fundraising lecture tours in America were marred by reports from the Indian government to the Department of State, discouraging foreign funds for his institution. His visits to Germany and Italy were viewed with suspicion and many applicants who wanted to teach at Shantiniketan, especially Jewish candidates, were denied entry. The proposal of planting informants among both female and male students at Tagore's institution was made as late as 1934 by the police department.[29] Tagore was aware of his letters being opened and the governmental watch on his institution and was often frustrated by the obstacles put in the path of his educational programme. As late as February 1935, when the Bengal governor, Anderson, visited Shantiniketan, he encountered an empty campus as the staff and students had been sent away as a precautionary measure.

Both Tagore and Gandhi, who were and still remain India's greatest intellectual and political minds, respectively, continued to depend on each other for mutual support until Tagore's death in 1941. Both believed that man needed to rely on his inner resources, on truth, love and compassion to find full freedom to realize himself and recognize fellow human beings as brethren. Their ideals were imbued with a sense of deep moral ethos and both worked from an inner core of spirituality. But while Gandhi was against technological advancement and science, Tagore, as a modernist, believed that science and the humanities were needed for a holistic education and social advancement.

Three leading scientists of the day, the physicist and biologist Sir Jagadish Chandra Bose, the chemist Sir Prafulla Chandra Ray and Sir Patrick Geddes, the Scottish botanist and environmentalist, were Tagore's close associates, who each held the poet in high esteem. He had long conversations with Albert Einstein, whom he met for the first time in Berlin in 1926 and again in 1930. Both Jagadish Chandra and Prafulla Chandra were Bramhos, the latter being an early initiate to the Bramho faith and the former belonging to a Bramho family, thus sharing Tagore's monotheistic background and liberal ideals. Prafulla Chandra came from a poor family, but since his father wanted one son at least to be educated in Britain, he studied on a Gilchrist Scholarship at Edinburgh and graduated with a BSc in Chemistry and was later awarded a DSc. Jagadish Chandra studied at Cambridge and was conferred a DSc in Physics. He was the second Indian to become a fellow of Britain's Royal Society. Acharya Prafulla Chandra Ray joined the faculty at Presidency College on his return. An ardent nationalist, he was a pioneer in the chemical industry and sought to alleviate the economic plight of India through the development of chemical industries in Bengal, establishing the Bengal Chemical and Pharmaceutical Works, with a view to making Indians self-reliant. While he was a staunch Gandhian who supported Gandhi's *charkha* movement and the making of *khadi*, he recognized in Tagore an iconic literary figure who had given Bengal, vis-à-vis India, a significant identity through his songs and literature.

Jagadish Chandra and Tagore were participants at Patrick Geddes's summer school in Darjeeling in 1918. While Geddes admired Gandhi and corresponded with him, he was averse to Gandhi's adoption of the *charkha* and his rejection of science, because he instead saw the introduction of science as the true path to the liberation of India. Geddes proposed the introduction of science and technology to improve Indian agriculture. At Visva-Bharati, he advocated the synthesis of disciplines, of mathematics, technics, physics and biology alongside logic, education, politics, economics, religion and ethics.[30] Jagadish Chandra was given a difficult time by physiologists who disapproved when he moved into plant physiology. Initially he worked on semiconductors and electromagnetic waves. It was in 1885 at the Asiatic Society that he made known the possibility of wireless transmission of radio waves over a distance of 23 metres (75 ft). In 1901 he announced his discovery of the responses of plants to external stimuli. The British Navy was a keen adopter of the Bose coherer, which they used to establish contact between a torpedo boat and friendly ships. Both Ray and Bose were in touch with Western scientists and Ray travelled to Europe to meet and discuss developments in his field with leading chemists of his time. In 1896–7, and again between 1900 and 1902, Bose went on lecturing tours throughout England and the Continent. During his later trip, he also lectured in America.

However, the resistance, disbelief and dismissal Jagadish Chandra encountered in some Western scientists made him give up his experimental work in the West and return to India to concentrate on his own research in Calcutta, establishing the Bose Institute for scientific research in 1917. What impressed Geddes was that Bose used local artisans in India to make his own instruments; both Geddes and Tagore respected Bose for refusing to patent his discoveries and therefore receive money for his inventions. Bose believed that knowledge should be free and not remain the domain of the initiated or exclusive groups, a belief that his close friends appreciated. In fact, at the Bose Institute his directive was 'no invention from this Institution should be patented'.[31] Both Bose and Ray were patriots, and deeply aware of their Indian heritage. Bose's model of the fusion of his spiritual roots with scientific experimentation resonated with both Geddes and Tagore. Like Geddes, Bose was an advocate for the global cooperation of the sciences.

Tagore and Bose had met regularly as friends in the late nineteenth century. On Tagore's invitation, Jagadish Chandra Bose and his wife Abala went to Shelidah for a holiday and spent some time enjoying Tagore's hospitality on the River Padma. It was here that Bose urged Tagore to write his prose narratives, which he did, and this began the great flowering of his short stories, which Rabi read to Bose every evening. Later Bose would translate 'The Hungry Stones' for publication in *Harper's Magazine*, but it was met with the refusal of the publisher who said that the West was not ready for Oriental themes. When Bose ran out of money in 1901 while he was abroad, his poet friend went on a fundraising mission, appealing to the Maharaja of Tripura, obtaining Rs 5,000 for Bose to continue his research in London (as mentioned earlier). On his return to India in 1896, after the first flush of his international successes, Tagore went to his house to congratulate Bose in person, but finding him absent, he left a magnolia blossom on his work table as a note of his appreciation. In 1931 Tagore dedicated his collection of poems on flowers, plants and trees, *Vanavani* (Voice of the Forest) to his friend. In the same year, Bose, with Romain Rolland, Gandhi, Albert Einstein and the Greek poet Kostis Palamas, sponsored *The Golden Book of Tagore*, which contained tributes to Tagore by famous people across the world who had known him personally, to celebrate the poet's seventieth birthday.

Tagore met Einstein through Dr Mandel, a friend in common. They met five times, their first meeting being in 1926 and the subsequent ones in 1930 between July and December, in Berlin and in New York. The conversations which took place during their second and third meetings at Einstein's house in Caputh and at Dr Mandel's house were on truth, beauty and realism, published in the *New York Times* in 1930, and as Appendix II in Tagore's lecture collection *The Religion of Man* (1931). Though they both respected each other, and their social ideals were similar, as Isaiah Berlin later said, their views remained distinctive. On the subjects of time and space, Tagore proposed that he himself had been looking beyond the temporal at a universal reality where man's personality enabled him to perceive and understand the universe. Einstein proposed two possible realities – a universe reliant on humanity and another abstracted from it and thus an independent entity. For Tagore, it

Tagore and Albert Einstein, 1930, Berlin.

was man's comprehension of the universe that affirmed its presence and thus it could not be divorced from man's existence and experience of it. Their second conversation was on music and the question of harmony. The raid by the Nazi Brownshirts on Einstein's residence led an angry Tagore to write to a Jewish journalist against the 'insults offered to my friend Einstein' which shook his 'faith in modern civilization'.[32] Tagore refused an honorary degree from Berlin University as a mark of protest against the persecution of Einstein in Germany. In 1931 Einstein wrote in *The Golden Book of Tagore*:

> thou hast served mankind
> all through a long and fruitful life,
> spreading everywhere a gentle and free thought
> in a manner such as the Seers of thy people
> have proclaimed as the idea.[33]

Another bonding thread between Geddes, Bose and Tagore was that of the previously mentioned Margaret Noble, an Irish woman, more popularly known as Sister Nivedita (the dedicated sister). She was a follower of Swami Vivekananda and later became a disciple of Sri Ramakrishna. In 1900 Geddes met Sister Nivedita and Vivekananda in New York. Vivekananda had addressed the World Congress of Religions in Chicago in 1893, where he presented Hinduism 'to the world at large as a major religion, emphasising its antiquity'.[34] He also lectured in London in 1895. The trio met again in Paris during the International Exhibition. It was here that Vivekananda delivered lectures in which he rejected the theory that Indian art had evolved from Hellenic influences; instead he argued that Buddhist art had shaped Indian artists' creations. This was a view that would be adopted and confirmed by Sister Nivedita too.[35] She was a social reformer, a champion of female education and a dedicated social worker. A Hindu convert, she became a staunch defender of Hinduism and authored several books on Indian art, culture, history and religion. Murdo Macdonald notes that while Geddes played an active role in the Celtic Revival in Scotland, Sister Nivedita was a vigorous participant in the Celtic Revival in Ireland.[36] After settling down in India, she became an active contributor to the Hindu Revival, publishing *Kali the Mother* in 1900. In Paris they met Bose, whose wife, Abala, would remain one of Sister Nivedita's closest and most supportive friends. Sister Nivedita was a dedicated Indian nationalist, who designed the first Indian flag and was an intrepid critic of the government in India. Tagore was critical of her religious views, but admired her love for India and Indians. As mentioned earlier, Sister Nivedita reacted angrily to Tagore's ending of *Gora*, where the hero parts ways with the love of his life, the cultured and liberal Sucharita, asking him why he had to continue to adhere to narrow patriarchal social norms when he had the freedom of a writer to ring in the changes. It was perhaps on Sister Nivedita's advice that Tagore changed the ending of *Gora* to a happier one of reconciliation and acceptance. Tagore wrote the Introduction to the 1918 edition of Sister Nivedita's *Web of Indian Life* (1904). As a perceptive and appreciative critic of Indian art, she was instrumental in creating a platform for the Bengal School of Modern Art and it was Nivedita who introduced Kakuzo Okakura to the Tagore household. Okakura's pan-Asian ideology resonated with Tagore, as did his vision for a continuity of India's association with her Eastern neighbours.

10
Waves of Nationalism and *The Religion of Man*

While Sister Nivedita set up home and carried on her work in India, Tagore's restless travels continued both within his country and internationally, as he was invited by people and institutions to take forward his mission of bringing the East and West closer. In 1923 Tagore visited Karachi, Hyderabad, Porbandar and Bombay between March and April and went to several princely kingdoms in western India in November that year, seeking funds for Kala Bhavana.

Between March and June 1924, he turned east, travelling to Burma (now Myanmar), China and Japan, to speak about Asian unity. He was accompanied by a diverse group in Leonard Elmhirst, the American nurse Gretchen Green, Nandalal Bose, the artist from Kala Bhavana who was studying Chinese art, and a Bengali student of Sylvain Lévi. The visit to China was significant for Tagore, as he hoped to revive the historic exchange between the two nations that had long elapsed in the nine centuries since the first missionaries had been sent by Emperor Ashoka in the 3rd century BC. He confided in Elmhirst that they would listen to Chinese students and meet the country's artists and writers to find out what they were thinking and feeling about their times. Tagore was conscious that he was trying to renew a tenuous link, inspired by Kakuzo Okakura's declaration 'Asia is one'.

On his way to China, Tagore received a warm, reverential letter of invitation from Sun Yat-sen, who was then in exile in Hong Kong. However, Tagore decided to proceed to China and travelled to Shanghai, Hangzhou and Nanking. He was the guest of General Ch'i, the military governor of Nanking, whom he advised on pursuing reconciliation and peace, a route that was readily agreed to by his host. This plan was broken, however, five months later, when the general attacked another military leader before the general took shelter in Japan. However, the civil governor, a Buddhist scholar, was overjoyed at Tagore's visit, as the poet brought with him from India the message that the Chinese authorities had been waiting centuries to receive. This was a great anniversary for the Chinese. Elmhirst commented that Tagore's lecture to 3,000 students was brilliant.[1] His journey to Peking with military escort in a private carriage on the Blue Express train was arranged by General Ch'i. On the way they stopped to pay respects at Confucius' tomb. The receptions and felicitations were accomplished in style and Tagore even had the privilege of meeting the former emperor in the Forbidden City, the first foreigner to be given this privilege.

Initially Tagore's promotion of the vernacular language against the stultified classical language, his reference to India's historic missions to China, and his account of his familial background and the socio-cultural and religious transformations in Bengal went down well. His reverence for Buddhism was welcomed by several Buddhist scholars and monks, and he was given a pair of seals and tablet inscribed with his Chinese appellation *Chu Chen Tan* (Thundering Dawn of India).[2] But the tide soon turned as his advice to China to desist from succumbing to the modernizing trends of the new era – of pursuing aggrandizing methods of conquest and coercion at the cost of forgetting China's historic civilizational roots, and abandoning a whole way of life steeped in Oriental aesthetics – was received with virulent opposition. The translation of a leaflet with this message from a section of China's youth shocked Tagore. The acute misunderstanding of his message was clearly spelled out, as they took Tagore's advice to value China's heritage as an urge to return to a feudal era, and his warning against competitive modernization as a directive to abandon modern advancement.

However, he was acutely conscious of the changing times, which he saw in the illuminated young faces of students at Tsinghua College in Peking. He told them, 'What a delight it may be for you, and what a responsibility, this belonging to a period which is one of the greatest in the whole history of man!'[3] Tagore had always admired Chinese culture and civilization, and had a deep sympathy for the Chinese people. In 1881 he had written a hugely critical article on the imposition of opium on the Chinese. Later he would voice his anguish at Japan's invasion of China in 1938, despite Yone Noguchi's efforts to win the poet over to Japan's imperialistic ambitions. He said, 'the reports of Chinese suffering batter my heart' as they filled him with 'sorrow and shame'.[4] In China, Tagore faced the same resistance he had faced in 1916 in Japan. Realizing that the core of his message had been lost in translation in a newly emergent climate of radical change in China, he decided to cut short his lecture programme and proceed to Japan, where he spoke of his earlier warning against aggressive nationalism which had proved prescient by the destruction caused by the First World War, where the spirit of the nation had been denounced, giving way to the 'collective egoism of the people'.[5] However, Indo–China collaboration would be effected in 1937 by Tan Yunshan through the establishment of China Bhavana at Visva-Bharati. Tagore's lectures in China were published in three versions as *Talks in China* in 1924, 1925 and finally in 1999, the last with an 'Introduction' by Liang Qichao.[6]

After the visit to China, Elmhirst had decided to leave for England. The sense of loneliness that seemed to pervade Tagore's life, in spite of those who thronged round him, seized him now. His age and state of health added to his tiredness. W. W. Pearson had died after falling from a train in Italy in September 1923. This was a severe blow to the poet and a great loss for his institution.

Tagore in the Forbidden City, China, 1924.

Tagore's long-time supporter, his eldest brother Satyendranath, had died in 1923. A sense of loss weighed heavy on Tagore.

Between September and October 1924, Tagore went to Paris, from where he set off for Peru on an invitation from the Peruvian government, who had invited the poet to their centenary celebration of their defeat of the Spanish. However, Tagore fell ill during the journey and was intercepted by the Argentinian writer and art curator Victoria Ocampo, who invited him to Buenos Aires to recuperate. Tagore was there until December 1924 and never picked up his aborted journey to Peru. Tagore was 63, Ocampo in her mid-thirties. She was impetuous, wealthy, generous and well-connected. She was later known internationally as the editor of the literary journal *Sur* (South).

Ocampo arranged for Tagore and Elmhirst, who was again with Rabindranath, to stay at the Villa Miralrio at San Isidro, overlooking the River Plate, quite close to Villa Ocampo. As a hostess, Ocampo was impeccable. Elmhirst wrote to Dorothy Straight, 'She was in love with him [Tagore]', and in her hurry to get close to him, she seemed to push the poet further away.[7] But Tagore was grateful for her solicitous affection. As he wrote to her later, he 'never failed to recognize that . . . [she] had a mind' which was 'like a star that was distant and not a planet that was dark'.[8] He was grateful for her friendship, but felt strongly that he needed his own space as he still had much to do and many responsibilities. The tensions between three strong personalities at Villa Miralrio are recorded in several letters and reminiscences; however, their friendship was cemented then and tested through time, creating a deep bond between them. Ocampo provided the poet with a comfortable easy chair, where he spent most of his time recovering. Here he wrote the poems that were collected in *Purabi* (The Easterner), dedicated to Bijaya, his name for Victoria, his devoted hostess. The chair was gifted to him when he returned, shocking a ship's crew who were coerced into taking off his cabin door and readjusting the furniture to accommodate this unwieldy piece of furniture. Tagore enjoyed its ample comfort on his journey back and it is now housed in Udayana, one of his Shantiniketan houses.

In the Spanish-speaking world, Tagore was well-known through the 22 volumes of his poetry, prose and plays translated by Juan Ramón Jiménez and his American wife, Zenobia Camprubi. Leading Chilean poets like Pablo Neruda and Gabriela Mistral were influenced by Tagore and a whole young generation read him avidly. Ocampo knew Tagore's work through Spanish translations. When warned by Andrews and Rolland that the Peruvian government was a dictatorship and he would be used for their own propagandist agenda, an embarrassed Tagore abandoned his journey to Peru, though he had been promised a donation of $100,000 for his university, his plea being doctor's orders. He had accepted Mussolini's invitation to Italy instead, where he would fall into this trap of political machinations. In February 1925 he returned to India via Geneva. He was in Dhaka the same month. His travels continued in a whirlwind of journeys in and outside India.

The following year, in May 1926, he travelled to Italy, answering Mussolini's invitation, accompanied by Professor P. C. Mahalanobis and his wife Rani, Rathindranath, Pratima Devi and their daughter, Nandini. Professor Carlo Formichi, who had taught for a year at Visva-Bharati, was entrusted with taking care of the Indian poet and his entourage. Elmhirst had come from England to meet Tagore when he landed in Naples, but when he went away to get his suitcase and buy a ticket to accompany Tagore to Rome, the Indian party was bundled quickly onto a train that left without warning – a frantic Formichi gesticulating to a surprised Elmhirst not to board it. The incident was a warning of what was to come. In Rome, however, Tagore was happy. He had old friends surrounding him: Elmhirst, Harriet Moody, Andree Karpeles and her Swedish husband, Dal Hogman. Mrs Moody wanted Tagore to meet the Italian philosopher Benedetto Croce, which Formichi thought was impossible. Croce was loyal to the king and virtually under house arrest in Naples. An Italian officer who knew Croce arranged a private talk between the Indian poet and the Italian philosopher, with a young officer bringing the philosopher by an overnight train to Rome so that Croce was in the hotel by 5 a.m., allowing him and Rabindranath to have a few hours of uninterrupted private talk before the entrance of Formichi at breakfast. Formichi was visibly flustered by the news of the one-to-one meeting between Croce and Tagore.

Tagore was charmed by Mussolini (as were many, like Ezra Pound, W. B. Yeats, T. S. Eliot and Winston Churchill), who told him that he had read all his translated books in Italian. The poet was given a grand reception at the Capitol and gave a public lecture where Mussolini was present.[9] Tagore was grateful for the library of Italian classics and books of art that Mussolini had sent earlier to Visva-Bharati with Formichi. Mussolini had written to Formichi that the 'gift' of books was most appropriate, as Tagore intended Visva-Bharati to be a university that was 'the main centre of Indian culture'; he hoped this 'offer' would 'help in strengthening more and more the cultural relations between India, the classical land and cradle of the world's civilization and Italy'.[10] Tagore was touched and his statement to the *Tribuna* was complimentary about Mussolini's person and his wish for Italy to emerge from 'the fire-bath' 'clothed in quenchless light'.[11] These words from Tagore were vague and poetic, but showed that Tagore was willing to gloss over signs of political unrest and repression that might have been evinced during his visit. However, Rathindranath noted that both Mahalanobis and he felt that Tagore was being given a rather sanitized view of the country's reality. Earlier, the poet and his group had been invited guests of the aristocrat scholar Duke Scotti in Milan in 1925, where Tagore's audiences were ecstatic and his host warm and welcoming. Here on 22 January 1925 he had given a lecture on 'People and Nation', which was published in the *Manchester Guardian* a month later on 23 February. He had compared the difference between people and nation to that between natural and professional man: 'The one being kind and hospitable . . . and the other grasping, deceitful and cruel.'[12] The feeling that all was not well in Italy is evident in the poet's response. Duke Scotti was a man looked on with suspicion by Mussolini for his popularity. In 1926 the political climate had changed as the fascists had gained power in the north and the people were gripped with fear. On this occasion, Duke Scotti paid a brief visit to Tagore, but later sent the king's sister as his emissary to explain his earlier stiff behaviour and also to hand over papers which documented the torture meted out to intellectuals who had not bowed down to fascist ideology.

Tagore honoured invitations from Turin and Venice, and after being given a grand welcome by the city fathers in the latter, he was able to fufil a personal wish to escape the public gaze and tour the canals incognito early in the morning, before he returned to an agitated Grand Hotel manager who had congregated the whole staff to enquire about the poet's disappearance.[13]

It was in Villeneuve, Switzerland, between July and September, that Tagore met Romain Rolland and others, and where he learned about the torture inflicted on dissenters of Mussolini's regime. This sent Tagore into a flurry of revision of his earlier view. It was a difficult decision, as he was aware of the hospitality shown to him by Mussolini and the generosity of his gift of books to his institution. The Indian idea of not betraying the one who gave you your life's nourishing salt must have irked him. He was torn from within, his sense of gratitude being tried by his sense of humanity and justice. His initial anodyne responses were met with frustration by the writer Georges Duhamel, whom Rolland had invited to talk to Tagore. But Rolland understood Tagore and brought more evidence to him: first-person accounts of horrific torture suffered by the Italian exiles Salvenini and Salvadori, presented by a lawyer, Modigliani. This had the desired effect as Tagore fired off his revised response to the *Manchester Guardian*, which the editor, C. P. Scott, published on 5 August. Here Tagore showed his awareness of 'a parody of greatness' and his own Eastern admiration of 'efficient organization' which had initially attracted him to Mussolini's 'creative mind'.[14] The response from the fascist press was decisively dismissive of someone who had 'profited from Italy's traditional and lordly hospitality', and concluded 'Who cares? Italy laughs at Tagore.'[15] Tagore was willing to revise his opinion as facts were revealed to him and as circumstances around him changed; he voiced his response with the humility of an intellectual whose integrity never faltered, unwilling as he was to bend to win public opinion.

Between mid-July and September 1926 Tagore travelled through Denmark, Switzerland and Germany, and between September and November he visited various European destinations: Zurich, Oslo, Stockholm and Berlin. He also made an extensive tour of German cities before going to Prague, Vienna, Budapest and Athens. Of the European tour Rathindranath wrote, 'it is impossible to imagine the immense popularity and the ovation with which he [his father] was received in every country'.[16] He came back to India via Cairo and Alexandria in December 1926.

The following year, between August and October 1927, he travelled to Southeast Asia – to Burma, Thailand, Malaya, Singapore, Penang, Bangkok, Sumatra, Bali and Java. His *Letters from Java* document his experiences there. His two main reasons for visiting this part of the world were to retrieve the voice of 'Old India' that had been 'stranded there [in Bali] for centuries',[17] and to collect material to reconstruct Indian history and 'establish a permanent basis for research'.[18] He had formal invitations from many British Malayan towns and from Kunstkring and the Java Institute, both leading art and literary bodies. His trip was funded by the Indian business magnate and philanthropist Jugalkishore Birla and Narayandas Bajoria (Rs 10,000 and Rs 1,000, respectively).

The translations of Tagore into Dutch by Frederik van Eeden, Henri Borel and Raden Mas Noto Soeroto were already available

Tagore, Mr and Mrs Prasanta Chandra Mahalanabis and others in front of St Gellert Hotel before the lecture, Budapest, 1926.

Java, 1927.

and widely read in what was then the Dutch East Indies. Soeroto and Soeriosoeparto, two leading aristocratic *littérateurs*, were great admirers of Tagore and their own work had been influenced by the poet's writing. They shared Tagore's dream of effecting a synthesis between the East and West through cooperation. Tagore was a guest of Mangkoenegoro VII at his Soerakarta palace. His *Letters from Java* spoke about the hospitality he and his party, consisting of Dr Suniti Chatterjee, the remarkable linguist, the artist and architect Surendranath Kar, Ariam Williams (a Malayali teacher at Shantiniketan) and the painter and musician Dhirendrakrishna Devbarman, received here. Arnold Bake and his wife joined Tagore in Indochina. It was in Java that Surendranath picked up the craft of batik, which he brought back to Kala Bhavana, Visva-Bharati's art institute, with various motifs and design elements. From Kala Bhavana, batik and various Southeast Asian designs have spread across India.

In 1930, Tagore visited Russia for fifteen days and his experiences are recorded in *Russiar Chithi* (Letters from Russia, 1931). By the late 1920s Tagore's poetry and prose had been translated into Russian. Nicholas Roerich was a well-known admirer of the poet. Ilya Tolstoy, Leo Tolstoy's second son, had described Tagore as one of the world's greatest living men and Konstantin Stanislavsky had undertaken the staging of *The King of the Dark Chamber*, putting Tagore alongside Aeschylus. Tagore saw a production of Tolstoy at the Moscow Art Theatre, and on his own request watched *Battleship Potemkin*, interpreted by Eisenstein's wife, Pera Atasheva, since the director was away in Hollywood. The mutiny in the film moved Tagore to comment, 'They are right'.[19] There were no meetings with high officials apart from the first deputy minister of foreign affairs in Stalin's Russia, perhaps as a result of Tagore's response to Mussolini's Italy. In a letter written on 3 October 1930 on ss *Bremen* on his way to America, Tagore wrote of how everything had been 'integrated and assimilated' to work for 'common man, common mind, common right . . . to create an uncommon entity', creating equal opportunities through education, discouraging greed and thus eschewing envy that comes from unequal distribution.[20] Tagore was not ready to question what he was shown in Russia. For example, Russia had just executed 48 professionals without trial.[21] However, in an interview with the Russian newspaper *Izvestia*, Tagore, gauging all was not well below the surface, did propose, 'Freedom of mind is needed for the reception of truth; terror hopelessly kills it . . . Why not try to destroy this one also?'[22]

Between October and December 1930 he paid his fifth visit to the USA, staying in both New York and Philadelphia. The British Ambassador to the U.S. arranged a private meeting with President Hoover for Tagore. During this visit the poet met Helen Keller. Carnegie Hall, which holds 4,000 people, was packed during his talk and several lecture-goers had to be turned away. Though this trip was not a successful one for fundraising, Ruth C. Denis did stage a dance performance on Broadway to raise money for Shantiniketan. Tagore's reception in the U.S. had met with high and low tides of enthusiasm on past visits. This time, the *New York Times* carried 21 reports on him during his 67 days in the country.[23] This was his farewell trip to the USA. He returned to England and, during this visit, he had some unsatisfactory meetings with Indian leaders who had travelled there to attend the Round Table Conference.

Tagore had started painting in the interwar years, and though his artist compatriots had praised his work at home, he was dissatisfied and sought Western opinion on this new genre to which he had turned his hand. It was again a reflection of his mistrust of opinion at home. Conscious of the fact that he had not had any formal training in art, he became a resident of the Calcutta Art College in 1928 and took lessons in drawing and painting. The result was that his paintings were exhibited in Paris, sponsored by Ocampo and curated by Andree Karpeles in May 1930. In England, he was a guest of the Elmhirsts at Dartington, where he spent a blissful month painting. Tagore's paintings were exhibited in various other European cities as well as in America: in Paris, Birmingham, London, Berlin, Copenhagen, Moscow, New York and Boston between March and December 1930, making quite a sensation. His countrymen were able to view his paintings for the first time in December 1931 at an exhibition in the Town Hall in Calcutta.

Tagore's bad health had caused him to delay his Hibbert Lectures at Oxford, which he finally delivered in May 1930. The rise of narrow nationalism in the interwar years in the East and the West had long troubled Tagore. He turned to his inner life for answers, and considered the unity between man and the universe to be a reliable source of sustenance; this unity could link the finite with the infinite through man's creativity. Tagore's spiritual journey was lifelong, as the artist in him evolved and he discovered the 'truth' in epiphanic moments of illumination. This realization was his 'Religion of Man', which was the subject of the Hibbert Lectures. The lectures were gathered together, added to, edited and published in 1931. He published *Manusher Dharma* in Bengali in 1933 and he gave a lecture in the same year at Andhra University on 'Man'. Inherent in *The Religion of Man* is his 'message of universal humanism'.[24] It 'reads like a modern version of the Book of Genesis, which provides a study of evolution and leads into Tagore's consideration of Man as the greatest miracle of creation with his mind and potential for creativity'.[25] Tagore postulated that in the universe there exist two great forces at work, creative unity and freedom. While mortality links man with other animals, humanity connects him to the everlasting. What distinguishes man from other animals is his 'surplus', a creative energy that makes him look beyond mere existence and sustenance, surmounting selfishness and greed, for there is in man a desire for freedom. This is because man possesses a mind which harbours not only reason, but emotional attachment and affection. Man has dreams and desires, facilitated by his imagination. His surplus, embodied in his knowledge, action and love, unites him to his universe. We realize ourselves in others through the spirit of empathy, the Spirit of Man. What makes man coterminous with the eternal is his innate creative principle, where the humanity of God is reflected in the divinity in man, the visionary principle or 'personality' which leads to 'transcendental Man'.[26] Great souls who have facilitated the unity of the finite with the infinite through 'sympathy and immeasurable love' are Buddha, Zarathustra, Christ and the Mahatma, who can thus realize the Bramha within themselves. What Tagore proposed was a life in the service of others, practised through his 'Religion of Man', which unites man with the divine in himself, as the outer life finds sustenance in the inner life and is replenished by it. Elsewhere he has spoken of 'the Lord of my Life', his *Jivan Devata*, the creative principle in man which allows him to represent his Creator as exemplified in the Music-maker and the Artist who act with responsibility and self-effacement, achieving true liberation through creativity, who, like the poet philosopher, say, 'We are the music-makers / We are the dreamers of dreams.'[27]

As Sabyasachi Bhattacharya points out, Tagore's own home experienced the winds of freedom from dogma and orthodoxy as the Tagores led the Bramho Samaj, which lent impetus to the religious reform movement.[28] Moreover, the cultural, educational and social practices and experiments at Jorasanko nurtured this atmosphere of freedom, which probably explains Tagore's own search and desire for freedom that defines his deep humanism. In the final section of *The Religion of Man*, Tagore uses the image of the 'Twice-born bird' to explain man's double birth: the bird emerges in life by breaking through its shell and is born again to true freedom once it has learned to fly; so too does man first experience a limited existence in mundane individualism, and only when he is in conjunction with the infinite through unity with the universe does he know true liberation.

Tagore saw the Passion Play at Oberammergau in Bavaria in July 1930, and was so moved by the performance that he composed his one long poem in English, *The Child* (1930), in a frenzy of composition. In this poem, the child embodies innocence, as he is born in the East, the source of light and life, the new birth signifying a fresh beginning, sending a message of hope from the East as the new dawn breaks – a message that Tagore endeavoured to take to the West through his various lectures and talks.

In April 1929, Tagore had been invited to lecture in Vancouver on education. In the small town of Victoria in British Columbia, in spite of anti-Asian racial sentiment, 2,000 people attended his lecture, while 3,000 waited outside the hall.[29] In Vancouver, where his passport had been misplaced, he was questioned and humiliated deliberately by an American immigration official who knew exactly who he was. Among the official's stock questions he asked the poet if he had been previously imprisoned and whether he could write.[30]

The experience made him cut short his lecture schedule and sail back from California to India, stopping at Yokohama and Saigon on the way.

He travelled abroad again in 1932 when he received an invitation from Reza Shah to visit Persia. On this trip he experienced his second plane journey. He told one of his hosts, who was an Arab Bedouin, that in one of his poems he had said, 'O that I were an Arab Bedouin!' Tagore was now able to fulfil his long-cherished desire of spending time in a Bedouin's tent. In a letter from Persia he wrote that the Bedouin leader said, 'Our ancient sage has said that the person whose words and actions do not threaten anyone is a true Muslim.' His host went on to remark, 'the seed of hatred among Hindus and Muslims in India lies in the minds of the educated'. It was a humbling moment for Tagore. At the end of this letter he concluded, 'My travels in various places are now over. I return with my foreign friends' love and respect.'[31]

Tagore at a Bedouin Camp, Baghdad, 1932.

Dartington Hall, 1930. Dorothy Elmhirst and Tagore are seated on the right, with Ariam Williams, Tagore's secretary, and an unknown companion seated to the left and far left respectively.

In 1934 he left India to visit Ceylon (now Sri Lanka), where he was impressed by Kandyan dance and desired it to be imbibed at Sangit Bhavana, his institute of music, dance and drama. This was his final foreign tour. In India he answered multiple invitations and enjoyed travelling with his dance dramas. Among his many travel activities over the next few years, he attended the Tagore Festival, organized by Sarojini Naidu in Bombay in November 1933; gave a lecture at Osmania University in Hyderabad in December 1933; received a D.Litt from Banaras Hindu University in Varanasi in February 1935; and that same month was conferred the Sikh saropa at Gurdwara Dera Sahib in the Punjab. From May to June 1937 he also visited an old favourite spot, the hill station of Almora in the Himalayas, where he had taken little Renuka to recuperate in 1903. After his last international trip to Ceylon, Rabindranath retreated to Shantiniketan, his abode of peace, but continued to accept national honours and invitations to deliver talks. In his country, he remained a national cultural icon and was recognized as an international figure.

11
Tagore's Modernity

After winning the Nobel Prize, Tagore stayed in the public eye on the global stage, where his reception would range from ecstatic to hostile. The renunciation of his knighthood (though never accepted) made him a suspect of the government in India, which affected his position at home, in England and in America. Aspersions claiming Tagore held 'anarchist' sympathies branded his institution and obstructed attempts to raise funds for it abroad. His unpopularity in certain circles affected the sales of his books, on whose returns his institution relied for its maintenance. His own inner urge to speak his mind against capitalism and materialism in America, militarization and nationalism in Japan, aggressive modernization at the cost of discarding one's heritage in China and fascism in Italy did not help to warm some of his audiences to him. At home, his differences with Gandhi on non-cooperation and passive resistance – strategies which gained popular support in the nationalist struggle – made him a misunderstood figure whose very patriotism was sometimes doubted. What held the poet firm in spite of his isolation was his integrity and his inner urge to continue what he felt was his duty: to protest in his writings, activism and his educational and practical projects against social evils, religious orthodoxy, political persecution and economic exploitation. The faith in him held by many leading intellectuals, artists and leaders of his time was a source of sustenance. As an artist, his creative output proceeded at a relentless pace, in spite of the many personal tragedies that afflicted him, such as the deaths of close relatives and friends.

While he was establishing and strengthening Shantiniketan and Sriniketan and partaking in his national debates with Gandhi, his creativity flowed in diverse streams. His novel *Chaturanga* (1916) went back to the humanist values which gave impetus to the Bengal Renaissance. Inspired by Japanese haiku, he had produced *Stray Birds* (1916) and *Fireflies* (1928). After the success of his translated prose poems in *Gitanjali*, Tagore introduced the genre in Bengali in his collection *Lipika* (1922), and instead of spiritual themes, they told simple narratives about people. His plays *Muktadhara* (Free Current, or The Waterfall, 1922, which incorporated sections from an earlier play, *Prayashchitta*, Penance, 1909) and *Rakta Karabi* (The Red Oleanders, 1926) were both allegories portraying state oppression and exploitation being challenged by humanist values. The idea of the monster machine against ordinary people echoes his distinction between the state and society: Nation with a capital 'N' and nation with a small 'n', respectively (the crushing effect of a mechanized Nation on subjects, as discussed in *Nationalism*). Yet the depiction of machinery as tyrannical is not a critique of science and technology per se, but of its misuse to the detriment of humanity.

His inner compulsion to carry his vision of peace and the message from the East often took him on his travels, lecturing, meeting and debating with leading intellectuals of his day. To say that all these lecture tours and meetings were just for raising money for his educational projects would be wrong, as his intellect and acute sensibility would have told him that his critique of socio-economic exploitative systems would not make him popular to would-be funders. Yet his adherence to 'truth' and his prescience made him deliver messages that he knew would alienate his audience and further isolate him. He was often the sole voice of reason facing hostility and anger.

Just as his letters, lectures and speeches were often against the grain of the political climate and the general public mood, the message in his writing, his use of irony, satire and allegory, his introduction of new forms and genres in literature, upset those who felt he was criticizing and compromising traditional forms. His use of spoken Bengali revolutionized the written form, but met with resistance and criticism among many of the Bengali literati, including at Calcutta University.

As the world was being transformed, new modes and forms of expression evolved to reflect the changing reality and carry the burden of the times, exemplified most in the modernist movement of the interwar years. Tagore, conscious of the marginalized and the suppression of freedoms and human rights at home and in the world, gave voice to his concerns in his writing and projects. In this he affirmed his modernity, and his willingness and power to evolve as he absorbed diverse creative experiments and expressions. He produced his own distinctive brand of modernity relevant to India vis-à-vis the world. As a liberal humanist and a deeply spiritual man, he had, 'All his life . . . lived by his faith in life, in humanity, in God.'[1]

In Peking (now Beijing) he had allied himself with the modern: 'The impertinence of material things is extremely old. The revelation of spirit in man is modern. I am on its side, for I am modern.'[2] 'Modern' for Tagore signified what was always relevant and hence new, signifying the spirit in man. For Rabindranath, the real test of what works of literature would survive the test of time was their continuing relevance; in his essay 'Modern Poetry', he speaks of the Chinese poet Li Po: 'It is more than a thousand years since [Li Po] . . . wrote his verse, he was modern, his eyes had freshly viewed the world.'[3]

During the Bengal Renaissance, there were two realities. On the one hand, there was the encounter with Western literature, culture and science which affected and influenced the thought, writing, education and sociocultural developments in Bengal/India. On the other, Indians, faced with a sense of inadequacy in the present politico-cultural climate, turned to their heritage and found sustenance and a sense of continuity in Sanskrit texts and tenets and in cultivating modern vernacular literatures. The past and the present presented, as Bhabatosh Chatterjee says, two loyalties which were not always reconciled, leading to 'confusion and amateurishness'.[4] However, in Tagore, the Indian tradition and Western reality were integrated through his eclectic intellect and sensibility. Uma Das Gupta describes this choice as that of the 'difficult middle path' between 'radical modernism and proud traditionalism'.[5] Tagore's vast reading and ability to dissect and analyse what he encountered in written texts, oral debates, conversations and written exchanges gave him a clarity that went into shaping his writing and practical projects and ideology. He was able to glean what was pertinent from India and the West and apply it to India's sociocultural context through his writing, his pragmatic social projects, his political stand and in education. His clear and comprehensive understanding of the Upanishads and Vedas; of Sanskrit literature; folk culture and folk traditions; Bengali literature, both medieval and contemporary; and his wide reading of English literature and world literature (for example, his acquaintance with Goethe in German or with Hafez in Persian) gave him a catholicity which framed and shaped his modernity.

Of modernity Tagore said, 'If you ask me what pure modernity is, I will say that it is to see the world with dispassionate absorption, free of personal attachment. The seeing is bright and pure, there is genuine joy in such undeluded vision.'[6] As a writer for all times, he evolved with the exigencies and demands. In a Europe devastated by a brutal war, age-old institutions and a stable social order had been disrupted. This fragmented world demanded a different response from its artists, who found expression in modernism. Tagore detected a restlessness as people were confronted with a sense of the world's fragility and an acute awareness of their powerlessness to revert the current reality. Of modernist poets, Tagore said, 'The world that they view and show is crumbling, dustblown, and choked with *rubbish*. Their minds today are morbid, discontented, unsettled. In such a state, it is impossible for them to disengage their minds totally from the world-as-object.'[7] Baudelaire had used the term 'modernity' to describe his poetry that responded to the times, referring to the modern in his essay 'The Painter of Modern Life' as an expressive mode rejecting the school of French Romantic poets (Victor Hugo, Théophile Gautier, Francois-René de Chateaubriand and Alexandre Dumas). Baudelaire's poetry in *Les Fleurs du mal* (The Flowers of Evil, 1857) abounded in morbid images. In Bengal, the Kallol and Parichay group of poets were deeply affected by Baudelaire's modernist response and the work of Yeats, Eliot and Pound. They advocated *adhunikata* (modernity) and since Tagore was the towering, overpowering literary figure in Bengal, they felt impelled to resist his artistic domination by giving impetus to *Rabindra-birodhita* (opposition to Tagore). Their exploratory poetics appeared in journals like *Sabuj Patra* and *Parichay*, founded by Pramatha Choudhury and Sudhindranath Dutta, respectively, in 1914. This youthful group created *Kalaraber sahitya* (literature of clamour). However, there were those who continued to respect and promote Tagore and remained his followers. They advocated *Rabindrikata* (Tagorean) and were dubbed *Rabindric*. However, the tide of *Rabindra-birodhita* worried Tagore. In 1921 he wrote to Edward Thompson, 'All along my literary career I have run against the taste of my countrymen, at least the vocal portion of my province [Bengal]. It has hardly been pleasant for me.'[8] His sense of loneliness at home drove him restlessly across the world, finding solace in being able to communicate with and find appreciation among intellectuals of his stature in his journeys in 1920–21, 1922, 1924, 1926, 1929 and 1930.

At home Tagore was drawn into the debate that erupted about the efficacy of modernism in Bengali poetry. Tagore disliked the poetry of Bishnu Dey and some of Dey's group who were prominent exponents of modernism in poetry. As Tagore saw it, events in the West led to the modernist response in Europe in literature and art, but the reality in India, with her imperial subjectivity and nationalist aspirations, could not be reflected in forms similar to European responses in literature.

Disturbed by the adverse comments against his poetry, which his opponents considered moribund, Tagore decided to speak out in his essay 'Sahitya Dharma' (The Dharma of Literature[9]), igniting debates and counter-debates which were finally concluded by Tagore himself in 'Sahitye Nabatya' (Modernity in Poetry[10]), confirming his unassailable position as Bengal's leading *littérateur* who could express the spirit of the age, its zeitgeist, while retaining his distinctive powerful voice. But having the last word in critical debates was not enough for Tagore to demonstrate his modernity.

Tagore arriving at Frankfurt railway station, 26 July 1930.

The prevailing conflict in literary circles in Bengal at this time was reflected in Tagore's own poetic conflict, famously embodied in the introduction of the section 'Rabi Thakurer Sabha' (Rabi Thakur's Assembly) from a second notebook which was interpolated in the third edition of his novel *Shesher Kabita* (Farewell My Friend, 1929).[11] This was suggestive of Tagore's aesthetic answer to the raging controversy raised by the Kallol group of Tagore's relevance.

In the novel, the youthful Amit, a new age poet, is vociferous in his denunciation of Tagore as a relic of Romanticism, his work unfit for the modern age. He and his circle feel Tagore should recognize that his time is over and retire graciously to give space to poets of the new era, like Nibaran Chakrabarty, Amit's alter ego, a pseudonym he has adopted to counter and vanquish Tagore's domination. The Oxford-educated Amit Ray comes from the anglicized world of Western sophistication; his Bengali friends are known as Katy, Lisi and Sisi. The reality of his home-grown culture, an alternative universe, as it were, to his circle, hits him when he meets Labanya and her aunt, who read and value Tagore and other Bengali stalwarts. 'Rabi Thakurer Sabha' is a gathering that takes place at the Ballygunge literary gathering where Amit Ray disparages Tagore's Wordsworthian antiquity and proposes that if the old poet does not retire of his own accord, they should all discard him. Curiously, what begins as a vilification of Tagore slowly takes on a tone of respect for the timeless elements in him, and previous poetic geniuses like Byron and Tennyson, acknowledging and reinstalling the efficacy of Tagore. Amit's love for Labanya's quiet beauty and intellect, his admiration for her integrity and acute literary sensibility, however, cannot find a place in his own fashionable world. They can meet on a Platonic plane, while their actual worlds remain separate. Labanya sums this up in a masterpiece of a poem, her farewell to Amit, in 'Shesher Kabita' (The Last Poem). Labanya's poem is Tagore's answer to the modernist poets, embodying the masterstroke of a true modern in a powerful poem which handles the new poetic idiom with the confidence and finesse of a poet whom his contemporaries have to accept as a poet for all times, capable of carrying the burden of the times. This trend in new forms and techniques was further explored by Tagore in the poems of *Punascha* (Postscript, 1932), *Mohua, Shesh Saptak* (The Last Chords, 1935), *Patraput* (Platter of Leaves, 1936) and *Shyamali* (The Dark Maiden, 1936), where the themes often relate to the mundane, to everyday reality.

Unlike poets like Sudhindranath Dutta, Bishnu Dey, Amiya Chakrabarty, Jibanananda Das and Samar Sen, who belonged to the twentieth century, Tagore traversed and belonged to two centuries, the Victorian and the modern. He was in a position to comprehend and appreciate the strengths and weaknesses of the earlier literary period and experience, and identify the transitions in the new century as he sought a synthesis of the two periods within himself through his own evolution as a creative artist. What is remarkable, as Jharna Sanyal says, is that Tagore could reinvent himself at seventy years old as a creative artist and write back to the centre of metropolitan dominance as waves of European 'standards' and forms swept across the literary milieu in India, while he maintained his distinctive voice, and remained representative of a modern nation.[12] In his prose poems, he liberated poetry from metrical strictures when necessary and faced much criticism from critics who felt that rhyme and metrical discipline, which formed the sacrosanct domain of poetry, were being displaced by Tagore's unwonted innovation.

As early as 1893 the young Tagore had read Alfred Russel Wallace's *Darwinism* (1889). He also retained an interest in science, believing that India's progress depended on the introduction and utilization of science and technology. With his young physicist friend Satyendra Nath Bose, Tagore was intent on making science accessible through the publication of a simple series of popular education books. He wrote the first booklet in this series, *Visva-*

Parichay (An Introduction to the Universe), towards the end of his life and dedicated the book to Satyendra Nath.[13]

Nandini, who in the drama *Rakta Karabi* embodies the power of women to change society, epitomizes Tagore's idea of the freedom which women need to facilitate social progress and the emancipation of men. This theme is portrayed in Rabindranath's fiction and the position of women in marriage, in the household and in society, all explored with Tagore's characteristic discernment and empathy: for example, in the walls marriage can build in a loveless relationship, which imprison Kumudini in *Yogayog* (1929). Tagore unpacked the intricacies of love and bonds in marital relationships in psychological novels like *Dui Bon* (Two Sisters) and *Malancha* (The Orchard), written between 1933 and 1934. His modernity is exemplified in his espousal of continuity as he reaffirms his criticism of casteism, sectarian politics and violence in *Char Adhyay* (Four Chapters, 1934), where he depicts the value of free love between man and woman in the characters of Atin and Ela. This story meets with an expected fatal end, as Atin's involvement with terrorism does not grant him an exit even when he wants to part ways with his comrades. This was the period of the Chittagong Armoury Raid led by Surya Sen, popularly known as Masterda, which, like Easter 1916, experienced a brief success in its expression of nationalist freedom before Surya Sen's betrayal by his uncle, his capture and execution probably haunting Rabindranath as a misguided endeavour. In *Char Adhyay*, Tagore is torn by his sympathy for the revolutionaries, though he remains doubtful of their means to freedom. In his soul-searching exploration of crime and punishment, Tagore continues to condemn violent acts of the revolutionaries and their incarceration and execution by the British Raj.

This was also the period when Tagore wrote some spectacular dance dramas. The cruelty of social ostracism engendered by casteism is portrayed in his *Chandalika* (The Untouchable Girl, 1933). In the same year he wrote *Tasher Desh* (Card Country), which shows how the liberating influence of the outer world is brought by strangers to a moribund society stifled by rules which have made its people behave like unquestioning robots. This is Tagore's answer to unimaginative social strictures which need to be challenged by innovative and imaginative rebellion. It is like a breath of fresh air which blows away the dried leaves, representative of a stagnant order. In the final dance drama in Tagore's last decade, *Shyama* (1939), Tagore explores the deeper questions of love that lead Shyama to transgress boundaries of right and wrong as she urges the youth Uttiya, who is enamoured of her, to sacrifice his life to free Bajrasen, the itinerant merchant who has been arrested and jailed for a crime he has not committed. More deeply, however, this musical play is about forgiveness and the limitations of human ability to condone – Bajrasen, who cannot forgive the penitent Shyama, is disturbed by the absence of mercy in himself.

Tagore had no training in art, though a drawing teacher was employed by the Tagore family. As in music and literature, he was open to different forms and able to assimilate diverse influences and emerge with his own recognizable style. His drawing started with his doodles in 1924 in *Purabi*, when instead of simply crossing words out in his writing, he transformed them into odd shapes of strange animals, birds and geometric forms. In 1928 he took up the brush and started painting in earnest. He continued to doodle both in his manuscripts and for the pleasure of the diversion and experimentation. His use of rhythm and movement as a writer and composer now entered his art. He was influenced by primitive art, European Expressionism and Japanese art, but in his around 2,400 paintings, produced over a period of seventeen years, of landscapes, portraits and pictures of strange creatures and shapes, a style was discernible which was his own, a new idiom which reflected the modern times in its surrealism, use of the grotesque and irony, which influenced modern Indian art as it took new directions. Just as he engaged in a discussion of modernism in poetry, he developed

Riverside View with Silhouetted Trees at Sunset, April 1937, coloured ink and poster colour on paper.

in own theory of art in 'What is Art?', a chapter in *Personality* (1917); a lecture, 'Construction and Creation' (1920); 'Religion of an Artist' (1924, 1926, 1936); 'The Meaning of Art' (1926) and his short essays on 'My Pictures' (1930).[14] Tapati Gupta speaks of his 'dreamworld atmosphere . . . a credible dreamland', as the poet-artist redefined beauty and ugliness in an exitentialist re-assessmemt, 're-discovering himself' during the high tide of modernism.[15] Tagore defied national borders and amalgamated Eastern and Western styles boldly in his art as an expression of his inner life.

In his fiction, both long and short, Tagore stressed women's resistance and women becoming agents of change, particularly in stories such as 'Streer Patra', in which Mrinal, who came as a child bride at twelve to her husband's house, became *Mejo Bou*, the second bride, expected to be obedient, devoted, self-sacrificing and self-effacing.[16] Fifteen years after a marriage of neglect and non-recognition, Mrinal writes her first and last letter to her husband,

Landscape with Stepped Structure, painted in Shantiniketan, August 1937, coloured ink and poster colour on paper.

detailing her loveless, stifling life in his household, ending with her declaration that she is to leave him. The nameless *Mejo Bou* regains her identity once more as she signs off as Mrinal, *Tomader Charanatalasroychhinno* – one who has now freed herself from under the feet of her in-laws.

In his final years, Tagore did not write many short stories, but in one story, 'Mussalmanir Galpo' (The Story of a Muslim Woman, 1941), he dealt with the complexity of interrelatedness of Hindus and Muslims in the Indian community. The divide-and-rule policy of the government which had allowed communal division and violence to escalate, fragmenting an interdependent society, continued to trouble Tagore. In 'Mussalmanir Galpo', the beautiful orphan girl Kamala, brought up by a loving uncle but shunned by her aunt, is married off to the second son of a wealthy businessman. The son is well-known for being debauched and Kamala is to be his second wife, much to the consternation of her helpless uncle. This is the time of *dacoits* (robbers), who infest the area, and as the marriage party proceed through a notorious field after an ostentatious wedding they are attacked by the robbers and the party disperses. Kamala is discovered hiding among bushes, but Habib Khan, a leader whom the community respects, stalls the advance of the *dacoits* and offers his home to Kamala, where she becomes a respected wife of a kind son of Habib's, Karim, and is allowed to continue practising her Hindu religion. By a curious turn of events, when her uncle's daughter, Sarala, has a similar encounter with the *dacoits* after her wedding, it is Kamala who stops the robbers and rescues her cousin and offers her a home in her house, knowing that her community will not accept Sarala after this encounter. The theme of mutual respect that Tagore saw as the only way forward for nations and communities remains a recurring theme in his work.

Tagore did not totally abandon rhyme in his poetry collections, for example it features in *Parishesh* (The End, 1932; poems mostly written in the 1920s) and *Bithika* (The Avenue, 1935). But an awareness of his approaching death coloured Tagore's later volumes, evident in their titles and subject matter: his 1938 collections *Prantik* (Terminal) and *Senjuti* (Evening Lamp), where many of the poems have a grave note, reflect Tagore's experience of a period of unconsciousness, hovering between life and death. The reaffirmation of his faith in life and humanity, his Romantic optimism, was his own brand of modernity, as expressed in his final lyrics in *Akashpradip* (Skylamp, 1939), *Nabajatak* (Newborn, 1940; dedicated to Sudhindranath Datta) and *Sehnai* (1940). Some of the poems celebrate a simple life – a sparrow at the window or a dog keeping watch with affection, witnessed from the author's sick bed – while other poems probe existential questions.[17]

In his last years Tagore was once again buffeted by the death of close friends and relatives. His long-standing friend Jagadish Chandra Bose died in 1937; his artist nephew Gaganendranath died the following year. His close friend C. F Andrews and his nephew, translator and writer Surendranath, as well as his dedicated associate Kalimohan Ghosh, died in 1940, leaving him once again a lonely man.[18]

As the world was plunged into a dark conflict of unmitigated destruction inflicted by nation on nation during the Second World War, an intensely disturbed Tagore lashed out in his essay 'Shabhyatar Shankat' (Crisis in Civilization) at the intransigence of the British Empire in India. This was written in 1941 for the occasion of the poet's eightieth birthday. In it he declared that he had believed that 'the springs of civilization would issue out of the heart of Europe', but now this faith was totally destroyed by unfolding events. He knew that one day British rule would end in India, 'But what kind of India will they leave behind, what stark misery?' His criticism is of British imperialism, but he reserves his admiration for individual Englishmen, evident in his endorsement of men like Andrews – his humanity, his generosity, 'his spirit of service and sacrifice'. He ends with a proposition: 'Perhaps that dawn will come from this horizon, from the East where the sun rises.' The final message is of Tagore's indomitable faith in 'unvanquished Man' who will 'win back his lost human heritage', asserting his undying faith in man's inherent humanity.[19]

Tagore's modernity does not share the disenchantment which characterized Western modernity. What signifies his modernity, both in his literary expression and his multiple social activities, is the freedom of choice to seek new forms, modes and spaces for creativity. In *Shesh Lekha* (Last Writing, 1941) there are three poems which he dictated from his deathbed in 1941 at Jorasanko, where he had gone to undergo an operation. In his poem of 25 July, the first and the last Sun asks the 'manifestation of being – Who are you? . . . There is no answer.' In the poem 'Through the Dark Night' of 29 July, the inevitablity of death is confronted, 'Sorrow's dark night' and 'Death's consummate art in scattered gloom'. His final poem,

'The Right to Peace' (30 July), is addressed to the 'guileful one' who has spread 'a net of varied wiles' over 'the path of [His] . . . creation' with 'cunning hands'. He who can 'with ease bear your deception, earns from you the impersishable right to peace'.[20] The direct communication with the Creator is reminiscent of Tagore's *Gitanjali* poems. There is at once an acceptance of this world of beauty, of *maya* (illusion) and a wish to find peace elsewhere. Tagore did not recover from his operation. He could not travel back to his beloved Shantiniketan. He breathed his last on 7 August 1941 at Jorasanko, the house where he was born.[21]

12
The Legacy: At Home and in the World

Tagore died in an upstairs room at his Jorasanko home, the place he had deliberately left four decades earlier. Thus he died where he was born and Calcutta could claim him back. It was an irony that he could not breathe his last under the open skies, among the rambling fields of his abode of peace, his Shantiniketan, where a sombre mantle of mourning and helplessness descended on the students and staff on receiving the news of their Gurudev's death. He who liked sobriety and organization and valued his privacy would have been horrified by the vast funeral cortège that accompanied his last journey to the burning *ghat* and the frenzied response of an unmanageable crowd.

Yet however much Tagore valued his own space – as evident in his retreats to his boat, *Padma*, on the mighty river where the family's agricultural lands were, or to Shantiniketan – he was very much a public figure in his life, owing to his national and global stature as a creative artist, a cultural ambassador for East–West understanding who was sought, utilized, feted, cherished (or dismissed as the case may be by political powers) and remained a significant voice during the nationalist struggle in India. This private/public dichotomy in Tagore's choices, attitudes and responses to events and people at home and in the world epitomizes his ambivalence and the diverse responses to the poet's person and work in his lifetime and after.

Jawaharlal Nehru, who would become independent India's first prime minister, was in Dehra Dun District jail when the news of Tagore's death reached him. Though the death of an ailing eighty-year-old was foreseeable, when it did happen, Nehru was as shocked as the nation, and sad that he would not be able to visit Gurudev again. In a letter to Kripalani (Rathindranath's son-in-law, dated 27 August 1941), he wrote that though he had met many great men in his life,

> I have no doubt in my mind that the two biggest I have had the privilege of meeting have been Gandhi and Tagore. I think they have been the two outstanding personalities in the world during the last quarter of the century . . . It amazes me that India in spite of her present condition (or is it because of it?) should produce two mighty men in the course of one generation.[1]

He goes on to say how different they were, yet how much they had in common, and how they represented India's 'many-sided personality'.[2]

What we have to remember is that Tagore wrote and achieved all that he did as a subject of a subject nation. Until the end, even when he wrote 'Crisis in Civilization' in 1941, he did not lose his faith in humanity. He continued to believe in India's resilience and India's position as a nation which could give much to the world, especially as the Second World War ruptured the globe after the two tentative decades of a tenuous peace in the West. India's image was enhanced, her dignity salvaged by his genius during colonial rule. His persona and work continue to sustain India, which thrives on the powerful appeal of his work, and as Atulchandra Gupta says, his compatriots have used his literary talents as the fortress of their dignity, which has provided them with a life breath.[3]

In *Rabindranath Tagore: An Interpretation*, Sabyasachi Bhattacharya has said

> actually, it is quite possible to argue that there are two Tagores.
> There is Tagore seen as a prophet and thus iconized by his
> admirers, especially in Bengal, who is like an oracle. And then
> there is also another Tagore, an intellectual who had a fair bit
> of knowledge of the history of the world in his own time.[4]

So there are two Tagores: the mystic sage of the East whom Bengalis adored (and almost deified), who was hailed and admired soon after the Nobel award in the West, and thus easy to brush aside when he proved to be a pragmatist and activist; and the other Tagore – the intellectual who was a rationalist thinker. One could go further and say that there were many Tagores, different personas for different people, depending on where his critic or admirer was positioned.

Thus there was the Eastern Nobel laureate – one from the subject races, who was startlingly vilified and despised for the adulation he received in the West by some prominent intellectuals and held with suspicion by some colonial administrators of his time. There was the peace warrior and socialist who inspired disappointment when he failed to live up to the image of the seer allocated to him by the West, as he proved to be a strong voice against aggressive and exclusive nationalism, alarming militarization, capitalism and expansionism. He displayed a tremendous courage in standing by his convictions, which often went against the grain. The fact that he was a pragmatist and not a romantic dreamer pricked the bubble of the romantic aura that surrounded the prophet-like figure. In Bengal he was a household name, mostly revered and loved, but also disparaged by certain intellectual sections who felt that he dominated the literary and cultural scene, drowning out new voices.

In India he was the Gurudev whom India's political leaders, such as Jawaharlal Nehru and Mahatma Gandhi, respected at the time of a nation's awakening. Nehru sent his daughter, Indira, to study at Tagore's ashram and Gandhi brought his Phoenix Ashram boys to Shantiniketan after he closed his settlement in South Africa. And there were Westerners and Easterners who came to his institution to give their time and service, believing in and taking forward his ideals and ideas.

Tagore was the poet whom leading poets across the world read and translated in various languages. *Gitanjali* has remained one of the most translated poetry collections that continues to be published – albeit mostly from Tagore's own prose version, rather than from the original Bengali edition.

So he was Tagore, the Eastern sage and Nobel Laureate, the peace warrior and socialist, the pragmatist and rural reconstructionist, a household name in Bengal, dominating her art and culture, a pan-Indian and global man of letters, an educationist, the poet of poets in Bengal and an international poet.

Can we bring the many Tagores together into a coherent, comprehensible whole – a versatile figure, a multifaceted genius, viewed as he is through diverse prisms, controversially positioned by his admirers and detractors on different planes of appreciation and comprehension in order to understand or dismiss him?

The question is, would some of the vituperative onslaught have been so persistent if Tagore had been a Westerner receiving the Nobel Prize? Would he need to be stereotyped and slotted if he was a European or American receiving the global prize for literature in English? Yet there were voices even in the West who were consistent in their veneration and affection for Tagore, such as William Rothenstein, Romain Rolland, Patrick Geddes, Arthur Geddes, Leonard Elmhirst, Maria Montessori, Maurice Winternitz, Vincent Lesny, C. F. Andrews and W.W. Pearson, to name a few. They knew Tagore from close quarters as they witnessed the astounding range of his creativity, encountering his work on the ground, and their respect for Tagore's person and his work remained unassailable. There were others like W. B. Yeats and Edward Thompson who were full of adulation at first, then deeply critical, but later came round to respectfully acknowledging his great artistic oeuvre. And like Edward Thompson and Esaias Tegner Jr, who was on the Nobel Committee, we have William Radice and Martin Kämpchen, both contemporary translators of Tagore, who read his work in Bengali and appreciate the original.

Prabhatkumar Mukhopadhyay noted that intellectuals like Tagore, Vivekananda, Bramhabandhab Upadhyay (a Catholic theologian), Ramendrasundar Trivedi (physicist) and Hirendranath Datta (lawyer), who were involved in resisting the Bengal partition and reinterpreting Hinduism, were not representative of orthodox Hindu society, as they were universalist and inclusive in their approach and attitude to society.[5] Tagore was the inheritor of Raja Rammohan Roy's ideals which propelled the sociocultural reform movement of the Renaissance. One sees the culmination of the spirit of the renaissance in Tagore's progressive ideas about education and sociocultural issues.

William Radice, looking forward to Tagore's legacy fifty years later while celebrating the end of the poet's 150th anniversary, at a conference said, 'He wrote so much, he did so much, he created so much. He was truly global.'[6] He was local as well as global and an architect of India's modern consciousness. As Asish Nandy has said, 'When Jawaharlal Nehru claimed that he had two gurus – Gandhi and Tagore – what he left unsaid was that the former was his political guru, the latter his intellectual. In rejecting Tagore, one rejects an important part of the modern consciousness of India.'[7] Tagore was wary of the 'foolish pride of narrow provincialism', and instead spoke of India's heritage and strength in her 'unity in diversity' (a slogan that one sees on billboards in India today) as the only way forward for a multicultural nation.[8] Gandhi too sought this unity of India's diverse people in his nationalistic campaign, condemning India's greatest social scourge, her casteism, and found the practice of untouchability her shame. Both saw a secure future in Hindu–Muslim unity, which, once jeopardized, would see the fragmentation of the nation, which mercifully Tagore did not live to see, but Gandhi witnessed with deep pain as Partition became a reality. Both believed that the means had to be stain-free in order to achieve a lasting and noble end, thus both condemned the use of violence during the freedom struggle – Tagore through his writing and lectures and Gandhi through his adoption of passive resistance as a political strategy. India's debt to these two great men is immense.

It is true that Tagore's family background, the lively and creative ambience provided by his family, the encouragement and recognition he received at home, helped him to develop a taste for creativity at all levels, value the urgency for positive change and nurture an unfaltering love of freedom, which he felt was essential for human expression and progress. This sense of freedom, so vital for holistic development of the individual, was something that marked the atmosphere in Shantiniketan. In fact, when asked what he had achieved at his institution, he remarked that he had created a *paribesh* (environment) conducive to creativity and self-development. Amartya Sen, winner of the 1998 Nobel Prize in Economics, a student

Rabindranath and Mahatma Gandhi, at Udayana, Shantiniketan, 1940.

of Tagore's school, comments on the attraction and pleasure of the outdoor classes amidst the natural surroundings, and the ease with which discussions in class could move from traditional Indian literature to Western thought, to Chinese and Japanese culture and beyond.[9] Sen also quotes from Satyajit Ray, who considered his three years in Shantiniketan to be the 'most fruitful' period in his life. Before this, Ray had been a votary of Western art, music and literature. Shantiniketan introduced him to Indian and Far Eastern art, making him what he was, 'the combined product of East and West'.[10] In spite of the vicissitudes of time, when one journeys from Kolkata to Shantiniketan, one has this inexplicable experience of an atmosphere of freedom pervading the place.[11] The love of and need for freedom is expressed in Tagore's famous poem no. 35 in *Gitanjali*, where he speaks of the ideal situation

> Where the mind is without fear and the head is held high;
> Where knowledge is free;
> Where the world has not been broken up into fragments
> by narrow domestic walls
> of petty distinctions, stifling customs and rituals.

In school education, Tagore, like Gandhi, believed that learning should take place in the mother tongue, rather than in a foreign language which the child had to be taught first before the joy of learning could begin. Moreover, Tagore argued that the culture depicted in the literature of a language was intrinsic to the understanding and experience of what was being conveyed. Indian children from the tropics, living under very different circumstances, would not understand the nuances and detail embedded in foreign literature or be able to visualize the picture of a snowball fight or haymaking which were relevant to a more temperate culture, far removed from their own. School education in a child's first language was a legacy of Tagore's educational philosophy which finds resonance in all cultures, especially in decolonized countries today. The reintroduction of Welsh, Scottish and Irish Gaelic and literature in local schools in Britain, for example, exemplify the need one feels to return to one's roots through the mother tongue. Realizing that primary education needed up-to-date primers, Tagore wrote *Shahaj Path* in two volumes, made attractive and accessible to children with beautiful illustrations and linocuts by Nandalal Bose – these books were rooted in their contemporary culture, in which children could identify their world in a language that brought home to them their own familiar way of life. The significance and urgency of a holistic education in which the arts (poetry, storytelling, plays, dance, painting and drawing) and sports make learning enjoyable and effective, alongside a knowledge of humanities and the sciences, are evident in schools like ones that adopt the Steiner method, which are very close to the ethos followed at Shantiniketan.

Tagore rationalized the Bengali language as he worked assiduously to narrow the gap between written and spoken Bengali, moving from *shadhu bhasha* to *chalit bhasha* (he was heavily criticized for this by some traditionalists), allowing the language on the page to reflect the language of contemporary conversation and thought. Literary doyens of Bengali literature, such as Michael Madhusudan Dutt in poetry and Bankimchandra Chatterjee in fiction, had given impetus to modern Bengali literature in their style, language and form, which Tagore took further forward as he shaped the Bengali language and literature by which his contemporaries were influenced. Bengali writers today continue to recognize their debt to Tagore.

As an innovator, he introduced the short story, the prose poem, short pithy imagist poems influenced by Japanese haiku and tanka and the dance drama to Bengali literature. In fact, he invented a new form of the dance drama – which combines songs, play-acting and expressive dancing, held together by a powerfully structured narrative – which remains unique and continues to have universal appeal at home and abroad. He created a distinctive brand of music called *Rabindrasangeet*, a repertoire of more than 2,200 songs in which Bengalis can find every mood, emotion and thought that human beings experience. Tagore did not like some classical traditions where the variations in tune dominated the song, stressing the virtuosity of the exponent, using a line or two of words in a repetitive manner. He valued the power of words and felt that the most appropriate music could convey the mood and meaning in a perfect marriage.[12]

In his dance form and songs we see the love of freedom to appreciate and assimilate tunes/forms from everywhere. Tagore's encounters with dance forms from Manipur, Indonesia and Ceylon had the positive effect of having these styles introduced at Sangit Bhavana and incorporated in Rabindra Nritya. The Tagore women had broken the gender boundaries of performance in plays staged at Jorasanko and in a theatre in Calcutta. Tagore took this revolution further when he urged the Tagore women and girls from respectable middle-class families to perform in his poetic play *Natir Puja*. This was the beginning of a freedom that would encourage girls and women to learn and perform dance, and even pursue dancing as a career. The stigma that had come to brand Indian classical dances in colonial times as *devdasi* (temple dancer) culture, marginalizing and distancing them from respectable society, was challenged by Tagore, who helped to restore them as art forms of acute sensibility practised by gifted professional artists through rigorous classical training. The founders of the Tagore Dance Academy in Coimbatore and the Kerala Kalamandalam, in Laxmana and Vallathoi, respectively, were given support and impetus by Tagore, which enabled them to reinstate, proudly reclaim and practise a whole rich tradition.[13]

In his songs, Tagore was inspired by the local and global, thus the Vaishnav hymns, the Baul repertoire, the classical purity of the Karnatak tradition, Hindusthani classical, Western music and Arabian tunes were incorporated in his songs, while they retained their *Rabindric* flavour.

However, the Nobel Prize brought home the necessity of communicating with the world and this urgency made Tagore transform himself into a bilingual writer, so that his lectures and essays, his translated creative writing and his message could reach a global audience. He thus travelled to the West and East on his one-man mission, urging the world to heed his ideas on the dangers of narrow nationalism and the need for internationalism/universalism, unity, mutual understanding and respect. International scholars like Michael Collins and Chris Marsh have found his prose writings in English a repository of thought and ideas that remain relevant to our post-colonial, transnational and ecological consciousness today.[14] Those with access to his Bengali writings find fresh aspects in his work which give impetus to their critical engagement with Tagore's contemporaneity and perspicacity. His reflections on history, education, feminism, nationalism and rural development continue to propel intellectual debates on these subjects among a global scholarship.[15]

Tagore's music, dance dramas and paintings have an appeal beyond linguistic borders in India and the world. Radice states that Tagore will live in popular memory in the next fifty years through the performance of his work through translations, adaptations and presentations, in creative productions of his plays, his songs and lyrical dramas and in exhibitions of his paintings, as has been evident in the fourth wave of interest in Tagore's work during the 150th anniversary of the poet's birthday (which prompted a creative showcasing of his work both at conferences and elsewhere around the world).[16] In Bengal, he remains an industry, with vocalists, musicians, dance troupes and elocutionists professing his art. The film industry in Bengal and Mumbai not only utilize his songs and music, but adapt his stories and his ideas, proving that he remains inspirational and saleable for a vast public in India and among the global Indian diaspora and their mainstream associates.

The lifting of the copyright at Visva-Bharati in 2001 has led to a plethora of new translations and edited volumes of Tagore's work, recordings of *Rabindrasangeet* and creative experiments with his music, dance dramas and plays in transcreations and adaptations which affirm a fresh approach to and appreciation of the poet's work, with a freedom the poet himself would have welcomed. His rural reconstruction work at Shelidah, Shantiniketan and Sriniketan, and his establishment of agricultural cooperatives in the rural backwaters, were the inspiration for Elmhirst's Dartington Trust in Devon, England, and his environmental schemes have resonance with the transition movement in Europe today. Visva-Bharati, his idea of an international university, was realized in his time, and set the tone and mode of knowledge exchange and transfer in motion for greater global interchange and interaction.

In a world of rising conflict, alarming friction and widening fissures, Tagore's syncretism remains a lasting legacy. He sought a positive outcome of the East–West encounter and exchange, so that the 'universal man' could meet and interact through a transnational dialogue. This syncretic culture imbues the vast oeuvre of his work; it has propelled his activism and lives in his pragmatic projects today. Tagore's faith in humanity stemmed from his belief in the creative potential of the individual, which needs to be identified, explored, exploited and allowed expression in order to contribute to life and the world. Freedom, creativity, syncretism and mutual respect are central to Tagore's ideas and work, and provide a blueprint for a world which can be brought closer together through mutual understanding, rather than be driven apart through ruthless competition, anger and greed. His conviction that truth, love and compassion can nurture an amicable future between nations for a sustainable world makes Tagore a man for all ages.

References

Introduction

1 Mijarul M. Quayes was the High Commissioner of Bangladesh for the UK, who gave a lecture at Edinburgh Napier University in 2014 as part of the Distinguished Lecture Series at the Scottish Centre of Tagore Studies (SCOTS).
2 Both Shantiniketan and Sriniketan are in Birbhum district in West Bengal, northwest of Kolkata.
3 In the tradition of the forest hermitage of India, the *tapovan*, where teacher and pupil lived together, close to nature, in a life of education, meditation and shared activities like gardening and cleaning.
4 See Bashabi Fraser, ed., *Rabindranath Tagore's Global Vision*, Literature Compass, XII/5 (May 2015).
5 See Kalyan Kundu, *Meeting with Mussolini: Tagore's Tour in Italy, 1925–1926* (New Delhi, 2015).
6 Ashis Nandy, *The Illegitimacy of Nationalism: Rabindranath Tagore and the Politics of Self* (New Delhi, 1994).

1 The Tagores of Jorasanko

1 *Prabashi*, 15 Poush 1338, Magh 1338, p. 501; see Tagore, *Atmaparichay*, in *Rabindra Rachanabali*, vol. X (Calcutta, Baishakh 1368), pp. 207–8.
2 In 1707 the English took over and conducted a survey of Kalikata, Gobindapur and Sutanuti and collected taxes from this area.
3 The use of the terms 'Muslim', 'Hindu' and 'English' in this sentence is not in reference to religious groups but the regional origin of the groups.

4 Prasantakumar Pal, *Rabijibani*, 2nd edn (Kolkata, 1993), vol. 1, p. 6. Pal notes that Nilmoni had five sons: Ramtanu, Ramratan, Ramlochan, Rammoni and Ramballabh. He also states that according to Byomkesh Mustafi, Nilmoni had three sons: Ramlochan, Rammoni and Ramballabh; his daughter was named Kamalmoni.
5 Ibid., p. 7. Prabhatkumar Mukhopadhyay puts his age down as twelve or thirteen; see Prabhatkumar Mukhopadhyay, *Rabindrajibani* [1934] (Kolkata, 2014), vol. 1, p. 5.
6 Sati actually means the good, devoted wife. The act of immolation of the good wife on her husband's funeral pyre was erroneously called 'Sati', where the noun was adopted for the act.
7 The Widow Remarriage Act was passed in 1856, supported by Debedranath and the Bramho Samaj.
8 Narayan Chaudhuri, *Maharshi Debendranath Tagore* [1973] (Delhi, 2010), p. 47.
9 Krishna Kripalani, *Rabindranath Tagore: A Biography* (New York, 1962), pp. 6–7. All references to Kripalani's biography of Tagore will be made to this edition unless otherwise specified. (A more recent edition of the same book has been published, with appendices, by Visva-Bharati Press, Kolkata, 2012.)
10 Ibid., p. 6.
11 In his autobiography he speaks of 'a peculiar sensation of disinterestedness . . . I was no longer my former self. There grew in me an intense aversion of riches. The coarse matting upon which I was seated seemed to be my fit place; the carpets and mattresses, etc., appeared detestable. My mind was filled with an intense joy hitherto unexperienced.' Quoted in Chaudhuri, *Maharshi Debendranath Tagore*, p. 13.
12 The Sanskrit text is: 'Ishabasyamidam sarvam jatkincha jagatyam jagat. / Tena tyaktena bhunjithah ma gridhah kasyasviddhanam.' Quoted ibid., p. 17.
13 Dr Radhakrishnan, ed. and trans., *The Principal Upanishads* (London, n.d.), quoted in Kripalani, *Rabindranath Tagore*, p. 12.
14 Puja is a ceremonial worship.
15 Sarada Devi's first born, a daughter, died soon after her birth without a name; she also lost her sixth son, Purnendunath (1851–1859), and her fifteenth child, a son. Her fourth son, Birendranath (1845–1915),

suffered from mental illness and her seventh son, Somendranath (1859–1925), was asthmatic, and he never married.
16 Satyendranath said about his father, 'with age he became somewhat conservative, with his deep philosophical thinking, he stepped carefully, testing the ground; I was young then, I was an extreme radical'. Satyendranath Tagore, *Aamar Balyakatha o Bombai Prabash* (Calcutta, 1915), p. 19.
17 Rabindranath Tagore, *My Boyhood Days* (New Delhi, 2004), p. 37.
18 Debendranath and Sarada Devi's second daughter was Sukumari (1850–1868), their third daughter, Saratkumari (1858–1920), and the fifth daughter was Barnakumari (1859–1948).

2 Growing Up in the Tagore Household

1 The Tagore men had their names ending with the suffix '-indranath' which means Lord Indra, the god of heaven.
2 Rabindranath Tagore, *Reminiscences* [1917] (Madras, 1987), p. 24.
3 Rabindranath Tagore, *Boyhood Days*, trans. Radha Chakravarty (New Delhi, 2007), p. 20. Originally published as *Chhelebela* (1940).
4 Ibid., pp. 12–13.
5 My translation does not reflect the captivating rhythm and rhyme of the original.
6 In Bengali, Tagore's *Shishu* (1904) and *Shishu Bholanath* (1922) are collections with poems in the voice of a child.
7 This house is mentioned in Sarala Devi's personal journal, *Jibaner Jharapata*. See footnote 4 in Prabhatkumar Mukhopadhyay, *Rabindrajibani* [1934] (Kolkata, 2014), vol. I, p. 31.
8 Rabindranath Tagore, *Reminiscences* (Madras, 1987), p. 32. (All references to texts by Rabindranath Tagore will henceforth be referred to by the book titles only.)
9 Krishna Kripalani, *Rabindranath Tagore: A Biography* (New York, 1962), p. 42.
10 See *Boyhood Days*, p. 44.
11 Ibid., p. 37.
12 Like much of his early writing, this translation is lost, but the section on the three weird sisters appeared later in *Bharati* (1880).

See Prasantakumar Pal, *Rabijibani*, 2nd edn (Kolkata, 1993), vol. 1, p. 183.
13 Ibid., p. 185.
14 *Reminiscences* (1987), p. 4. He recalls, 'Whenever the joy of that day comes back to me, even now, I realise why rhyme is so needful to poetry. Because of it the words come to an end, and yet end not; the utterance is over, but not its ring . . . Thus did the rain patter and the leaves quiver again and again, the live-long day in my consciousness.' Ibid.
15 Ibid., p. 3.
16 This poetry was published serially in the monthly magazine *Sadharani*, edited by Akshaychandra Sarkar. This is where Tagore encountered work by Chandidas, Govindadas and Vidyapati. See Pal, *Rabijibani*, vol. 1, p. 196.
17 Later Rabindranath carefully read and inscribed George A. Grierson's *An Introduction to the Maithili Language of North Bihar containing a Grammar, Chrestomathy and Vocabulary* (Calcutta, 1882).
18 Kripalani, *Rabindranath Tagore*, p. 71.
19 Mentioned in Pal, *Rabijibani*, vol. 1, p. 198.
20 Ajitkumar Chakrabarty, trans., *Maharshi Debendranath Tagore* (Allahabad, 1916), p. 19.
21 The aim was to create a platform for the arts and crafts of the motherland and give voice to India's diversity.
22 The *Indian Daily News* reported on 15 February 1875 that at the ninth anniversary of the Hindu Mela 'Baboo Robindra Nath Tagore, the youngest son of Baboo Debendra Nath Tagore, a handsome lad of some 15, had composed a Bengali poem on Bharat [India] which he delivered from memory; the suavity of his tone, much pleased his audience.' Mukhopadyay, *Rabindrajibani*, vol. 1, p. 49.
23 Mukhopadhyay, *Rabindrajibani*, vol. 1, p. 55.
24 Satyendrnath's 'Mile shabe Bharatsantan, ekataan monopran' (Unite children of Bharat in one voice, with one heart'), Ganendranath's 'Lajjae Bharat josh gayibo kemon kore' (How can we sing of Bharat's glories when we suffer from shame?) and Dwijendrenath's 'Milon mukhchandrima Bharat tomari' (Yours is the face of the Moon which unites us) are examples of patriotic songs. Ibid., p. 50.
25 Ibid., p. 53.
26 Pal, *Rabijibani*, vol. 1, p. 195.

3 English Interlude

1. Prasantakumar Pal, *Rabindrajibani* [1984], 2nd edn (Kolkata, 1990), vol. II, p. 6.
2. Prabhatkumar Mukhopadhyay, *Rabindrajibani* [1934] (Kolkata, 2014), vol. I, pp. 84–5.
3. Rabindranath Tagore, *Boyhood Days*, trans. Radha Chakravarty (New Delhi, 2007), pp. 83–4.
4. Pal, *Rabindrajibani*, vol. II, pp. 4–5.
5. In *Boyhood Days*, when Tagore was eighty he recalled Ana listening to his rendering of a song he dedicated to her, composed in the Bhairav raga and telling him 'O Poet! Your song would always give me renewed life, I think, even on my dying day.' p. 85.
6. Mukhopadhyay, *Rabindrajibani*, p. 75.
7. Letter to Jyrorintranath dated 26 November 1878, written in Bombay. Quoted in full by Pal in *Rabindrajibani*, vol. II, p. 12. Ana married Harold Littledale, a Scotsman who was vice principal of Baroda High School and Rajkumar College in Baroda. She went on to live with him in Edinburgh, where she died quite young from illness. See Pal, p. 30.
8. Ibid., p. 14.
9. Rabindranath Tagore, *Reminiscences* [1917] (Madras, 1987), p. 156.
10. 'Muslims' here is a reference to traders from West Asia.
11. Krishna Dutta and Andrew Robinson, *Rabindranath Tagore: The Myriad-minded Man* (New York, 1996), p. 68.
12. Pal, *Rabindrajibani*, vol. II, pp. 59–60.
13. Tagore's niece, Hrinmoyee Devi, notes that her mother regrettably lost this letter.
14. Raga Behag is a Hindusthani Classical raga sung/played in the second quarter of the night, reflecting a romantic mood.
15. *Reminscences*, pp. 162–5.
16. As recorded in the *Journal of the National Indian Association*, XXI/13 (March 1927). See Pal, *Rabindrajibani*, vol. II, p. 46.
17. *Reminiscences*, p. 179.
18. 'Beauty is Truth' is from John Keats's poem 'Ode on a Grecian Urn' (1819), from the final section where the Urn speaks: 'Beauty is truth, truth beauty, – that is all / Ye know on earth, and all ye need to know.'; The next two quotations are from Keats's reflection on 'Negative

Capability' in a letter to his brothers, George and Thomas, written on 22 December 1817.
19 See Krishna Kripalani, *Rabindranath Tagore: A Biography* (New York, 1962), p. 75.
20 *Reminiscences*, p. 170.

4 Loss and the Journey to the Banks of the Padma

1 Prasantakumar Pal, *Rabindrajibani* [1984], 2nd edn (Kolkata, 1990), vol. II, p. 56.
2 Rabindranath Tagore, *Reminiscences* [1917] (Madras, 1987), p. 187.
3 Ibid., p. 188.
4 Ibid., pp. 187–8.
5 Ibid., p. 187.
6 *Sunday Mirror*, XX/134 (June 1880), p. 5, quoted in Pal, *Rabindrajibani*, vol. II, p. 53.
7 Krishna Kripalani, *Rabindranath Tagore: A Biography* (New York, 1962), p. 96.
8 This meeting (in 1786–7) at Scienne's House, Edinburgh, hosted by Professor Adam Fergusson is recorded in an engraving based on a painting by Charles Martin Hardie. Scott was fifteen and studying classics at Edinburgh University.
9 *Reminiscences*, p. 208.
10 Raga Purabi is a Hindustani Classical raga suitable for the early evening, which is serious and mystical in mood.
11 Ibid., pp. 217, 219.
12 Rabindranath Tagore, 'The Vision', in *The Religion of Man: The Hibbert Lectures for 1930* (London, 1931), pp. 93–4.
13 *Reminiscences*, p. 247.
14 See Sabyasachi Bhattacharya, *Rabindranath Tagore: An Interpretation* (New Delhi, 2011), p. 84.
15 *Chithipatra*, vol. XIII, p. 49, letter 95; *The Bengalee*, XXX/2 (12 January 1889), p. 19; Prasantakumar Pal, *Rabijibani* (Kolkata, 1988), vol. III, p. 106.
16 See Pal, *Rabijibani*, vol. III, pp. 75–6.
17 See ibid., pp. 84–5.

18 Ibid., p. 173.
19 Ibid., p. 128.
20 See ibid., p. 152.
21 Kripalani, *Rabindranath Tagore*, pp. 111–12.
22 From a letter written from Shelidah on 29 November 1889: Rosinka Choudhuri, trans., *Letters from a Young Poet* (New Delhi, 2014), p. 51.
23 Ibid.
24 Krishna Dutta and Andrew Robinson, *Rabindranath Tagore: The Myriad-minded Man* (London, 1995), p. 110.
25 Ibid., pp. 110–11.
26 Rabindranath Tagore, *Glimpses of Bengal* [1921], trans. Krishna Dutta and Andrew Robinson (London and Basingstoke, 1991), p. 85.
27 Ibid.
28 Ibid., pp. 83–4.
29 Rabindranath Tagore, 'City and Village', in *Rabindranath Tagore: Towards Universal Man*, ed. Humayun Kabir (London, 1961), pp. 302–22 (pp. 318–20).
30 Ibid., p. 320.
31 'Samsya Puran' was translated by Shiela Sen Gupta in Bashabi Fraser, ed., *Bengal Partition Stories: An Unclosed Chapter* (London, 2006, rpt 2008), pp. 93–9.
32 Pramanath Bishi quoted in Pal, *Rabijibani*, vol. III, p. 181.
33 *The Bengalee*, XXVIII/37 (10 September 1887), p. 439, quoted in Pal, *Rabijibani*, vol. III, p. 71.
34 Rabindranath Tagore, *Chithi Patra* [1942] (Shantiniketan, 1993), vol. I, July 1901, pp. 62–3.
35 Ibid., December 1900, p. 36.
36 Ibid., December 1900, p. 43.
37 Ibid., December 1900, p. 41.
38 Ibid., August 1890, p. 3.

5 The Abode of Peace

1 Quoted in Rosinka Choudhuri, trans., *Letters from a Young Poet* (New Delhi, 2014), p. 294.
2 Ibid., p. 298.

3   Krishna Dutta and Andrew Robinson, *Rabindranath Tagore: The Myriad-minded Man* (London, 1995), p. 135.
4   Introduction to Rabindranath Tagore, *Gitanjali* [1912], trans. William Radice (New Delhi, 2011), p. xvi.
5   Rabindranath Tagore, *Gitanjali*, songs 39, 3 and 72, respectively.
6   Rabindranath Tagore, 'A Poet's School', in *Towards Universal Man*, ed. Humayun Kabir (London, 1961), pp. 285–301. Also in Bashabi Fraser, Tapati Mukherjee and Amrit Sen, eds, *Confluence of Minds: The Rabindranath Tagore and Patrick Geddes Reader on Education and Environment* (Shantiniketan, 2017), p. 85.
7   Ibid.
8   Rathindranath Tagore, *On the Edges of Time* [1958], 2nd edn (Calcutta, 1981), p. 46.
9   Rabindranath Tagore, 'My School', in *The English Writings of Rabindranath Tagore*, ed. Sisir Kumar Das (New Delhi, 1996), vol. II, pp. 389–403. Also in Fraser et al., eds, *Confluence of Minds*, pp. 36–7. Included in Rabindranath Tagore, *Personality* (London, 1917).
10 Rabindranath Tagore, *Letters to a Friend*; See Sisir Kumar Das, *The English Writings of Rabindranath Tagore* (New Delhi, 1996), vol. III, p. 228.
11 Tagore, *On the Edges of Time*, p. 49.
12 Rabindranath Tagore, 'Smaran 3', in *Rabindrarachanabali* (Calcutta, 1962), vol. III, p. 912.
13 This collection should not be confused with Tagore's English poem 'The Child' (1930).
14 The first Durbar in Delhi was held under Lord Lytton's viceroyship on 1 January 1877.
15 See Sabyasachi Bhattacharya, *The Mahatma and the Poet*, reprint (New Delhi, 1999), p. 55, published earlier in the *Modern Review* in May 1921.
16 Quoted by Rathindranath Tagore, *On the Edges of Time*, p. 62.
17 Ibid., p. 63.
18 Tagore, 'My School', p. 394; Fraser et al., eds, *Confluence of Minds*, p. 37.
19 Uma Das Gupta, ed., *My Life in My Words* (New Delhi, 2010), p. 142.
20 The poem is a father's thoughts on his little girl's innocent declaration, 'I won't let you go', when he is ready to journey forth, and there is his

realization that though everything wants to hold on to life, to this earth, nothing is infinite in this life. All have to let go.
21 Tagore, 'My School', p. 394; Fraser et al., eds, *Confluence of Minds*, p. 37.
22 Quoted in Das Gupta, *My Life in My Words*, p. 144.
23 Rabindranath Tagore, *Chithi Patra*, vol. VI, p. 84; Das Gupta, *My Life in My Words*, pp. 143–4.

6 From Shantiniketan to the World Stage

1 Krishna Kripalani, *Rabindranath Tagore: A Biography* (New York, 1962), pp. 217–18.
2 Prabhatkumar Mukhopadhyay, *Rabindrajibani* [1934] (Kolkata, 2014), vol. II, p. 388; see also Kripalani, *Rabindranath Tagore*, p. 218.
3 Tagore's letter to his niece Indira Devi Chaudhurani, in *Indian Literature*, II/1 (October 1958–March 1959), pp. 3–4; quoted in Uma Das Gupta, ed., *My Life in My Words* (New Delhi, 2010), p. 162.
4 See Rabindranath Tagore, *Gitanjali*, trans. William Radice (New Delhi, 2011), 'Introduction', pp. xvi–xvii.
5 See ibid., footnote 129.
6 Kripalani, *Rabindranath Tagore*, p. 218.
7 Ibid.
8 Krishna Dutta and Andrew Robinson, *Rabindranath Tagore: The Myriad-minded Man* (London, 1995), p. 165.
9 Ibid.
10 Ibid.; Mukhopadhyay, *Rabindrajibani*, vol. II, p. 393.
11 Quoted in Kripalani, *Rabindranath Tagore*, p. 203.
12 *The Times* in its coverage of the dinner (13 July 1912), mentions J. W. Marshall, Herbert Trench, R. B. Cunninghame Graham, J. D. Anderson, E. B. Havell, T. W. Arnold and T. W. Rolleston as present. See Kalyan Kundu et al., eds, *Imagining Tagore: Rabindranath and the British Press (1912–1941)* (New Delhi, 2000), p. 5.
13 Yeats's Introduction to Rabindranath Tagore, *Gitanjali* (New Delhi, 2008), pp. 263, 265.
14 Dutta and Robinson, *Rabindranath Tagore*, p. 169.
15 Kundu et al., *Imagining Tagore*, pp. 8–9.
16 Lascelles Abercrombie, 14 January 1913, quoted ibid., p. 16.

17 Ibid., p. 17.
18 Ibid., 29 October 1913, p. 73.
19 Kripalani, *Rabindranath Tagore*, pp. 278–9; the full letter is quoted in Rathindranath Tagore, *On the Edges of Time* [1958], 2nd edn (Calcutta, 1981), p. 111.
20 *Fortnightly Review*, March 1918; Harriet Monroe, *A Poet's Life: Seventy Years in a Changing World* (New York, 1938), p. 262.
21 Kripalani, *Rabindranath Tagore*, p. 226.
22 Ibid.
23 See Nobel Award Speech by Harald Hjärne, Chairman of the Nobel Committee of the Swedish Academy, 10 December 1913, www.nobelprize.org, accessed 20 March 2019.
24 Dutta and Robinson, *Rabindranath Tagore*, p. 176.
25 William Rothenstein, *Men and Memories: Recollections, 1900–1922, Part II* (London, 1932), p. 301. Also quoted in Tagore, *Gitanjali*, trans. William Radice, p. xxix.
26 See Edward John Thompson, *Rabindranath Tagore: His Life and Work* (Calcutta and London, 1921), p. 44.
27 See Mita Sarkar, '*Geetanjali*; Nobel; And Backdrop', *Folklore and Folkloristics (Rabindranath Tagore Special Issue)*, IV/2 (December 2011), pp. 130–33; Michael Collins, *Empire, Nationalism and the Postcolonial World: Rabindranath Tagore's Writings on History, Politics and Society* (London and New York, 2012), p. 57; Bashabi Fraser, 'Beyond Binarism', *Scottish Affairs*, LXXXIV (2013), pp. 1–16.
28 Edward Thompson, *Rabindranath Tagore, His Life and Work* (Calcutta and London, 1921), p. 44.
29 Letter 73 in Krishna Dutta and Andrew Robinson, *Selected Letters of Rabindranath Tagore* (Cambridge, 1997), p. 131.
30 There are letters addressed to 'My dear friend' from Rothenstein to Rabindranath. See Mary Lago, *Imperfect Encounter: Letters of William Rothenstein and Rabindranath Tagore, 1911–1941* (Cambridge, MA, 1971).
31 Quoted in Kripalani, *Rabindranath Tagore*, p. 304.
32 Ibid., p. 184.
33 Dutta and Robinson, *Rabindranath Tagore*, p. 183.
34 Tagore had earlier written his famous song 'Ei manihar aamay nahi shaje' (This jewelled necklace does not suit me, / When I wear it, it hurts me / When I tear it, it mocks me.), which epitomized his response

and was to be sung. However, on the occasion, he indicated to Santosh Majumdar not to sing the song. Both Sita Devi and Charles Freer Andrews who refer to this incident are quoted in Prasantakumar Pal, *Rabijibani*, 2nd edn (Calcutta, 1993), vol. VI, p. 449.
35 Ibid.
36 Dutta and Robinson, *Selected Letters of Rabindranath Tagore*, pp. 196–7.

7 The Renunciation of Knighthood

1 Krishna Kripalani, *Rabindranath Tagore: A Biography* (New York, 1962), p. 204.
2 Edward Thompson, *Rabindranath Tagore: His Life and Work* (Calcutta and London, 1921), p. 22.
3 Krishna Dutta and Andrew Robinson, *Rabindranath Tagore: The Myriad-minded Man* (London, 1995), p. 197.
4 Kripalani, *Rabindranath Tagore*, p. 246.
5 Women's responsibilities and freedoms remained themes in Tagore's work as he pondered on the position and role of women in his own society.
6 *Fireflies* (1928) was written in the same vein as *Stray Birds*.
7 Dutta and Robinson, *Rabindranath Tagore*, p. 202.
8 Ibid., p. 204.
9 Ibid., p. 212.
10 Ibid., p. 213.
11 Ibid., p 211.
12 Sabyasachi Bhattacharya, *The Mahatma and the Poet: Letters and Debates between Gandhi and Tagore, 1913–1941* (New Delhi, 1997), letter written on 12 April 1919 from Shantiniketan, p. 49.

8 Where the World Meets in a Nest

1 Quoted in Uma Das Gupta, 'Santiniketan: Continuity and Change', in *Rabindranath Tagore: A Celebration of his Life and Work* (Oxford, 1986), p. 33.

2 See Uma Das Gupta, ed., *My Life in My Words* (New Delhi, 2010), p. 197.
3 Krishna Kripalani, *Rabindranath Tagore: A Biography* (New York, 1962), p. 326. See Mandakranta Bose, 'New Horizons of Dance and Drama in Rabindranath Tagore's Creative Practice', in *Rabindranath Tagore: A Timeless Mind*, ed. Amalendu Biswas et al. (London, 2011); and Mandakranta Bose, *Speaking of Dance: The Indian Critique* (New Delhi, 2002).
4 Rabindranath Tagore, 'Bani' 2, in *Lipika*, in *Rabindrarachanabali* (Calcutta, 1962), vol. VII, p. 783, translation author's own.
5 Quoted by Rathindranath Tagore, *On the Edges of Time* (Calcutta, 1958), p. 109.
6 Ibid., p. 110.
7 Ibid., p. 125.
8 Ibid.
9 Ibid.
10 Ibid., p. 126.
11 Krishna Dutta and Andrew Robinson, *Rabindranath Tagore: The Myriad-minded Man* (London, 1995), p. 207.
12 See Kripalani, *Rabindranath Tagore*, p. 285.
13 Ibid., p. 286.
14 Tagore, *On the Edges of Time*, p. 131.
15 Kripalani, *Rabindranath Tagore*, pp. 288, 286.
16 Tagore, *On the Edges of Time*, p. 132.
17 See Martin Kampchen, 'Rabindranath's German Publisher Kurt Wolff', in *A Timeless Mind*, pp. 179–89 (p. 183).
18 Tagore, *On the Edges of Time*, p. 131.
19 Ibid., p. 135.
20 Ibid.
21 Ibid., p. 127.
22 To Kshitimohan Sen, 30 November 1920, see Das Gupta, ed., *My Life in My Words*, p. 197.
23 See Bashabi Fraser, *A Meeting of Two Minds: The Tagore Geddes Letter* (Edinburgh, 2005).
24 Kripalani, *Rabindranath Tagore*, p. 302.
25 See Uma Das Gupta, *Rabindranath Tagore: A Biography* (Kolkata, 2004), p. 70; Fraser, *A Meeting of Two Minds*, fn 41, p. 26.
26 Das Gupta, *Rabindranath Tagore: A Biography*, p. 70.

27 Leonard Knight Elmhirst, *Poet and Plowman* [1975] (Kolkata, 2008), p. 4.
28 Ibid., p. 4
29 Ibid., p. 5.
30 Ibid.
31 See Sabyasachi Bhattacharya, ed., *The Mahatma and the Poet: Letters and Debates between Gandhi and Tagore, 1913–1941* (New Delhi, 1997), p. 20, letter dated 19 February 1940.

9 'The Call of Truth' and 'The Great Sentinel'

1 Rabindranath Tagore in the *Modern Review*, quoted in Sabyasachi Bhattacharya, ed., *The Mahatma and the Poet: Letters and Debates between Gandhi and Tagore, 1913–1941* (New Delhi, 1997), p. 58.
2 Ibid., p. 4.
3 Ibid., p. 49.
4 Ibid., p. 55.
5 Ibid., p. 91.
6 Ibid.
7 Rabindranath Tagore, 'The Call of Truth' (*Satyer Ahaban*), ibid., p. 83.
8 Gandhi, 'The Great Sentinel', in *The Mahatma and the Poet*, p. 90.
9 Tagore, 'The Call of Truth' , p. 84.
10 Gandhi, 'The Great Sentinel', p. 90.
11 Rathindranath Tagore, *On the Edges of Time* (Calcutta, 1958), p. 152.
12 Ibid.
13 Ibid.
14 Ibid., p. 158.
15 Krishna Dutta and Andrew Robinson, *Rabindranath Tagore: The Myriad-minded Man* (London, 1995), p. 240.
16 'The Call of Truth', *Modern Review*, August 1921, in Bhattacharya, *The Mahatma and the Poet*, pp. 68–87.
17 *Young India*, October 1921, ibid., pp. 87–92: p. 87.
18 From 'The Poet and the Charkha', ibid., p. 123.
19 Ibid., p. 91.
20 Ibid., p. 23.

21 Bhattacharya, ed., *The Mahatma and the Poet*, p. 138.
22 Quoted in Uma Das Gupta, ed., *My Life in My Words* (New Delhi, 2010), p. 248.
23 Quoted in Krishna Kripalani, *Rabindranath Tagore: A Biography* (New York, 1962), p. 369.
24 Bhattacharya, ed., *The Mahatma and the Poet*, pp. 158 and 159.
25 Ibid., p. 6.
26 Uma Das Gupta, *Rabindranath Tagore: A Biography* (New Delhi, 2004), p. 42.
27 The Intelligence Bureau records are available at the National Archives in Delhi.
28 Bhattacharya, *Rabindranath Tagore: An Interpretation* (New Delhi, 2011), p. 138.
29 Ibid., p. 139.
30 See Biswanath Banerjee, 'The East Writing Back to the West: Acharya Prafulla Chandra Ray and Postcoloniality', in *Scottish Orientalism and the Bengal Renaissance: The Continuum of Ideas*, ed. Fraser et al. (Shantiniketan, 2017), p. 194.
31 Quoted in Amrit Sen, 'The Scientist as Hero', ibid., p. 204.
32 Bhattacharya, *Rabindranath Tagore*, p. 176.
33 Ramananda Chatterji, ed., *The Golden Book of Tagore* (Calcutta, 1931), p. 19.
34 J. L. Brockington, *The Sacred Thread: A Short History of Hinduism* (Edinburgh, 1997), p. 182.
35 Murdo Macdonald, 'Education, Visual Art and Cultural Revival: Tagore, Geddes, Nivedita and Coomeraswamy', *Gitanjali and Beyond: Tagore and Spirituality*, 1/1 (2016), p. 41.
36 Ibid.

10 Waves of Nationalism and *The Religion of Man*

1 Krishna Dutta and Andrew Robinson, *Rabindranath Tagore: The Myriad-minded Man* (London, 1995), p. 249.
2 Ibid., p. 250.
3 Sisir Kumar Das, ed., *The English Writings of Rabindranath Tagore* (New Delhi, 1996), vol. II, p. 653.

4 Tan Chung et al., eds, *Tagore and China* (New Delhi, 2011), p. 5.
5 Dutta and Robinson, *Rabindranath Tagore*, p. 252.
6 See also Das, *The English Writings*, vol. II, pp. 639–86.
7 Dutta and Robinson, *Rabindranath Tagore*, p. 257.
8 Ibid.
9 Ibid., p. 267.
10 Prasantakumar Pal, *Rabijibani* (Kolkata, 2003), vol. IX, p. 259.
11 Dutta and Robinson, *Rabindranath Tagore*, p. 267.
12 Pal, *Rabijibani*, vol. IX, p. 310.
13 Rathindranath Tagore, *On the Edges of Time* (Calcutta, 1958), p. 140.
14 Dutta and Robinson, *Rabindranath Tagore*, p. 271.
15 Ibid.
16 Tagore, *On the Edges of Time*, p. 140.
17 In letter to C. F. Andrews, 12 July 1915, Rabindra Bhavana Archives at Visva-Bharati.
18 In a letter to Ramananda Chatterjee, 28 May 1927, quoted in Rabindranath Tagore, *Letters from Java* (Shantiniketan, 2010), p. 11.
19 Dutta and Robinson, *Rabindranath Tagore*, p. 296.
20 Rabindranath Tagore, *Russiar Chithi*, letter 7 (1931), in *The Essential Tagore*, ed. Fakrul Alam and Radha Chakravarty (Shantiniketan, 2011), pp. 727–9.
21 Dutta and Robinson, *Rabindranath Tagore*, p. 296.
22 Quoted ibid., p. 297; the interview was not published until 1988.
23 Ibid., p. 298.
24 Sabyasachi Bhattacharya, *Rabindranath Tagore: An Interpretation* (New Delhi, 2011), p. 184.
25 See Fraser, 'Rabindranath Tagore on the Creative Principle', in *Tagore's Vision of a Contemporary World*, ed. Indra Nath Choudhuri (New Delhi, 2015), pp. 161–72.
26 Rabindranath Tagore, 'The Surplus in Man', in *The Religion of Man: Being – The Hibbert Lectures for 1930* (London, 1931), p. 60.
27 Rabindranath Tagore, 'The Music Maker', ibid., p. 122.
28 Bhattacharya, *An Interpretation*, p. 185.
29 Dutta and Robinson, *Rabindranath Tagore*, p. 284.
30 Ibid.
31 See 'Letter from Parasaye', in *The Essential Tagore*, ed. Fakrul Alam and Radha Chakravarty (Shantiniketan, 2011), pp. 729–30.

11 Tagore's Modernity

1. Krishna Kripalani, *Rabindranath Tagore: A Biography* (New York, 1962), p. 394.
2. Sisir Kumar Das, ed., *The English Writings of Rabindranath Tagore* (New Delhi, 1996), vol. II, p. 667.
3. Sisir Kumar Das and Sukanta Chaudhuri, eds, *Selected Writings on Literature and Language by Rabindranath Tagore* (New Delhi, 2001), p. 288.
4. Bhabatosh Chatterjee, *Rabindranath Tagore and Modern Sensibility* (New Delhi, 1996), p. 2.
5. Uma Das Gupta, 'Rabindranath Tagore and Modernity', in *Tagore and Modernity*, ed. Sen and Gupta (Kolkata, 2006), p. 1.
6. Das and Chaudhuri, *Selected Writings*, p. 288.
7. Ibid., p. 290.
8. Krishna Dutta and Andrew Robinson, *Selected Letters of Rabindranath Tagore* (Cambridge, 1997), letter of 20 September 1921, p. 276.
9. 'Sahitya Dharma', *Bichitra*, Sravan, 1927.
10. 'Sahitye Nabatya', *Probashi*, Agrahayan, 1927.
11. For a critical analysis of this literary debate, see Sivany Biswas, 'Tagore's *Punasca*: The Challenge of Nibaran Chakrabarty', in *Studies on Rabindranath Tagore*, vol. I, ed. in Mohit K. Ray (New Delhi, 2004), pp. 122–71.
12. See Ashis Nandy, *The Illegitimacy of Nationalism: Rabindranath Tagore and the Politics of Self* (New Delhi, 1994).
13. See Sabyasachi Bhattacharya, *Rabindranath Tagore: An Interpretation* (New Delhi, 2011), p. 197.
14. See ibid., p. 151.
15. Tapati Gupta, 'Unifying Experience: Rabindranath the Poet-Artist', in *Tagore and Modernity*, ed. Sen and Gupta, pp. 153 and 154.
16. See Sanjukta Dasgupta, 'Three Modern Women: Tagore's Transgressive Texts', in *Tagore and Modernity*, ed. Gupta and Sen, p. 121.
17. Bhattacharya, *An Interpretation*, p. 228.
18. Ibid.
19. See Sisir Kumar Das, ed., *The English Writings of Rabindranath Tagore* (New Delhi, 1996), vol. II, pp. 722–6.

20 See Humayun Kabir, ed., *Poems of Rabindranath Tagore* (Kolkata, 2005), pp. 250–52.
21 Sraban on the Bengali calendar is remembered by Bengalis every year in commemorative events.

12 The Legacy: At Home and in the World

1 Krishna Kripalani, *Rabindranath Tagore: A Biography* (Delhi, 2012), Annexure 1, p. 399.
2 Ibid.
3 Atulchandra Gupta, 'Rabindranath', in *Rabindrayan*, ed. Pulin Behari Sen (Calcutta, 1963), vol. I, pp. 1–4.
4 Sabyasachi Bhattacharya, *Rabindranath Tagore: An Interpretation* (New Delhi, 2011), p. 174.
5 Prabhatkumar Mukhopadhyay, 'Puratan or Natun Shatabdi', in *Rabindrajibani* [1934] (Kolkata, 2014), vol. II, p. 1.
6 See William Radice, 'William Radice: The Next 50 Years', in *Tagore's Global Vision, Literature Compass*, ed. Bashabi Fraser, XII/5 (May 2015), pp. 238–48 (p. 238).
7 Ashis Nandy, *Return from Exile: The Illegitimacy of Nationalism* (New Delhi, 1994), p. 4.
8 Kripalani, *Rabindranath Tagore*, Annexure 1, p. 423.
9 Amartya Sen, *The Argumentative Indian: Writings on Indian History, Culture and Identity* (Harmondsworth, 2006), p. 115.
10 Ibid.
11 See Christine Kupfer, 'Atmospheres in Education: Tagore and the Phenomenology of Sphere', in *Tagore and Spirituality, Gitanjali and Beyond*, 1 (2016), pp. 59–81.
12 The translations of some of Tagore's songs into English by Arthur Geddes and Alain Danilou for rendition illustrate their continuing universal appeal.
13 Uma Das Gupta, *Rabindranath Tagore: A Biography* (New Delhi, 2004), p. 79.
14 Michael Collins, *Empire, Nationalism and the Postcolonial World: Rabindranath Tagore's Writings on History, Politics and Society* (London and New York, 2012); Chris Marsh, *Tagore Speaks to the*

Twenty-first Century (Devon, 2016).
15 For a comprehensive website of Tagore and his circle, see www.scots-tagore.org, accessed 10 December 2018.
16 The first 'wave' of interest was after the Nobel Prize, the second during the centenary celebrations in 1961, and the third during the 1980s and '90s leading up to fifty years after Indian independence in 1997.

Select Bibliography

Writings by Tagore published in English

Boyhood Days [1940], trans. Radha Chakravarty (New Delhi, 2007)
The English Writings of Rabindranath Tagore (New Delhi, 1996), vol. II, and vol. III
The Essential Tagore, ed. Fakrul Alam and Radha Chakravarty (Shantiniketan, 2011)
Glimpses of Bengal, trans. Krishna Dutta and Andrew Robinson [1921] (London and Basingstoke, 1991)
The Home and the World [1915] (London, 1985)
I Won't Let You Go: Selected Poems, trans. Ketaki Kushari Dyson (Newcastle upon Tyne, 1991)
Letters from Java: Rabindranath Tagore's Tour of South-east Asia 1927, ed. Indiradevi Chaudhurani and Supriya Roy (Kolkata, 2010)
Letters from a Young Poet, 1887–1895, trans. and ed. Rosinka Chaudhuri (New Delhi, 2015)
Nationalism [1917] (New Delhi, 2010)
Omnibus, vols I–IV (New Delhi, 2003–5)
Rabindranath Tagore: Gitanjali, trans. William Radice (New Delhi, 2011)
Rabindranath Tagore: My Life in My Words, ed. Uma Das Gupta (New Delhi, 2010)
Reminiscences [1917] (Madras, 1987)
Selected Letters of Rabindranath Tagore, ed. Krishna Dutta and Andrew Robinson (Cambridge, 1997)
Selected Poems [1985], trans. William Radice (Harmondsworth, 2005)
Selected Poems, ed. Sukanta Chaudhuri (New Delhi, 2004)
Selected Short Stories [1991], trans. William Radice (Harmondsworth, 2005)
Selected Short Stories, ed. Sukanta Chaudhuri (New Delhi, 2000)

Selected Writings for Children, ed. Sukanta Chaudhuri (New Delhi, 2002)
Selected Writings on Literature and Language, ed. Sisir Kumar Das and Sukanta Chaudhuri (New Delhi, 2001)
Shades of Difference: Selected Writings of Rabindranath Tagore, ed. Radha Chakravarty (New Delhi, 2015)
The Religion of Man (London, 1931)
Towards Universal Man, Preface and Intro. Humayun Kabir (London, 1961)

Writings by Tagore in Bengali

Kalanukramic Rabindra-Rachanabali (Shantiniketan, 2014)
Nijer Katha (Letters to Nirmal Kumari Mahalanobis), compiled and ed. Amritasudan Bhattacharya (Kolkata, 2011)
Rabindra Rachanabali (Calcutta, 1986–92), vols I–XV
Rabindra Rachanabali (Shantiniketan, 1939), vols I–XV
Rabindra Rachanabali: Achalito Sangraha (Calcutta, 1991–2), vols I and II

Other Writings on Tagore, his Family and Associates in English

Andrews, Charles Freer, *Letters to a Friend* [1928] (London, 1931)
Ayyub, Abu Sayeed, *Modernism and Tagore* (New Delhi, 1995)
Bangha, Imre, ed., *Tagore: Beyond his Language* (Delhi, 2017).
Bhattacharya, Sabyasachi, ed., *The Mahatma and the Poet: Letters and Debates Between Gandhi and Tagore, 1915–1941* (New Delhi, 1997)
—, *Rabindranath Tagore: An Interpretation* (New Delhi, 2011)
Biswas, Amalendu, Kalyan Kundu and Chris Marsh, eds, *Rabindranath Tagore: A Timeless Mind* (London and New Delhi, 2011)
Chakrabarty, Ajitkumar, *Maharshi Debendranath Tagore* (Allahabad, 1916)
Chakravarti, Aruna, *Jorasanko* (New Delhi, 2013)
—, *Daughters of Jorasanko* (New Delhi, 2016)

Chakravarti, Sudeshna, Sanjukta Dasgupta and Mary Matthew, *Radical Rabindranath: Nation, Family and Gender in Tagore's Fiction and Films* (Hyderabad, 2013)
Chatterjee, Bhabatosh, *Rabindranath Tagore and Modern Sensibility* (New Delhi, 1996)
Chatterji, Ramananda, ed., *The Golden Book of Tagore* (Calcutta, 1931)
Chaudhuri, Narayan, *Maharshi Debendranath Tagore* (New Delhi, 1973)
Choudhuri, Indra Nath, ed., *Tagore's Vision of a Contemporary World* (New Delhi, 2015)
Collins, Michael, *Empire, Nationalism and the Postcolonial World: Rabindranath Tagore's Writings on History, Politics and Society* (London and New York, 2012)
Dasgupta, Sanjukta, and Chinmoy Guha, eds, *Tagore at Home in the World* (Kolkata, 2013)
Das Gupta, Uma, *A Difficult Friendship: Letters of Edward Thompson and Rabindranath Tagore, 1913–1949* (New Delhi, 2003)
—, *Friendships of 'Largeness and Freedom': Andrews, Tagore, and Gandhi, An Epistolary Account* (Oxford, 2017)
Dutta, Krishna and Andrew Robinson, *Rabindranath Tagore: The Myriad-minded Man* (London, 1995)
Elmhirst, Leonard, *Poet and Plowman* [1975] (Kolkata, 2008)
Fraser, Bashabi, *A Meeting of Two Minds: The Geddes–Tagore Correspondence*, 3rd rev. edn (Edinburgh, 2005)
—, ed., *Tagore's Global Vision*, Literature Compass, XII/5 (May 2015)
—, ed., *Tagore and Spirituality*, Gitanjali and Beyond, 1 (November 2016)
—, ed., *Tagore and the Environment*, Gitanjali and Beyond, 2 (November 2018)
—, T. Mukherjee and Amrit Sen, eds, *Confluence of Minds: The Rabindranath Tagore and Patrick Geddes Reader on Education and Environment* (Shantiniketan, 2017)
Gosling, David L., *Science and the Indian Tradition: When Einstein Met Tagore* (London, 2008)
Kämpchen, Martin, Imre Banghe and Uma Das Gupta, eds, *Rabindranath Tagore: One Hundred Years of Global Reception* (New Delhi, 2014)
Kripalani, Krishna, *Rabindranath Tagore: A Biography* (New York, 1962). Also see new edition (Delhi, 2012)
—, *Dwarkanath Tagore, a Forgotten Pioneer: A Life* (New Delhi, 1981)

Lago, Mary, *Imperfect Encounter: Letters of William Rothenstein and Rabindranath Tagore, 1911–1941* (Cambridge, 1972)
—, and Ronald Warwick, *Rabindranath Tagore: Perspectives in Time* (Basingstoke, 1989)
Majumdar, Sirshendu, *Yeats and Tagore* (Palo Alto, CA, 2013)
Marsh, Chris, *Tagore Speaks to the Twenty-first Century* (Devon, 2016)
Mukhopadhyay, Ramkumar, and Sanjukta Dasgupta, eds, *Towards Tagore* (Kolkata, 2014)
Nandy, Ashis, *The Illegitimacy of Nationalism: Rabindranath Tagore and the Politics of Self* (New Delhi, 1994)
Radhakrishnan, S., Humayun Kabir et al., eds, *Rabindranath Tagore: A Centenary Volume* (New Delhi, 1961)
Radice, William, *Particles, Jottings, Sparks: The Collected Brief Poems of Rabindranath Tagore* (New Delhi, 2000)
Ray, Mohit. K., ed., *Studies on Rabindranath Tagore* (New Delhi, 2004), vols I and II
Sen, Amartya, *The Argumentative Indian: Writings on Indian History, Culture and Identity* (London, 2005)
Som, Reba, *Rabindranath Tagore: The Singer and his Song* (New Delhi, 2009)
Tagore, Rathindranath, *On the Edges of Time* [1958] (Calcutta, 1981)
Thompson, Edward, *Rabindranath Tagore: His Life and Work* (Calcutta and London, 1921)
—, *Rabindranath Tagore: Poet and Dramatist* [1948] (New Delhi, 1989)
—, *A Difficult Friendship: Letters of Edward Thompson and Rabindranath Tagore, 1913–1940* (New Delhi, 1993)
Tuteja, K. L., and Kaustav Chakraborty, *Tagore and Nationalism* (New Delhi, 2017)

Other Writings on Tagore in Bengali

Mukhopadhyay, Prabhatkumar, *Rabindrajibani* [1934] (Kolkata, 2014), vols I–IV
Pal, Prasantakumar, *Rabijibani* (Kolkata, 1982–2003), vols I–IX
Sen, Pulin Behari, ed., *Rabindrayan* (Kolkata, 1961), vols I–II

The Rabindra Bharati Archives and Library at Visva-Bharati in Shantiniketan have the full archives of Rabindranath Tagore's papers, which include his correspondence with his family members and friends, many of which have been digitized and hence made accessible to visiting scholars.

Some valuable Tagore family documents are held in Jorasanko Thakur Bari, the Tagore family home in Kolkata.

Acknowledgements

I am hugely indebted to my late mother, Professor Anima Bhattacharya, and my father, Professor Bimalendu Bhattacharya, for kindling the love of Rabindranath's work in me.

I am grateful to Reaktion Books for commissioning me to write this biography.

The research for this book could not have been conducted without the generous International Senior Research Fellowship awarded by the Indian Council for Cultural Relations (ICCR) and without Edinburgh Napier University allowing me to divide my year between intensive teaching in Edinburgh and research in India.

The support of the Consulate General of India in Scotland, especially the Consul, Vishnu Sharma, and the efficient management of the fellowship by the regional director, Goutam De, ICCR (Kolkata), and the cooperation of his staff members are much appreciated.

I spent many happy periods delving into the rich archives and library of Rabindra Bhavana at Rabindranath's university, Visva-Bharati, Shantiniketan and have had unstinting support from the staff, the director, Tapati Mukherjee, the superintendent of archives, Utpal Mitra and the Reprography department. My multiple trips to Shantiniketan were made comfortable by the staff at Ratan Kuthi Guest House and the sustaining friendship of many friends at Shantiniketan.

My affiliation to Visva-Bharati and Rabindra Bharati Universities as an ICCR Fellow was supported by the vice chancellors of both these universities, who smoothed the way for the research for this book. Professor Srabani Pal at Rabindra Bharati and the director and staff of the Jorasanko Archives at Rabindranath's family house helped with accessing valuable research material.

Director Dr Jayanta Sengupta provided me access to the Victoria Memorial Library, Kolkata. The Nehru Memorial Library and Archives and the Sahitya Akademi Library in Delhi proved to be powerhouses of resources made available through the cooperation and help of the librarians and staff members.

In Delhi, the warm hospitality extended by Profs Indra Nath and Usha Choudhuri in their family home and their personal introductions to libraries and providing a car and driver for long trips across the sprawling city made the research possible during the hot summer weeks.

I have had productive meetings with scholars, translators and publishers like Professor Malashri Lal, Dr Radha Chakravarti, Dr Reba Som, Aruna Chakravarti, Professor Alok Bhalla and Esha Beteille.

I have benefitted from the vast scholarship of biographers and critics of Rabindranath like Krishna Dutta and Andrew Robinson, Krishna Kripalani, Edward Thomson, Uma Das Gupta, to name a few writing in English, and to Prasantakumar Pal, Prabhatkumar Mukhopadhyay, Professor Shankha Ghosh and Professor Pabitra Sarkar writing in Bengali.

The rich resources of the library and archives of the Scottish Centre of Tagore Studies (SCOTS) at Edinburgh Napier University generously donated by Dr William Radice, Professor Indra Nath Choudhuri and Professor Bimalendu Bhattacharya, provided a great impetus to the project.

I am immensely grateful to established Tagore scholars for their valuable work in the field and their constant support. I would particularly like to mention Dr Uma Das Gupta, Professor Sabyasachi Bhattacharya, Dr Martin Kampchen, Professor Tapati Mukherjee, Professor Tapati Gupta, Professor Krishna Sen, Professor Sanjukta Dasgupta, Professor Ramkumar Mukhopadhyay, Professor Swapan Majumdar, Professor Kumkum Bhattacharya, Professor Amrit Sen and Professor Somdatta Mandal.

Mr Amalendu and Mrs Swapna Dasgupta of Dasgupta & Sons took on the personal task of locating books and shipping books to me. Dr Saptarshi Mallick worked tirelessly to find rare books and manuscripts for me and Professor Pulin Das, with his encyclopaedic knowledge, clarified many points during the writing process.

And thanks to my family members: my father for his amazing level of scholarship; my husband, Neil Fraser, with his astounding intellect; my aunt, Reba Chakrabarty, for a sustaining ambience in our Kolkata home, and my daughter, Dr Rupsha Fraser, for her continuing faith in me.

My final gratitude is to the dawn chorus, the songsters who sang from the leafy branches of trees outside my Kolkata study window while our household slept, whose music was like a symphony played especially for me, encouraging, inspiring and urging me to write and finish this book. And of course, behind it all, there has been Rabindranath, who has remained a sustaining presence and impetus behind this work.

Photo Acknowledgements

Courtesy of Benjamin Boardman and Marion Geddes (photo Philip L. Boardman): p. 191; courtesy of Library of Congress Prints and Photographs Division, Washington DC: p. 6. All other photographs in the book are courtesy of the Rabindra-Bhavana Archives, Visva-Bharati University, Shantiniketan, West Bengal.